Large-Scale, Component-Based Development

ISBN 0-13-088720-X

9 780130 887207

90000

OBJECT AND COMPONENT TECHNOLOGY SERIES

Bertrand Meyer, *Series Editor*

FORTHCOMING

MAUGHAN and SIMON, *Windows Programming Made Easy*
2001—0-13-028977-9

MEYER, *Design by Contract*
2001—0-13-088921-0

CURRENT

BROWN, *Large-Scale, Component-Based Development*
2000—0-13-088720-X

COLMAN, et al., *Object-Oriented Development: The Fusion Method*
1994—0-13-338823-9

COOK and DANIELS, *Designing Object Systems: Object-Oriented Modelling with Syntropy*
1994—0-13-203860-9

HENDERSON-SELLERS, *Object-Oriented Metrics: Measures of Complexity*
1996—0-13-239872-9

HOPKINS, *Smalltalk: An Introduction to Application Development Using VisualWorks*
1996—0-13-318387-4

JOYNER, *Objects Unencapsulated: Java, Eiffel and C++*
1999—0-13-014269-7

KRIEF, *Using Object-Oriented Languages for Rapid Prototyping*
1996—0-13-014713-3

LORENZ, *Object-Oriented Software Development: A Practical Guide*
1993—0-13-726928-5

LORENZ and KIDD, *Object-Oriented Software Metrics*
1994—0-13-179292-X

MEYER, *Object Oriented Software Construction*, 2/e
1997—0-13-629155-4

MEYER, *Eiffel: The Language*
1990—0-13-247925-7

MEYER, *Object Success: A Manager's Guide to Object-Oriented Technology and Its Impact on the Corporation*
1995—0-13-192833-3

MEYER and BEZIVEN, *Tools 4: Technology of Object-Oriented Languages and Systems*
1992—0-13-923160-9

NIERSTRASZ and TSICHRITZIS, *Object-Oriented Software Composition*
1995—0-13-220674-9

POMBERGER and BLASCHEK, *Object Orientation and Prototyping in Software Engineering*
1996—0-13-192626-8

WEINER, *An Object-Oriented Introduction to Computer Science Using Eiffel*
1996—0-13-183872-5

WEINER, *An Object-Oriented Introduction to Data Structures Using Eiffel*
1997—0-13-185588-3

LARGE-SCALE, COMPONENT-BASED DEVELOPMENT

ALAN W. BROWN

PRENTICE HALL PTR
UPPER SADDLE RIVER, NJ 07458
WWW.PHPTR.COM

Library of Congress Cataloging-in-Publication Data Available

Editorial/Production Supervision: *MetroVoice Publishing Services*
Acquisitions Editor: *Paul Petralia*
Marketing Manager: *Bryan Gambrel*
Editorial Assistant: *Justin Somma*
Cover Design: *Talar Agasyan*
Cover Design Direction: *Jerry Votta*
Buyer: *Maura Goldstaub*
Project Coordinator: *Anne Trowbridge*

© 2000 Prentice Hall PTR
Prentice-Hall, Inc.
Upper Saddle River, NJ 07458

Prentice Hall books are widely used by corporations and government agencies for training, marketing, and resale.

The publisher offers discounts on this book when ordered in bulk quantities.
For more information, contact Corporate Sales Department, phone: 800-382-3419;
fax: 201-236-7141; e-mail: corpsales@prenhall.com
Or write: Prentice Hall PTR
Corporate Sales Department
One Lake Street
Upper Saddle River, NJ 07458

Printed in the United States of America
10 9 8 7 6 5 4 3 2 1

ISBN 0-13-088720-X

Prentice-Hall International (UK) Limited, **London**
Prentice-Hall of Australia Pty. Limited, **Sydney**
Prentice-Hall Canada Inc., **Toronto**
Prentice-Hall Hispanoamericana, S.A., **Mexico**
Prentice-Hall of India Private Limited, **New Delhi**
Prentice-Hall of Japan, Inc., **Tokyo**
Pearson Education Asia Pte. Ltd.
Editora Prentice-Hall do Brasil, Ltda., **Rio de Janeiro**

CONTENTS

FOREWORD

The Internet, business magazines tell us week after week, changes everything. Software professionals, who have a long tradition of helping automate all trades but their own, had better get it right this time, to keep pace with the speed of business-style innovation.

Do we know how to do it? Not quite. If we did, software wouldn't have the kind of reputation it has gained in business circles—always being late, over budget, and under function. Managers wouldn't be so preoccupied with the shortage of developers; and we would all go home earlier. But we have a few clues, and can also draw some hope from recent advances in tools, techniques, and standards.

Alan Brown's book does an excellent job of summarizing these advances clearly and comprehensively. Most software books belong to one of two categories: technical presentations directed at developers or management analyses intended for superiors. Although there is nothing wrong with either of these, the present work distinguishes itself by bringing elements of interest to both audiences while studying the confluence of three trends: application development, the Internet, and the rise of components.

Application development today is subject to considerable pressures. On the business side, the rule of thumb is to support the kind of constant, institutionalized change that has become the norm in much of the corporate world. On the user side, everything must be available all the time everywhere to everyone through the World Wide Web—without endangering the integrity and security of the critical business processes thus exposed to the whole wide world. On the human resources side, we must do with the limited pool of software talent available, and survive if the competition steals our best developers overnight. And, as if this weren't enough, we can seldom afford to do what we have been taught in Software Engineering 101. Even though the dream of any self-respecting software professional is to build a beautiful system from scratch, much of what we actually do is to wrap, rewrap, and wrap again some "legacy" code bequeathed to us by our predecessors.

The Internet doesn't just mean instant global connectivity; it also raises the stakes in almost all enterprise development today, requiring every application to include all the possible components—business logic, one or more (commonly several) Graphical User Interfaces, middleware, distribution, database, security, scalability, a built-in plan for evolution, and interfaces with many other systems from within and without the company.

Component-based development seems a required part of any solution. Born of the marriage between the high-flying software engineering principles of object technology and the initially humble "user controls" of the Windows world, components bring, to the legacy issue, the promise of clean, disciplined rewrapping; and, to new developments, the promise of modular, pluggable, evolutionary elements with impeccable interfaces to the rest of the world. Bring in intercommunication standards, and we are on our way to a new era of application development.

On our way only, since we must still master a dizzying variety of technologies, standards, metastandards, and standards on interconnecting standards, so numerous in fact as to make the old joke ("We love standards, and what we love most about them is that there are so many to choose from") lose any irony and become an objective description of the daily reality in the world of components and middleware. Alan Brown does a marvelous job of guiding the reader through the forest of technologies and acronyms, from EAI to ERP, EJB to RMI, UML to XML, RPC to MOM, and many more. Throughout the discussion, he brings together the technology and its application to business needs, illuminating component-based Internet enterprise application development to those of us who are developers, those of us who are managers, and those of us who are a little of both.

—Bertrand Meyer

PREFACE

Software engineering is entering a new era. The Internet and its associated technologies are changing the way customers, suppliers, and companies interact to conduct business, communicate, and collaborate. The result is the creation of huge opportunities to expand existing businesses, the delivery of greater variety and depth of information in a timely manner to those who need it wherever they need it, and the rise of completely new forms of commerce unthinkable without the business and technology advances fostered by the onset of the Internet age. As succinctly stated by the U.S. Commerce Secretary William Daley:

> *"Technology is reshaping this economy and transforming businesses and consumers. This is more than e-commerce, or e-mail, or e-trades, or e-files. It's about the 'e' in economic opportunity."*

This impact has been confirmed in a recent study conducted by the Economist Intelligence Unit (EIU) of Booz-Allen & Hamilton.[1] They surveyed the opinions of more than 500 senior executives with respect to how the Internet is changing their corporate strategy. The results showed that more than 90 percent believed that the Internet will transform or have a major impact on their corporate strategy within the next three years. Furthermore, many of these

---

[1] C.V. Callahan and B.A. Pasternack, *Corporate Strategy in the Internet Age*, Booz-Allen & Hamilton, June 1999.

executives recognized the need to restructure their businesses to take advantage of fundamental changes in their business environment.

However, with these changes come a number of threats. Many organizations are intimidated by the new technologies, unsure of how to take advantage of them, and wondering how these technologies will align with existing investments in skills and infrastructures. What they require is a conceptual framework for understanding software solutions in the Internet age, coupled with a realistic view of the technologies that will drive this revolution.

Components and *Component-Based Development* (CBD) are the approaches that satisfy these needs. More and more we see organizations turning to components as a way to encapsulate existing functionality, acquire third-party solutions, and build new services to support emerging business processes. The latest technologies for distributed systems support and encourage a component view of application integration and deployment. Furthermore, component-based development provides a design paradigm well suited to today's eclectic Internet-centric software solutions. This book examines components and component-based development, and their role in provisioning enterprise-scale solutions for the Internet age.

THE ORIGINS AND ROLE OF COMPONENT-BASED DEVELOPMENT

At its root, component-based development (CBD) is application development primarily carried out by composing previously developed software. Many people in the software industry are beginning to see CBD as an exciting new approach to application development which offers the promise of reducing cycle time for software development, and improving the quality of delivered applications.

Interest in reuse of previously developed components is nothing new. Ever since software was developed there have been efforts to reduce the amount of work involved in creating new software, ranging from small-scale efforts such as macro languages to large-scale efforts such as process asset libraries. While each of these efforts has had some impact on the reuse of software, none of them has had the overall impact expected or required.

Recently, however, a number of important advances in computer-based technologies have taken place. These have made the software industry rethink how software is developed, and offer new opportunities with respect to computer-based support for reuse of software artifacts. The impact of these advances is directly affecting everyone in the software industry. Three of these advances are of particular note.

First, the rapid evolution of hardware technologies has continued for more than a decade. The result has been a continuing improvement in the price/performance ratio of computer technologies. Organizations have much more computing power today than only a few years ago, embodied in a large number of desktop computers distributed throughout all levels of the organization.

Second, distributed access to remote information is now less expensive to develop, less cumbersome to maintain, and more user-friendly and responsive. This is a consequence of a number of advances in distributed infrastructure technologies supporting client/server architectures, high throughput networks, and distributed data management. Many distributed infrastructure technologies are now commonplace, supporting a collection of underlying protocols and standards that includes *transmission control protocol/Internet protocol* (TCP/IP), *remote procedure call* (RPC), *hypertext transmission protocol* (HTTP), the *Common Object Request Broker Architecture* (CORBA), and the *Internet inter-ORB protocol* (IIOP).

Third, unbounded excitement in the World Wide Web, Internet, and intranet technologies has changed the way people think about information access and availability. This has led to many new tools, processes, techniques, and technologies to support this new way of thinking and working. What an end user expects from an application is quite different now than it was only a few years ago.

Building on these advances, a new approach to solution provisioning, called component-based development (CBD), is being promoted. In its purest form, CBD takes advantage of these advances to provide an infrastructure for future applications that increases the ease with which separately developed software artifacts can be connected. As a result, it provides greater opportunity for integrating available software artifacts within your own organization or anywhere in the world, and uses available computing power to implement intelligent assistance to reduce the burden of evaluating, converting, and integrating software artifacts acquired from many sources.

All aspects of software design, implementation, deployment, and evolution are affected when a CBD approach is followed. As a result, a software project can be transformed from a development-intensive grind of code writing and bug fixing, to a more controlled assembly process in which new code development is minimized and system upgrade becomes the task of replacement of well-bounded functional units of the system. This is the goal of a variety of approaches and technologies gaining a great deal of attention in the software industry, which is now being referred to collectively under the banner of Enterprise Application Integration (EAI).

The needs and the rewards of taking a component-based approach are compelling. However, as with any new software approach, there is currently a significant gap between the aspirations of CBD visionaries, and the tools, processes, and techniques that support their vision. CBD has many hurdles to overcome to be considered a well-tried, repeatable process for developing large-scale, robust solutions for every application domain.

The most pressing needs facing software practitioners at present is to understand the business drivers encouraging the move toward CBD, to obtain a grounding in the underlying technologies from which it is built, and to gain the insight needed to understand how and when to apply CBD technologies within their particular context. These are the needs addressed by this book.

SCOPE OF THIS BOOK

This book provides the context necessary to understand CBD and to apply it successfully to enterprise-scale solutions. CBD is a new approach to software development that will significantly affect software development practices over the coming years. As a result, the goals of this book are threefold:

► It provides an introduction to the fundamental technologies of CBD. There are a number of different technologies that contribute to this approach. Each of these is examined in terms of how that technology has come to be, its major strengths and weaknesses, and the directions in which it is likely to evolve.

► Rather than simply enumerate individual technology advances, this book provides a holistic view of how each technology contributes to the larger goal of CBD. Readers can then put each technology advance into the context required for a more complete understanding of its relevance and impact.

► While the academic background of these technologies is discussed, the book is predominantly practical in nature. Wherever possible, the technologies are discussed with respect to their impact on current and future software engineering practices as experienced by a wide range of practicing software engineers.

Having read this book, readers will understand the key technology advances in software engineering as they affect CBD, and therefore be in a better position to take advantage of them in their organization.

TARGET AUDIENCE FOR THIS BOOK

The primary audience for this book is Information Technology (IT) managers, practicing software engineers, and software project managers interested in improving software engineering practices within their organization. Additionally, students in advanced software engineering courses will gain a valuable perspective on modern software engineering practices and techniques. The book provides such readers with the background information necessary to understand the convergence of a wide range of technologies. Armed with this information, the reader will be better able to conduct detailed studies in individual technologies of relevance and interest.

The descriptive text is aimed at informing managers, analysts, and programmers alike. The book does not attempt to justify CBD using detailed business cases, nor does it produce coded examples to type in at your workstation. The book's approach is essentially discursive, providing ample material of interest to all classes of readers, and providing references to other documents that contain detailed material in each of these areas.

OUTLINE OF THIS BOOK

The book is organized into four parts. Each part has been designed so that it can be read independently by different audiences depending on their background and interests. The four parts are as follows:

- ▶ **Part 1** contains background information on e-Business, the driving force of enterprise-scale solutions in the Internet age. This part can be considered the foundation that should be useful to anyone interested in gaining a deeper understanding of current software engineering trends and technologies.
- ▶ **Part 2** reviews the key elements of component-based approaches and the role of CBD in the overall software solutions life cycle. Three basic questions are answered in this part: What is CBD? What is a component? How is component behavior defined?

▶ **Part 3** describes the practice of CBD. It considers various CBD technologies in more detail, provides an illustration of the application of CBD technique, and considers how these ideas will impact future enterprise-scale solutions.

▶ **Part 4** provides some final commentary and advice on enterprise-scale solutions in the Internet age. It contains a view of current and future directions in CBD, and provides final reference material for further reading on the topics of this book.

Acknowledgments

This book could not have been completed without the hard work, support, and insights of a number of people. It is my pleasure and privilege to acknowledge their contributions.

Many of the ideas in this book have been based on work from a number of current and former colleagues at Sterling Software.* I have benefited greatly from written work and numerous discussions with Balbir Barn, Bill Barnett, John Cheesman, Doug Conley, John Daniels, John Dodd, David Helffrich, Mike Jones, David Marshall, and Doug McCammish. In addition, Bill Gibson, Keith Short, Desmond D'Souza, and Alan Wills made significant early contributions to the direction of this work. In particular, the work of John Cheesman and John Dodd has had significant impact on the form and content of this book.

The text of this book has been improved with the help of a number of people. I particularly wish to thank Paul Allen, Scott Farris, and Fred Long for their helpful reviews of draft material during the writing of this book. I thank them for their friendship, insight, and patience.

Finally, the biggest thanks of all to Moira West-Brown. Her endless support and encouragement was essential to the completion of this book.

—Alan W. Brown
alan@CBDEdge.com

* Note: *In March 2000 Sterling Software became a wholly-owned subsidiary of Computer Associates International, Inc. Further details of this acquisition can be found at http://www.cai.com/sterling.*

E-Business and the Changing Role of Application Development

INTRODUCTION

Much has been written about the impact of computer technology on all of our lives. As the availability and use of computers has increased, so have the valuable and innovative ways in which computer technologies have been employed to improve every aspect of the way we live, conduct business, and communicate with each other.

While this background is well-known and well-documented, a key aspect of this story is much less frequently highlighted; the challenges this brings to organizations tasked with developing, deploying, maintaining, and evolving software-intensive solutions designed to make use of this technology. In this chapter we examine the challenges software development organizations are facing in the context of current computer technology developments. This leads us to consider the primary business drivers motivating those organizations relying on computer-based technologies to carry out their activities. In this way, we are able to distill the primary requirements placed on software development organizations and the techniques they employ to develop, deploy, maintain, and evolve the systems they build.

1.1   MOTIVATION

We all frequently interact with software-intensive systems. The impact of their availability (and failure) is of everyday concern to large parts of the world's population. However, what is often ignored is that the software industry involved with the development and maintenance of software systems is increasingly becoming a strategic aspect of many countries' economies. The software industry has an important and compelling impact on economic, safety, and employment aspects of the world. For example:

- ▶ In 1998 it was estimated that the worldwide market for programmer development tools was in excess of $24 billion, and is continuing to grow at a rate of over 11% per year [1].
- ▶ Computer systems are at the heart of many safety-critical systems such as aircraft control, hospital patient monitoring, and power station management. The consequences of failure of these systems are severe. For example, in 1996 the uninsured loss due to the crash of the European Ariane 5 launcher was estimated at $500 million, and was subsequently traced to a single error in the Ariane's control software [2].
- ▶ By the end of 1999 there were almost 200 million Internet users worldwide. By 2003 it is estimated that more than 500 million will be "surfing the web" [3]. This offers a huge potential market for goods and services, and a significant base of employment opportunities.

While the ubiquity and importance of software is not in doubt, and certainly the consequences of software-induced failures are well-documented, perhaps most worrisome to many of those involved in the software industry is the lack of control and predictability of many software projects. Many surveys attest to the difficulties organizations have in predicting software costs, in identifying suitable target technologies to use during software development and maintenance activities, and in gaining visibility and control throughout the software life cycle.

As a consequence, the last decade has seen the promotion of software development as an engineering discipline, encouraging the use of more rigorously defined software development methods based on sound mathematical principles and supported by a strong experience base. This has been backed up by initiatives with titles such as the "software experience factory" [4] and the software capability maturity model (CMM) [5], by software certification efforts such as ISO 9000 [6], and by a host of new software development methods, tools, and techniques. While each of these initiatives has improved our capability to develop and maintain software, there is little indication that the problems faced by software development organizations are either reduced or less frequent.

A major reason for these ongoing problems is that the scale and complexity of software-intensive systems is constantly growing. Throughout the past three decades there has been increasing use of computer technology in a growing number of areas. We can identify at least three important reasons for this.

First, there has been a dramatic increase in readily available computing power. Computer main memories are now measured in hundreds of megabytes, secondary memories in gigabytes, and personal computer central processing unit (CPU) speeds in hundreds of millions of instructions executed per second. Furthermore, despite predictions to the contrary, new technology advances indicate there is no immediate end to the trend of increasing computing power. Moore's law (that processor speeds double or prices halve every 18 months) continues to prevail.

Second, there has been a continuing fall in the real cost of this computing power. The availability of powerful desktop computers at low cost has made computer technology available to most businesses, and to many individuals. This, coupled with advances in computer networking (including intranets and the Internet), has allowed organizations to harness the computing power they have with less concern for its physical distribution across the organization.

Third, there has been a growing acceptance that information technology is a pivotal component of many business functions. Computer technology is seen not only as a significant business enabler, it is now frequently considered an integral part of an organization's competitive advantage, significantly impacting the way they do business, compete in a crowded market, and differentiate their products and services.

1.2   SOFTWARE DEVELOPMENT CHALLENGES

This rapid increase in the power, availability, and use of computer technology has had a number of important consequences. For those responsible for provisioning and maintaining software-intensive systems, the most compelling of these are:

▶ the demand for computer software has not been met by software producers at the rate required (the so-called "software crisis");

▶ the complexity of computer software is constantly growing, both in the size of developed systems, and the intricacy of its operation to meet the extensive functional and non-functional requirements placed upon it;

▶ the rate of change of computer technology has increased the risk that projects with a long life cycle can have early technology decisions made obsolete by later technical advances;

▶ the significant investment made in developing and deploying computer technology cannot easily be thrown away when business requirements change—many organizations have mission-critical systems in place that were developed over a decade ago.

Clearly, as software-intensive systems reach this scale and complexity, the problems of software production become significant. Producing such systems within budget and on time is problem enough. Designing a system so that it can easily evolve as the operating environment changes, as user requirements are modified, and as errors (which inevitably occur in such systems) come to light, makes this an even more difficult task. Yet these are the challenges faced by any organization involved with the development, deployment, maintenance, and evolution of software-intensive systems.

1.3   THE KEY TO THE FUTURE: MANAGING COMPLEXITY AND RAPIDLY ADAPTING TO CHANGE

Organizations that deploy software-intensive systems face pressures from many sides in their efforts to improve the way they carry out their business activities. The biggest challenge they face is how to manage the complexity inherent in the systems they are deploying, while at the same time being able to rapidly adapt to change. This combination of complexity and change provides the greatest risk to successful system deployment.

To investigate this challenge further, it is useful to examine the sources of both of these key ingredients: complexity and change.

Managing Complexity

To be successful, the systems being developed and deployed must meet a variety of requirements. The complexity of any software-intensive system naturally tends to increase as these requirements grow in quantity, diversity, and difficulty. While there has always been a range of complex systems being developed, the past few years has seen a marked increase in system complexity. The source of this complexity lies in at least four classes of requirements being placed upon them.

Functional Requirements

Software-intensive systems are being deployed in a much wider set of application domains than ever before. Increasingly, computer-based solutions are at the heart of innovative technology approaches in domains as diverse as the aerospace, manufacturing, financial management, and entertainment industries. Each of these industries brings a range of new functional requirements to software developers, frequently pushing the boundaries of capabilities previously offered.

Furthermore, as technologies evolve, whole new domains of business are opening up to take advantage of them. One prime example is the impact that electronic commerce has had on the retail industry. As a result of technology improvements such as the Internet, completely new forms of trade between suppliers and users of retail goods are possible. This has resulted in significant changes to the requirements for many systems being developed for those industries. For example, order management systems must now be concerned with a variety of nontraditional means of order entry, payment, and delivery of retail goods for people making online orders over the Internet, making payment using electronic forms of cash, and allowing real-time tracking of delivery, inquiry, and order amendment.

Nonfunctional Requirements

A software-intensive system that performs the functions it was designed to do is necessary but not sufficient. It must also do so accurately, reliably, predictably, securely, and quickly to support the volume of use expected. These required attributes of a system are often referred to as the system's nonfunctional requirements. As a consequence of the ubiquity and importance attached to the operation of software-intense systems, nonfunctional requirements are becoming ever more important to the systems being developed and deployed.

Many organizations rely heavily on computer-based systems to carry out their daily activities. For such organizations there are costly consequences if those systems are unreliable, unavailable, or unusable. Hence, mission-critical applications are typically specified with stringent requirements for mean time between failures, startup times in the event of problems, number of simultaneous users, transaction throughput, and so on. Meeting these requirements typically results in a great deal of additional complexity in the provisioned solution. Approaches employed include the use of duplicate hardware and software, fault-tolerant designs for exception handling, transaction logging and rollback to enable hot standbys, and various multilevel security schemes. Each of these approaches will add significant complexity to the solution.

Technology Requirements

In recent years there have been many improvements to the technologies available for developing and deploying software-intensive systems. Consider one aspect of this new technology, namely, the platform on which applications are deployed.

The availability of low-priced personal computers has accelerated the requirement for software-intensive systems to target distributed networks of computers as the platform on which they must execute. Whether this results in a central computer running most of the business logic accessed by remote desktop machines, or true peer-to-peer systems of interconnected machines, significant complexity is introduced to the applications to allow them to execute in such an environment. Indeed, as the move to distributed computing accelerates, these requirements become more severe, and may lead to more and more complex solutions.

As an illustration, consider the variety of target execution platform options that may be available to a typical application. One such configuration is illustrated in Figure 1.1. As a result of this architecture, any application designed to execute on it must devise some approach to handling communication among the various pieces, synchronization of the actions performed across the pieces, and graceful degradation in the event of failure of any piece.

Organizational Requirements

The organizations developing and deploying software-intensive systems are themselves distributed across organizational boundaries and, increasingly often, also distributed geographically. For any project distributed in this way the development process for software must cope with, and if possible take advantage of, this situation. Going back to the earliest days of software development projects such as the IBM/360 operating system, Fred Brooks noted that the way the development team is organized could have significant impact on the structure and complexity of the applications being developed [7]. This complexity is only likely to increase given recent moves toward distributed development teams, telecommuting, and offshore development.

External Software

An additional source of complexity imposed on many organizations is the need to make use of significant third-party products and packages as an integral part of any application. The last few years has seen a swift rise in the number of

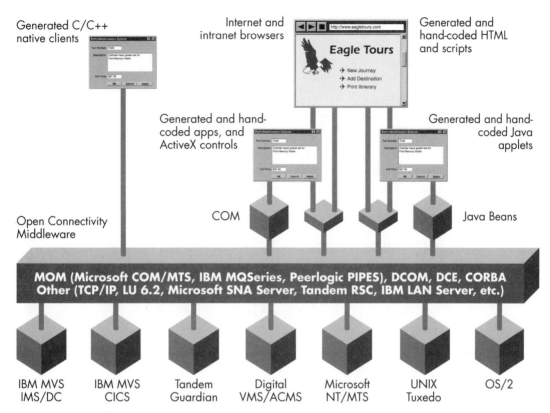

FIGURE 1.1. An example set of target deployment technologies for an application.

organizations deploying third-party developed systems, often driven by expected long-term economic benefits in reduced maintenance costs. However, the majority of organizations also maintain development and maintenance control of some aspects of their mission-critical application systems. As a result, these systems typically must interact with the third-party systems in ways unanticipated by their developers. These requirements can greatly increase the complexity of the applications portfolio as a whole. Unfortunately, lack of accessibility to details of third-party products means that the resulting requirements for integration are all too often a problem to define, difficult to specify, and very time-consuming to implement and maintain.

Adapting to Change

Change is endemic to any large system. Change can bring risks to those unprepared, or open up new avenues of business to those best able to take advantage of the opportunities it brings. Whether an organization manages change in an effective way is a major discriminator among organizations. Those organizations able to anticipate change, predict its likely impact on the way they do business, and implement effective measures to take advantage of it, are likely to be those that flourish. The other organizations will be left to deal with the resultant chaos that ensues when the effects of change leave their well-intentioned plans and approaches rendered inefficient and impractical.

While change is inevitable, recent years have seen increased levels of change driven by a variety of forces. We distinguish three forces of change here: business, technology, and organizational change.

Business Change

As organizations compete in a market economy, those able to provide the best services at the most competitive price are likely to succeed. This requires that an organization understand the business context in which it operates, and enhances that business with the computer systems it uses to support it. As changes occur in the business environment, the computer systems themselves must change to continue to provide appropriate functionality.

Recently, a number of organizations have faced unprecedented changes to their business, driven by at least three significant trends.

First, a number of industries have recently faced changes in government policies and practices resulting in major changes to the business practices in those industries. For example, in both the United States and the European Union the banking, insurance, telecommunications, and electricity supply industries have all dealt with government deregulation at a state or federal level. This deregulation has had a major impact on business practices by introducing new forms of competition, breaking down traditional supply chain monopolies, and providing consumers with greater choice in the kinds of services they can acquire and from whom.

Second, the business community has been faced with an increasing number of acquisitions, mergers, and takeovers of organizations. While each such event results in major changes to the business practices within the organizations involved, there are also frequently changes required by a large number of organizations who partner, trade, supply, or compete with those organizations. This can impact tens if not hundreds of organizations, particularly for some of the larger mergers in the banking, defense electronics, and telecommunications industries. As the merged organizations move forward, there is typically a complete reassessment of the business practices to be enacted, a redefinition of the markets served, and new products and service offerings to be developed, marketed, and supported.

Third, a number of major political and economic events will continue to cause many organizations to review and upgrade their computer systems. The most publicized global event affecting computer systems was the Year 2000 (Y2K) problem that forced many organizations to repair many of their existing systems. To deal with Y2K, many computer systems were examined and suitable changes put in place. This is only one of many events, however, that require computer systems to be upgraded. Events such as the European Monetary Union (EMU), the creation of the North American Free Trade Agreement (NAFTA), and the expansion of the members of the North Atlantic Treaty Organization (NATO) are being faced by specific industries, or in particular regions of the world. Each such event may require significant changes to be made to mission-critical systems in response to changes in taxation, tariffs, currencies, laws of competition, and so on.

Technology Change

Some of the most far-reaching changes being faced by organizations are as a result of significant advances in technology. The rapid pace of change of computer technology is something that many people are aware of, yet for which most are largely unprepared.

Typically, an organization embarking on a large-scale software development or upgrade effort has to make a number of choices concerning how they intend to deal with the technological changes that will undoubtedly occur as the project proceeds. Almost inevitably, technology choices made early in the project life cycle will be made obsolete by technology advances that take place before the results of the project can be deployed. This is particularly evident with the latest wave of Internet-based technologies such as Java, web-browsers, and application servers. In some situations, particularly government-funded projects, one can argue that the typical life of advanced technologies is shorter than the procurement process that is needed to purchase those technologies!

This rapid pace of change is not limited to the computer industry. Many application domains being supported by computer-based systems are themselves undergoing significant technological change. Particular examples of such domains include the telecommunications, manufacturing, and entertainment industries. This leads to a curious tension between the domains in which the software is used, and the software industry itself. On the one hand, as these industries evolve they are forcing major changes to the software systems that form an essential part of their infrastructure. On the other hand, the ability of these industries to make changes is severely constrained by the difficulties of updating the software-intensive systems required to manage and support their day-to-day activities. This dichotomy is at the heart of many of the battles currently taking place in the boardrooms of large corporations across the world.

Organizational Change

Many organizations are facing unprecedented change as they adopt new work practices and management styles encouraged and supported by the changes in business practices in those domains. Many examples of this exist—from the rise of home offices and remote working, to the relocation of call centers to reduce costs and enable around the clock operation. The dynamic, flexible way in which organizations are structured is the cause of significant kinds of change. Such change can indirectly have a major impact on the software-intensive systems being developed, and the techniques that are used for their development, deployment, and maintenance. Three particular sources of organizational change can be identified.

First, modern management tends to emphasize a much more flexible approach to structuring an organization. Many of these approaches introduce sources of change within the organization to allow appropriate teams to form, complete a task, and disperse. Typical of these approaches are techniques that emphasize matrix management, project-based integrated product teams, and "just-in-time" delivery of skills, resources, products, and services. While the dynamic nature of the organizational structure is considered an advantage in allowing projects to quickly engage in a task, it also represents a major challenge to the support technology used by that organization.

Second, the workforce employed over the past few years has needed to be much more mobile and willing to change organizations than ever before. Certainly, the days when someone was employed by one organization throughout his or her working life have all but disappeared. This phenomenon is fueled in part by what Alan Greenspan calls "creative destruction"—many organizations, in the rush to reinvent themselves or seize new opportunities, are in a constant state of rebuilding their staff and skills base. Consequently, it is not unusual for organizations to see significant turnover of staff in a given year. As a result, much of the continuity and knowledge gained by the organization may be lost whenever an employee leaves. This staff turnover is a significant source of change and becomes a major source of instability without careful management.

Third, to improve flexibility in work practices there is a renewed interest across the software industry in greater use of outside contractors and third-party service providers. The market for these services has grown in response to the business and organizational changes previously highlighted. This has led to a host of new companies offering specialized software solutions to vertical industries, focusing on specific technologies, or providing skills in particular development techniques. An example is the set of organizations acting as systems integrators (SIs) to create custom solutions based on commercially available systems and packaged software. This is one of the main ways that organizations are looking to overcome the problems of hiring and retaining skilled staff, and the difficulties of honing those skills over time.

1.4   BUSINESS DRIVERS AND IT STRATEGY

The previous discussion highlights the challenges being faced today by the IT department of any organization responsible for the development, deployment, maintenance, and evolution of software-intensive systems. Their ability to manage complexity and rapidly adapt to change is a major determinant in whether such organizations are able to compete and succeed in the industries in which they operate.

However, it is also useful to consider the challenges as they are perceived by the various business units within an organization. In particular, consider two separate aspects of their perception.

The first is the business context in which they operate and the business objectives that drive their information technology needs. In a Software Productivity Group (SPG) Analyst Services' recent annual market survey of the Fortune 1000 IT community, respondents collectively identified their companies' top five business objectives. These results are summarized in Figure 1.2.

FIGURE 1.2.   The top five IT business drivers (Source: SPG Analyst Services).

Interestingly, the highest priority objectives based on this survey are to improve the quality of the services offered in support of customers' needs, and to do so in as efficient and effective manner as possible. These results are interesting because they indicate that quality and fitness for purpose are by far more important drivers than speed of execution per se. This has important implications for the software-intensive systems supporting these businesses. Based on the discussion earlier, the key considerations in achieving these goals are the ability to:

▶ understand the business domain in which they operate;
▶ produce systems which accurately model some part of that domain;
▶ maintain the integrity of the system as the business domain evolves.

The second aspect of the organizations' perception is how they have translated the business objectives into specific, actionable initiatives that will have an impact on the software-intensive systems used to run their businesses. The same SPG Analyst Services' annual market survey also asked the Fortune 1000 IT community to identify their top five IT initiatives and mandates. The results from those who responded are summarized in Figure 1.3.

The results summarized in Figure 1.3 reveal that exploiting intranet and Internet technologies is the highest priority IT initiative in these organizations. Improving the quality and speed of delivered applications are also considered important. However, this is overshadowed by the need to use new technologies to reduce costs and drive new business opportunities.

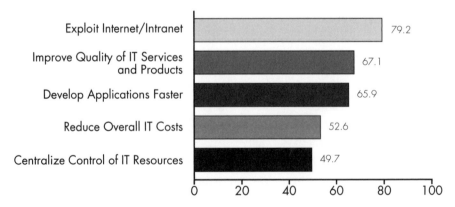

FIGURE 1.3.   The top five IT initiatives and mandates (Source: SPG Analyst Services).

This survey indicates that the need to adapt to technology changes in support of improved customer satisfaction is the preeminent IT strategy today. Use of Internet-based technology is typically expected to improve the availability of desktop services to customers, increase access to corporate information sources, and reduce management effort for delivered services through thin clients and "just in time" delivery of services from the server to the desktop.

Currently, this emphasis is most often seen in two main areas. The first is in analysis, mining, and wrapping of "back-office" data and services. These are often tied up in enterprise resource planning (ERP) systems, or held in an assortment of database files. These data and services represent key corporate assets that must be made available for use with new, web-based systems. The second is in the renewed attention being paid to "front-office" customer-focused solutions. A new generation of call center management and customer relationship management (CRM) systems are being installed to offer improved response and greater personalization of interactions between an organization and its customers.

The greatest challenge facing many organizations, however, is the integration of the results of these two initiatives. This brings the whole supply-chain together, and offers the possibility of major improvements in efficiency and customer service.

1.5   SUMMARY

From its earliest days the software industry has been characterized by rapid and continual change in the domains in which software is applied, and in the underlying technologies they target and use. Coping with these changes has been a struggle for every software engineer and every software-intensive system that has been built. However, in the past few years the speed and depth of these changes has begun to increase. These changes are completely reshaping both the software industry and many of the business communities it serves. Many people believe we have seen the start of a new era of computing—the Internet age.

In this new era, software is a dominant factor in many of the current business initiatives. Software is essential for driving new Internet appliances, managing networks of computers, and supporting the businesses on which we all depend. In this capacity the software industry plays an interesting dual role. Software-led initiatives are a major catalyst for change in many domains, and provide many opportunities for new kinds of commerce or information sharing. Yet at the same time the major inhibitor faced by many organizations as they try to embrace this change is the speed at which the IT infrastructure can evolve. In the face of these changes their systems are often found to be inflexible, brittle, and poorly documented.

The challenge to the current generation of software engineers is to build systems that enable and support the kinds of business initiatives typical of the Internet age. This requires approaches that:

▶ Make the most of previous investments in software or hardware infrastructure;
▶ Exploit new technologies to their full potential;
▶ Drive new business initiatives to provide a competitive advantage in an increasingly crowded marketplace of solutions.

Meeting these needs is the main challenge faced when provisioning enterprise-scale solutions in the Internet age.

THE EVOLUTION OF
APPLICATION DEVELOPMENT

The previous chapter discussed the changing characteristics of application systems. Technology advances lead us to conclude that future software-intensive solutions in almost all domains will be distributed across many sites, access data from multiple sources, and have web-based interfaces [1, 11]. Furthermore, users expect robust, high-performance systems in the face of constant change of underlying technologies, reconfiguration of the system, and the occasional failure of any pieces of the system. These expectations are coupled with the parallel need for reducing overall development and maintenance costs, typically by consuming more third-party software rather than building all software in-house from scratch for each new project. Consequently, traditional approaches to software development and maintenance are under increasing pressure to evolve in ways that provide better support for these kinds of needs.

Unfortunately, even relatively recent innovations such as rapid application development (RAD) and object-oriented analysis and design (OOAD) are falling short of the mark. They have much to offer in support of many kinds of application development, but exhibit a number of limitations when faced with challenges such as modeling externally-developed pieces of a system, facilitating flexibility in the design of system architectures, and encouraging reuse of analysis patterns, design templates, and code fragments.

New approaches are needed to support these requirements—approaches that encourage appropriate ways of thinking about the solutions being provisioned, and which foster a wide range of skills in distributed systems, databases, and web-based technologies.

In this chapter we examine the evolution of application development and the tools required to support it. This establishes a base for subsequent chapters analyzing current and future enterprise-scale application development approaches in general, and component-based technologies in particular.

2.1   INTRODUCTION

The software industry is constantly in a state of change. One area where change is particularly evident is the area of automated tool support for application development. A key message over the past two decades has been that automation has a major impact on productivity and quality in any large-scale software engineering effort [21]. Most systems are now sufficiently complex that automated support for many tasks is essential, from managing the thousands of user requirements to recording which variant of a product was delivered to each customer. As a result, automated tools for designing and provisioning application solutions are essential. In fact, as we face the new challenges of the Internet age, the need for automation only increases.

In response, a new generation of tool support is becoming commercially available. We can identify three major sources of such tools:

► A plethora of small start-up companies have recently appeared, producing a wide variety of tools that aid application developers in many aspects of web-based software development. Frequently, their goal is to offer innovative approaches to improvements in individual developer productivity. However, these tools tend to suffer from typical first-generation software problems: instability, poor support, and concentration on single-user, small application development.

► The vendors of infrastructure technology (operating systems, middleware, databases, messaging systems, browsers) have produced their own tools to facilitate the creation of software-intensive solutions targeting that infrastructure technology. Often, the availability of these tools is a major drawback in the purchasing decision among a set of similar infrastructure offerings. The main limitation of these tools is that they tend to be very closely tied to a particular infrastructure product, and may not allow use of a competitor's product, or a combination of products.

► The established application development tool vendors are evolving their existing product bases to address the problems of falling sales in their established markets, and to embrace the opportunities opened up by the new distributed, web-based applications market. Initially, this involved a repositioning of existing products targeted at new opportunities and markets. But, it has also led to large-scale redesign of many of the current tool capabilities to support the needs of web-based solutions. The main problem with these tools is that they are slow to reach the marketplace. The application development vendors are performing an interesting balancing act between evolving their products quickly to address market needs while maintaining their existing product base and customers.

In this chapter we review the application development world and look at the pressures that are currently being placed upon it. We discuss the source of these pressures, ways in which the pressures might be relieved, and the likely future directions of interest for the application development community.

The focus of our analysis is primarily on the third category above: the challenges facing established application development tool vendors as they attempt to address the distributed, web-based solutions market. At first sight, this community is perhaps in the best starting position of the three categories of tool producers, with an established customer base and marketing channels, experience in tool development, and a large body of development, maintenance, and research staff. However, on closer analysis, the challenges to this community are particularly severe.

Over the past few years established tool vendors have taken a number of steps to adapt their solutions in light of the changing kinds of applications being developed. Most notably these have been with respect to supporting client-server applications and object-oriented techniques and languages. In most cases these changes have been provided as natural evolutions of existing tool functionality. However, this evolutionary approach is facing many challenges as we move to Internet-based solutions. Established application development tool vendors must not only completely revolutionize their tools to support the creation and maintenance of distributed, web-based applications, they must also reengineer their own toolsets to be similarly architected. They must achieve this in conjunction with:

► an existing code base of many millions of lines of code;
► supporting a wide variety of development styles and techniques including structured design, object-oriented analysis and design, and rapid application development;
► running on a variety of platforms that range from MVS to many flavors of Unix;

▶ using established methods and consultative business based on 1980s-style structured methods producing traditional mainframe and client-server applications.

2.2   EVOLUTION OF APPLICATION DEVELOPMENT SUPPORT

Given the changing technological infrastructure available to software developers, it is not surprising that application development support has been required to evolve substantially to generate applications that are able to take advantage of these changes. Here, we illustrate the evolution of application development tools as they try to keep up-to-date with application developers' needs. We do this by contrasting application support tool support of the past (in the early 1990s) with a new generation application support tool support (in the late 1990s), and speculating on the support that will be needed in the future (post year 2000).

Past—Client/Server Applications

Enterprise-level application development in the early 1990s was characterized by a move away from monolithic, single-machine applications toward client-server computing. In most cases this meant using the graphical capabilities of a user's desktop personal computer (PC) to provide remote access to an application across a local area network. Typically, the desktop client programs provided local display processing and command interpretation, while the central server program performed the compute-intensive activities, maintained shared databases, and so on. This has sometimes been called the "thin client, fat server" model of computing [13].

However, over a short period of time the rapid improvement in performance and reduced cost of PCs began to change the kinds of processing that were performed on the client versus the server. The client PCs could now be used for operations such as query optimization, and could be customized to perform user-specific data visualization and analysis. This approach resulted in more of a "fat client" architecture, now typical of most client/server solutions. This migration of functionality from server to client, together with increasingly more reliable, high bandwidth networks, led to software architectures that provided a great deal of flexibility over what functionality was performed on which machine. This architecture is illustrated in Figure 2.1.

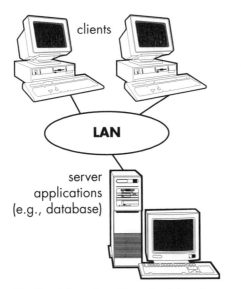

Typical Tool Functions

- Generate database schema
- User interface design
- Database optimization
- Data distribution and replication

Typical Application Architecture

FIGURE 2.1.   Past application architectures and application support tool functions.

Tool support for client/server architectures typically revolved around the generation and maintenance of the database on the server side, and a series of user interfaces to access and update that database on the client side. Some application support tools also provided support for database optimizations, interoperation between databases from different vendors, and synchronization of replicated data sources.

Present—N-Tier Distributed Systems

By the mid 1990s the advent of the Internet and the World Wide Web had placed a number of stresses on traditional client/server solutions. These had an important impact on both the client and server aspects of these architectures.

In terms of the client aspects of a system, the use of the Internet as a deployment infrastructure resulted in two major inefficiencies with client-side technologies. In the first, the use of the Internet as a public infrastructure for communication between client and server led to a number of concerns with respect to performance and reliability. The "fat client" architecture typical of most client/server applications was found to be inappropriate for many kinds of Internet-based solutions. Second, the growing variety in client technologies raised another concern with respect to installation and upgrade of the client software. A more cost-effective means for supporting many clients was required. This became a more important issue with the growing popularity of the Internet, and the availability of non-traditional client devices such as network computers, Internet appliances, and handheld devices.

As a result, application developers demanded two major changes to the way in which client aspects of current applications were developed:

- ▶ Use of web browser-style interfaces to data retrieval and update. As a consequence of the popularity of the web, browser interfaces became a familiar and comfortable metaphor for accessing all types of data. This provides a common look and feel for all applications.
- ▶ Commonality of interfaces across heterogeneous client platforms. Organizations have a large investment in a variety of desktop machines and other client devices running different operating systems and support software. Applications need to execute on any of these without requiring custom changes for each client target.

On the server side of a distributed application there were also pressures forcing changes in traditional client/server approaches. The business logic supporting many back-office functions is encoded in a variety of legacy systems, purchased packages, and custom developed software. Throughout the 1980s, as the diversity of these solutions continued, it became more difficult to manage and evolve enterprise solutions involving collections of these systems. The notion of a single layer of server functionality was found to be unrealistic and unworkable. More typically, multiple layers of server functionality were supported. Architectures of systems needed to recognize and support the design, implementation, deployment, and management of these multitiered solutions.

In particular, an important division was defined between the client-focused processing necessary to support the new thin client parts of an application, and the back-office-focused processing capturing the business rules of the application. The client-focused processing is typically managed within a web server, while the back-office-focused processing is handled by an application server.

To support these kinds of n-tiered architectures, application development tool vendors extended their products to combine the enterprise-level services of client/server architectures, with the platform independence and commonality of interfaces provided by a web server. An example of such an approach, adapted from [15], is illustrated in Figure 2.2.

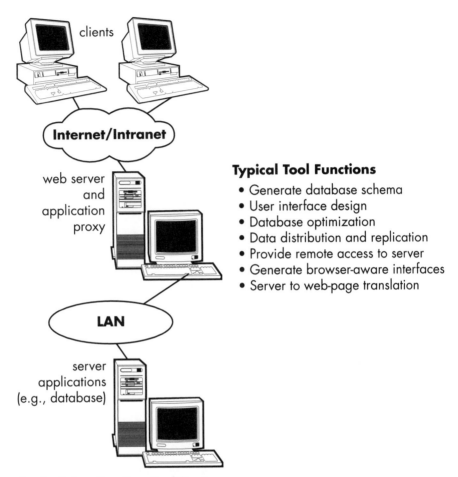

Typical Tool Functions

- Generate database schema
- User interface design
- Database optimization
- Data distribution and replication
- Provide remote access to server
- Generate browser-aware interfaces
- Server to web-page translation

Typical Application Architecture

FIGURE 2.2.   Current application architectures and application support tool functions.

In the example illustrated in Figure 2.2, an application end user views an application as a series of interconnected web pages from a browser on any machine connected to the Internet/intranet. The user interacts with the web browser by selecting links or by entering information into fields on a web-based form. This information is transmitted across the Internet to the web server which recognizes requests for external data and passes the request to an application proxy on the web server whose task is to map data requests to application queries on the server. The application server services the request, and the proxy converts the returned information into a web page that it passes to the web server for display to the end user.

In this example, the application support tool is now responsible for providing the proxy application server that maps between web-based requests and application services, and vice-versa. Typically, the application support tool provides a set of templates for this which the application developer can then use to create user dialog screens in HyperText Markup Language (HTML) or Java.

The result of this approach is more than just an application that can be accessed from a browser anywhere on the Internet (security restrictions permitting). Additionally, high-performance local clients can still be developed using the client/server approach illustrated in Figure 2.1.

Future—Nomadic, Service-Oriented Solutions

Although many changes in software technology have been seen over the past few years, many believe that we are only in the early stages of a period of explosive change as computer-based technologies are combined with low cost, highly-available broadband communications technology. Major changes in software development tools and techniques will be needed to support and keep pace with these changes. Looking to the future, there are many interesting directions for the architectures of applications. Three directions are of particular note:

▶ The need for faster time-to-market solutions is having an enormous impact on the kinds of systems being developed. Many organizations believe that the only way these solutions can be produced at the required rate is by reusing existing functionality. As a result, there is a growing emphasis on assembly and integration techniques for tying together legacy systems, packages, and newly developed systems.

▶ Advances in telecommunications systems and broadband networks are creating many new possibilities for distributed applications. Internet appliances and handheld devices are significantly altering perceptions of how information systems deliver information and allow access to services. With reduced memory and screen size devices frequently disconnected from the network, it is difficult to see how common approaches of delivering web-based applications through screen-scraping and emphasis on web-browser technology can be applied. New approaches are needed.

▶ New kinds of solutions and businesses are changing the face of many aspects of our society. As the "bricks-and-mortar" companies look to add web-based interfaces to their services to offer their goods online, completely new ways of doing business and delivering services have arrived. These typically involve innovative approaches to collating disparate services, personalizing interaction with existing systems, or supplying information in more timely, actionable ways. This often requires sophisticated brokering and intelligent information management using agent-based techniques.

As a result of these changes, many new tools and techniques for software development will be required. One key aspect of this are those organizations that would like to move toward greater reuse of the results of previous development efforts, leading to application development primarily through assembly of existing services to support new business processes. Achieving this requires a number of changes both in the way applications are developed and in the resultant architecture of developed applications.

Applications must be developed as independent sets of interacting services offering well-defined interfaces to their potential users. Similarly, supporting technology must be available to allow application developers to browse collections of services, select those of interest, and assemble them to create the desired functionality. Such an approach is illustrated in Figure 2.3.

The illustration in Figure 2.3 shows a supply of reusable components available to the application developer. These may be drawn from local sources such as previous development projects, acquired externally by browsing the Internet, or purchased from a third-party supplier. In any case, having gathered the components, an application support tool must provide support for browsing, querying, and assembling the components within the context of the current application.

Note that the architecture of the applications may be significantly more complex than the simple client/server model of the late 1980s. In particular, as shown in Figure 2.3, is an example in which a service provider is accessible somewhere across the Internet. In this example, the application makes use of external components from that service provider, perhaps on a fee-for-service basis. Such approaches to distributed systems may become common as a marketplace for distributed components is established.

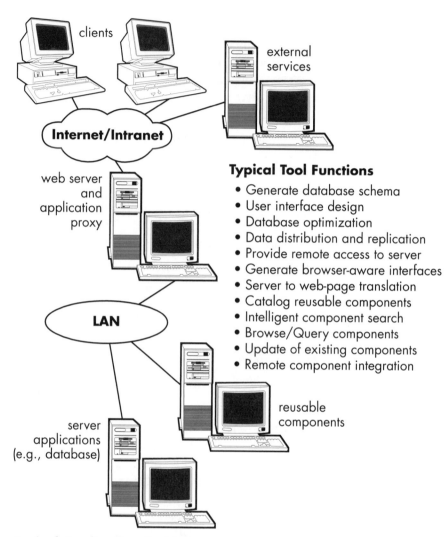

Typical Tool Functions

- Generate database schema
- User interface design
- Database optimization
- Data distribution and replication
- Provide remote access to server
- Generate browser-aware interfaces
- Server to web-page translation
- Catalog reusable components
- Intelligent component search
- Browse/Query components
- Update of existing components
- Remote component integration

Typical Application Architecture

FIGURE 2.3.   Future application architectures and application support tool functions.

2.3   KEY ISSUES FOR FUTURE APPLICATION DEVELOPMENT

In summary, future enterprise-scale applications will exhibit a number of key characteristics. These applications will typically be distributed over many sites, access commercial database management systems (both relational and object-oriented), interact with legacy applications and data, and be web-enabled to allow a browser interface for display and query on heterogeneous machines across the Internet. This seems to be true whatever the application domain, whether the system is a real-time command and control system, an enterprise management system, or a material tracking system.

These characteristics pose some important challenges for architects, designers, and implementers of these systems. Most notably, developing these systems requires decisions to be made in a wide area of technologies. Among the questions to be addressed are the following:

► Which architectural possibilities exist for a distributed system, and what are their advantages and disadvantages?

► What should the architecture of my solution look like, given the specific requirements of my domain, expected throughput, planned number of simultaneous users, etc.?

► How do I create a flexible architecture for my system to allow it to be easily updated as the system's use evolves?

► What is a good method of designing my system? Should I use an object-oriented analysis method? A structured method? Do these work for developing web-based distributed applications?

► How can I make use of the existing data and applications I have around? Can I reuse them? How do I wrap them?

► I've heard that all the functionality I need is available either somewhere on the Internet, or as commercial packages. How do I find them, evaluate them, integrate them, and test them as part of my system?

► What support tools and technologies are around to help me? Are there good toolkits? Good libraries of design templates? Useful examples?

Developers of application support tools and technologies must provide solutions that directly address these questions. These solutions must be well-crafted and provide a reasonable return on investment for a software purchasing community that is increasingly becoming used to buying and installing low-cost, shrink-wrapped software over the Internet, or from their local computer superstore.

These questions raise many issues to be addressed by future application support tools. There appears to be three key aspects of future software applications that application support tools must directly address to be successful: explicit representation of the architecture of large-scale distributed systems, modeling of reusable pieces of system functionality, and improved methods appropriate for the development and maintenance of this new generation of applications.

Representing Large-Scale Distributed Software Architectures

As a consequence of recent advances in network technology and distributed infrastructures, future applications will more frequently be constructed from collections of discrete functionality distributed across a range of machines. For application developers, this can bring about a number of new problems. In particular, application development tools supporting future enterprise solutions must address the challenge of simplifying the task of designing, managing, and evolving appropriate architectures for large-scale distributed systems.

Making things more concrete for a large-scale distributed system, an application developer typically has to make decisions at three levels of abstraction [16]:

▶ At the most abstract level, often called the architecture level, the developer must decide on the basic "shape" of the solution. That is, the architectural style of a solution that determines the primary characteristics of the application's non-functional properties [2]. While Garlan and Shaw analyze these styles based on their inherent qualities, pragmatic factors seem to play a preeminent role in a developer choosing among them. Typically, the fact that the developer has previously built a similar system dictates that the new system will have a similar style, or will differ in response to that experience. The resulting architecture must be examined with respect to the required functional (i.e., what the system must do) and non-functional (e.g., fault-tolerance, usability, portability, performance) attributes, as dictated by the specific application domain, the users' needs, and what the users are willing to pay to get them. A number of analysis techniques aimed at assessing the qualities of the architecture of a distributed system have been developed based on these ideas. Most notable among them is the System Architecture Analysis Method (SAAM). This attempts to assess a system architecture in response to the qualities of known architectural styles [22].

► At a services level, the developer has to consider the interfaces among the major architectural pieces and how they will interact. There are at least two different perspectives in this kind of analysis. One focuses on the logical architecture of the solution. From this perspective, the system consists of abstract services made available through interfaces. For each such service one must consider the operation through which that service is made accessible, their signatures, and their abstract behavior. From a different perspective, these services are collaborating agents working together to provide some required behavior. From this perspective, the major concern is with the coordination, or structure, of the way in which those services interact. For example, it may be determined that two components of the architecture (regardless of their function) must synchronize in a particular way, communicate results via certain channels, or allow access to intermediate results through a shared persistent data area (i.e., blackboard). Also dealt with at this level are issues such as replication of service, tolerance to certain faults, and unavailability of data.

► At a mechanism level, the implementation, deployment, and runtime management aspects of a distributed system are considered. Ultimately, the developer really does have to choose specific products, languages, platforms, etc., and make the system work. In making these choices there are many considerations with respect to performance, reliability, ease of use, available skills, and vendor stability. Even then the choices are numerous. For example, having chosen, say, to use a particular vendor's middleware, database, web-browser, etc., the simple question of "where do I start?" is far from straightforward. Each of these products claim some sort of integration with some subset of the others. Yet each does so on its own terms—"I integrate with ABC as long as I am in charge, you don't use features XYZ, and you compile in exactly this order!" As a result, many complex product integration issues must be assessed and overcome.

One of the most intriguing and challenging problems is that the designer of a large-scale distributed system must think at these three levels *at the same time*. Each level directly influences and shapes the others. For example, choosing to use an infrastructure product such as a particular implementation of the Common Object Request Broker Architecture (CORBA) has a significant impact on the services to be designed and how they interact. While software is sufficiently malleable so that you can do almost anything with any product, the products make some things so difficult that the system designed is just too brittle, too hard to build, or too complex to maintain.

The topic of software architecture is currently a major research area, with many technologies being developed including architectural description languages (ADLs), collections of specific styles and their inherent properties, and analysis techniques for determining appropriate architectures given a set of specific domain needs [12]. Much of this work is still in the research and prototyping stage. However, there is the promise that these ideas will be supportable by application support tools in the very near future [4].

Modeling Reusable Pieces of a System

For more than a decade the dream of software engineering managers has been to have "software factories" where standard components are selected from a catalog, assembled with some value-added local pieces or customizations, and sold to a willing public. In the 1980s this vision was pursued by considering relatively broad application domains, gathering components (or more generally "assets"), and waiting for a flood of customers to make use of them [4, 5]. It didn't work. The majority of "reuse initiatives" did not succeed, and in hindsight it was for all of the obvious reasons: cataloging was hard, the assets were diverse and of varying quality, the interfaces and behavior of assets were poorly defined, and the culture of reuse was undervalued and insufficiently rewarded by organizations.

The mid-1990s saw a massive revival of reuse initiatives under the banner of "component-based development" [10]. There appear to be two separate stimuli to this. First, the economic push of moving toward greater use of commercial off-the-shelf (COTS) products. Particularly in federal and local government, the use of COTS products is seen as a way to reduce costs, speed up technology refreshment, and improve interoperability of solutions [6]. Second, the popularity of the World Wide Web and easy-to-use browsers lead to the belief that "if you want it, it will be somewhere on the net!" Indeed, a great deal of free software is available over the Internet, in many programming languages, and in every application domain.

Of course, responding to these stimuli presents major challenges. Composing a system from COTS products often requires a great deal of specialized integration code, and in many examples has led to systems that are brittle, impossible to upgrade, and therefore very expensive [23]. Similarly, obtaining software from the Internet can be a hit-and-miss affair. There is some very good software available at low cost, but after a lot of effort to find, download, and evaluate, most of it is found to be inappropriate, incomplete, or unsupported.

But all is not lost. There are some reasons why the current generation of reuse-oriented approaches may be more effective than earlier attempts. These reasons include:

▶ Object-oriented languages have a better structure for facilitating CBD than traditional 3GLs. C++, Eiffel, and (to a lesser extent) Ada95 are in the best position to have an impact. These OO languages have a foothold in the mainstream software development community, with increasing numbers of libraries of classes available.

▶ Into this we must also factor in Java. Its OO structure makes it ideal for creating Java component libraries, and building Java applets and applications from them. Java has the added advantage that Java byte code is portable and contains sufficient information for interface and inheritance details to be determined from a Java component even when the component's source is not available. Standards concerning the structure of Java applets, such as JavaBeans, further increase the ease with which Java components can be interchanged and assembled.

▶ Domain-specific libraries and frameworks are starting to appear. Concentrating on domain-specific component libraries means that a number of assumptions can be made about the likely architectures of applications in the domain and the ways in which components usually interact. This will make the cataloging and composition of components much easier to manage. It may also mean that the integration code can be predefined to some extent to include some intelligence about its tasks. Examples of recent framework-based initiatives include IBM's San Francisco Framework [24] and Microsoft's Digital InterNet Architecture (DNA) initiative [25].

▶ The current reuse-oriented initiatives are being vendor-led and supported. This inevitably means some of what is produced is hype and market positioning. However, this also means that robust technology support, an established market and distribution channels, and near-term orientation will provide usable tools in a reasonable timeframe. These will underwhelm the research community, but are likely to provide some measure of simple, effective tools and techniques for developers writing applications. Reuse-oriented strategies and tools have already been announced by companies such as Sterling Software, PowerSoft, Centura, and NeuronData.

▶ The web infrastructure is maturing. While there is a great deal of chaos and competing technology, there is also some basic shape to the infrastructure that allows collections of independently-developed software applications to be searched and remotely invoked, and for users of the web to communicate and share data. There is at least a hope that the technologies will converge, or at least interoperate fairly well, so that selecting among them will be based on price and performance rather than which integration strategy you want to be tied to.

► There finally appears to be some real interest and research from the academic community that is leading toward a deeper understanding of component interfaces, component integration, and the ways to detect, avoid, and repair mismatches among components. Papers by Garlan [2], Wallnau and colleagues [8], and Kaiser [9] are good examples.

For established application development tool vendors, the move to reuse-oriented approaches will be an evolution from their current strategy and tool base. This is far from straightforward, and will probably proceed in an iterative fashion. For example, a first step may consist of simply trying to "componentize" existing applications generated using the application support tool by reengineering them to conform to a set of "component integration guidelines." This may simply be a set of naming conventions, specific required annotations on design elements, and so on. However, this will be sufficient to allow users of the application support tool to share and exchange application designs. Additionally, this will allow users to develop new discrete pieces of applications that can be cataloged and reused (although purely within the context of that specific application support tool).

The second step may be to take one of the major competitor's applications and allow it to be imported into that application support tool by automatically converting it to conform to the integration guidelines, then add another competitor's application, and try to make the guidelines and the solution more general. The result of this evolution will be a set of translation filters for the component integration guidelines that will have been proven to work with a reasonable set of applications, and experience with the processes that are carried out when developers follow a component assembly approach involving a "select and integrate" rather than a "design and build" philosophy.

Improved Method Support for New Kinds of Applications

Structured methods as defined today are rarely used in any consistent, concerted way by the majority of software developers. Studies have found that such methods use abstractions that don't relate to the designers' perceptions of the system. Furthermore, they are frequently found to be too inflexible with respect to changing the design, require too much effort to maintain once coding begins (so, consequently, are not maintained), and do not tell maintainers of the system what they need to know to evolve the applications.

Unfortunately, these problems are becoming more acute with rapid changes to the technology used for software development and the need to assemble large-scale distributed systems with significant reuse at every stage of development. The challenge for method definers is to more closely couple the methods to a development approach that:

► encourages and supports reuse of existing artifacts as the primary approach to building an application. Hence, the component interfaces, interactions, and dependencies are the focus for the method.
► is more closely aligned to what designers really do when they design: a continuous cycle of "conjecture, explore, evaluate" based on experiential knowledge of what has worked before. (This cycle concludes when the money runs out, the deadline is reached, or the requirements are sufficiently scaled-back to claim you are done—whichever comes first!)
► documents what maintainers really need to know: how to design rational and decision points rather than graphical representations of call graphs and inheritance trees (which can more accurately be generated from the code).

These challenges are beginning to be addressed. There is a growing recognition of the need for pragmatism in the way in which application solutions are produced for web-based infrastructures [26, 27]. It is encouraging to see some recent technology advances that directly address each of these challenges.

Addressing the first challenge, the Unified Modeling Language (UML) is proving to be an interesting focus for creating a notation that can accommodate the modeling of components and interfaces as first class objects [17]. As the UML develops, it is likely that there will be even greater pressure for it to become the standard for component modeling, responding to the influential voices of contributors to UML such as Sterling Software and ICON Computing.

Addressing the second challenge, a new wave of development methods is being defined centered upon the notions of component-based development, modeling component interconnections, and reusing patterns of component collaboration. Methods such as Catalysis [18] and Synopsis [19] exemplify these new approaches.

Addressing the third challenge many developments in multimedia and hypermedia can now produce tools which weave documentation, code, audio, and video artifacts to create a complete picture of a product's design and manufacture. Some of these features are now available in most software development tools. The n-dim system at Carnegie Mellon University is an innovative research example of a system modeling and design environment that captures many aspects of the design process for later analysis and review [20].[1]

However, in addition to these challenges, any practical reuse-oriented method must exhibit another important set of characteristics essential to their success. These are based on lessons from the design, application, and use of application development tools over the past decade. From this experience, a number of key practical aspects of the methods and their support tools are essential to their adoption and success. It would seem that any such method and its associated tools must support at least the following:

► *Multiple entry points.* The method must support the full life cycle from software design, construction, testing, and so on. It must also support organizations starting an application development from scratch in a traditional development, those involved in a series of rapid application developments, and those wishing to update a large existing system.

► *Scalability to different size tasks.* There is a wide variety of possible usage scenarios for reuse-oriented development, ranging from small-scale reuse of class libraries, to large-scale mission-critical solutions provisioned from commercial off-the-shelf (COTS) packages. Applying the method for either of these extremes (and at points in between) must be possible.

► *Documentation of engineering decisions and trade-offs.* Any approach based on reusing existing artifacts is based on selection, integration, and evolution of available components. The method must therefore support the documentation and analysis of the engineering decisions that form the heart of such an approach.

► *Specification and analysis of component interfaces.* Understanding and controlling the interfaces among components is key to component integration. Rather than simply allowing interface signatures (i.e., input and output parameters) to be defined, a reuse-oriented method must allow modeling of component interfaces to include modeling of behavior. Some formal language may be required to allow reasoning about the behavior and about compatibilities among different component behaviors.

Viewed from a high level, a method satisfying these needs would involve at least the activities illustrated in Figure 2.4.

---

[1] These advances, and many others, will be discussed in detail in later chapters of this book.

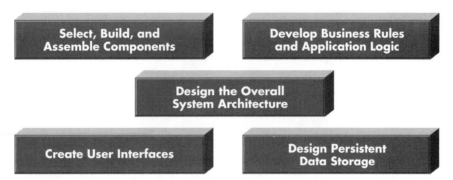

FIGURE 2.4.   Activities in a reuse-oriented method.

The activities in Figure 2.4 could be carried out in any order. In fact, for a reuse-oriented method the user may engage in all of these activities simultaneously throughout the project. The key to such a method (and any tools supporting such a method) is the support it provides for managing this concurrent design, the decisions that are made, and the impact of a decision made in one activity on the other activities.

Another key idea from Figure 2.4 is that business rules and logic are separate entities that should be managed and maintained in their own right. While the expert systems initiatives of the 1970s and 1980s may have been greatly oversold, their basic notion of separately managing business logic as a key corporate resource is very valuable. This is a concept that has been heavily used in the technologies of the 1990s, providing improved flexibility to the systems that have been developed.

A final comment on Figure 2.4 relates to the central role played by the system architecture. As illustrated in this figure, the system architecture forms the backbone of any application. The choices made in defining this architecture dictate to a large extent many of the system's properties (e.g., performance, fault-tolerance, and modifiability). If this architecture is poorly chosen, inadequately documented, or unstable, then the resulting application will likely be poorly suited to its task, and difficult to maintain and evolve. Many research efforts over the past few years have concentrated on improving our understanding of architectural design and analysis methods, and providing heuristics that can lead to improved system design.

Any application support tool for reuse-oriented methods must provide explicit support for these features. However, the situation is more complex because it is unlikely that a single method will be appropriate for all situations. It may well be that there are at least three different kinds of such methods:

► Single language, reuse-oriented methods that involve building relatively small applications from component libraries that reside locally or that you purchase off the shelf. Examples are C++ widget libraries and Java applet libraries.

► Multilanguage, reuse-oriented methods that involve building medium-sized applications from components written in multiple languages. The sources to the components are probably available, and there is likely some documentation or local expertise on what the components do.

► Large-scale, reuse-oriented methods based on integrating a variety of locally developed components, external components, legacy systems, and large COTS applications. The issues here involve the scale of the applications, how to understand and interface to components for which only executable code exists, and how to wrap and adapt legacy components to mask unwanted or untrusted behavior.

Of course, it is in this final area that many of the complexities of enterprise-scale solutions are encountered. Not only are the demands of the target application domain more difficult to comprehend and address, the range of technologies required to provide a solution are themselves more complex to master and apply. This occurs within the difficulties inherent to managing any large-scale engineering effort involving large numbers of people with a diverse set of skills, goals, and objectives.

Pragmatic Concerns for Established Application Development Tool Vendors

In discussing enterprise application solutions, it is clear that the established vendors of application development tools have an important role in the success or failure of many development projects. Their tools, technologies, and approaches have a major influence on the development practices in use. Decisions within any enterprise development project are greatly influenced by the technologies they choose to support. Consequently, an important dimension of the discussion on the evolution of application development must be the pragmatic concerns being faced by these vendors.

In addition to the three primary technical areas of concern for future application support tools discussed earlier, there are some particular challenges facing established application development tool vendors as they seek to improve their product offerings. These are essentially pragmatic issues that inhibit an established application development tool vendor from competing in a new market. A few of them are highlighted here.

Competing with the Small Tool Companies

There seems to be an endless stream of small (2 to 10 person) companies that can quickly produce new application support tools for the latest languages, technologies, and development methods. These companies provide an essential source of new ideas, and innovation. In contrast, the life cycle for an established application development tool vendor from concept to product is traditionally much longer—measured in years and in millions of dollars. At first sight, competing in such a market seems impossible.

Of course, what the established companies trade on is their reputation, the marketing and support infrastructures they have in place, and the "software engineering" aspects of the tools they develop—support for multiple users, versioning, and so on. Unfortunately, this important separation between the tools is diminishing as the technology changes. In particular, on the surface it seems that the whole premise of reuse-oriented methods and the move toward components is to eliminate that separation completely!

Defining appropriate marketing strategies for tools is a major challenge. This is illustrated by the current approach in many organizations where some pieces of the tools cost many thousands of dollars, smaller versions of those tools (which consist of the main product with some features switched off!) cost only hundreds, and other add-ons are given away free. Simply deciding which part of the tools to sell, which to give away, and in which markets to compete is becoming even more difficult.

There is also an interesting change in development, testing, and release policy that is taking place. Organizations such as Netscape and Microsoft are under such pressure to release new versions of their tools that they reduce their beta testing and field testing to a minimum. Their policy of "release now, fix later" may infuriate some users, but it allows them to continually add new functionality to their tools (even at the cost of robustness). Releasing a tool as soon as possible in a narrow window of opportunity is paramount. For established application development tool vendors, commitment to quality may be a drawback in obtaining initial market sales!

Dealing with Legacy Platforms and Code

In developing new tools, having an established user base is both an asset and a hindrance. While the user base provides a ready market for new products, it also brings obligations with respect to supporting existing methods, platforms, deployment architectures, and so on. The organization may wish to invest heavily in developing new tools that support component-based approaches, new implementation languages, and web-based input and display. However, the established application development tool vendor has an obligation to make bug fixes to existing products running on MVS, OS/2, and a myriad of Unix operating systems.

The result is that established application development tool vendors cannot commit as much resources to developing new products as they would like. Furthermore, any new products must provide a migration path for existing customers. Not doing so severely dents the reputation of the organization in the eyes of existing customers. This dichotomy—providing functions aimed at new platforms and techniques while supporting existing users and their needs—is at the heart of many challenges facing established application tool vendors today. The compromises made to address these challenges may be deciding factors in the organizations' long-term success or failure.

Taking on a New Mindset

In any walk of life there is always a tendency to stick with what you know. Moving away from familiar surroundings is difficult. This form of "separation anxiety" is particularly true in the software industry. For established application development tool vendors there is a vast corporate knowledge of how to build, maintain, apply, and consult using the existing tools and techniques. Changing that involves a massive reeducation of the workforce.

This problem is amplified if the organization is trying to move into new markets. For example, moving from the enterprise-scale application support tool market to the individual application development market requires a completely different approach to how designers work, how the tool is marketed, and what is important to long-term revenue. A significant amount of reeducation is required to overcome these problems.

For established application tool vendors there are two different levels of concern with changing practices. The first is that the vendor's organization itself must change. The people, processes, and business practices must evolve in line with the software industry directions. These changes can be difficult to execute, as the application tool vendors must compete for skilled resources from an inadequate pool of available talent.

At a second level, the organizations making use of the tools are also evolving both their business and IT practices. This presents a number of problems for established application tool vendors. In particular, these vendors must attempt to support those organizations as they evolve, walking a fine line between offering tools and services that are ahead of their customers needs, versus moving more slowly and being viewed as out-of-date or irrelevant.

2.4   SUMMARY

This chapter has examined the future profile of application developers' needs and the changing technology base that will be used to develop and maintain the resultant applications. It has described the kinds of applications that will be developed in the future, and the implications for established tools and tool vendors. The response to these challenges will be a major determining factor in the future success of established application development tool vendors.

While the rapidly evolving technology of the Internet age poses many threats, there are also many opportunities for established application development tool vendors. Such vendors have an excellent base of tools, knowledge and skills, distribution and marketing channels for future products, and an existing user base that can be an important provider of requirements and new ideas for future products.

There are also significant unanswered challenges to be addressed. In particular, established application development tool vendors must address the challenges of:

▶ understanding the distributed systems design life cycle, the skills required to build large-scale distributed systems, and the requirements for subsequent tool support;
▶ investigating how reuse-oriented methods based on components can be realized in practice through appropriate methods and tools;
▶ analyzing and comparing existing methods and tools, both as a showcase of technology for the software engineering community and as a basis for determining competitive advantage for future application support tool offerings.

As the application development tool industry continues to consolidate, each of these challenges must be addressed to create a more mature, robust marketplace for the rapid creation of high quality, large-scale, distributed applications.

With this background, we now look more specifically at the business practices and technology needs of the Internet age. We look at the business needs driving organizations in the use of IT services, and provide a more detailed analysis of the kinds of software architectures being planned and implemented to support these needs.

T   H   R   E   E

ENTERPRISE-SCALE SOLUTIONS IN THE INTERNET AGE

The previous chapter highlighted the changing role of application development. The last vestiges of the old Computer-Aided Software Engineering (CASE) days of the 1980s have all but disappeared. Yet, in the Internet age organizations delivering large-scale software solutions for the enterprise still require powerful tools that enable them to manage costs, be productive, reduce time-to-market, and enable maintenance and evolution of those solutions over extended periods of time.

The increasing heterogeneity, complexity, and distributed nature of deployment architectures only serves to compound the problems faced by today's software solutions providers. One of the major driving forces for these changes over the past decade has been the massive adoption of the Internet as a deployment target for many systems. From its origins as a means to share documents and perform collaborative research in academia, the Internet (and its related technologies of intranets and extranets[1]) has become a primary target for highly-interactive systems of all kinds, supporting commercial transactions, information gathering and dissemination, and many forms of education and entertainment.

Today it is clear that the Internet is having a major impact on the way business is conducted. Many new business opportunities are being created. A

---

[1] For ease of discussion, we shall refer to all of these technologies simply as "the Web."

recently published U.S. government report, *The Economic and Social Impact of Electronic Commerce,* estimates business-to-business electronic commerce will grow to more than $1 trillion within three to five years. Additionally, existing business are being transformed. Economic efficiencies of electronic commerce are resulting in lower cost distribution, tighter inventory control, increased productivity, and improved customer service.

Supporting these changes is a wide collection of web-based technologies, spawning a revolution in the way in which systems are designed, deployed, and evolved. Many organizations see the need to take advantage of the Web using these technologies. Fewer of those organizations have the knowledge, technology, or skills necessary to do so. Arguably, this mismatch between the needs of organizations and their ability to execute those needs represents the greatest challenge to organizations since the dawn of the computer age more than 30 years ago. Those that have succeeded have been rewarded with more efficient services meeting the needs of a growing customer base, the flexibility to support the move into new markets, and inflated stock evaluations based on their future potential to dominate their chosen domains. Those that have not embraced this technology have at best been sidelined as niche players, or at worst have failed to survive at all.

The challenges faced by organizations assembling software-intensive solutions also provide the greatest opportunity for enterprise application solution vendors. Recognizing the strategic importance of these new technologies to their businesses, many organizations have raised the importance and stature of their IT departments to levels not seen in the past 20 years. Organizations understand that their ability to compete is substantially limited by their IT department's ability to execute using web-based technologies. Consequently, IT managers are frequently well positioned within the organization to have a voice in strategic decision making, and to obtain funding and support for new ventures. However, with this visibility comes responsibility, and IT managers require partners to help them to succeed. They are looking for an enterprise solution vendor with the following qualities:

- ► A knowledge and understanding to help them navigate the uncharted waters of web technologies;
- ► The tools to help them be productive and efficient;
- ► Educational and consulting services to enable their organization to be effective;
- ► Experience with building business mission-critical solutions.

In this chapter we provide an overview of the evolution of enterprise application solutions and the technology that supports them. It provides a basis for understanding enterprise-scale solutions in the Internet age.

3.1   INTRODUCTION

Organizations face many pressures as they seek to improve the services they deliver to their markets. By far the most compelling motivation for many organizations is the need to participate in the e-business revolution.

The e-Business Revolution

Much has been written about the current changes taking place in the business practices of many organizations as a result of the e-business revolution [1, 2]. Taken in its broadest sense, e-business is the transformation of key business processes through the use of Internet technologies. The hype around this transformation is so extreme that it is essential to ask the question, "Is the Internet really revolutionizing the business world?"

The answer is an emphatic *"yes!"* Organizations recognizing the impact of e-business are reaping astonishing rewards. Those left behind are in great danger of becoming niche players in an expanding market. What makes the Internet so important is that it enables new kinds of business to be conducted and completely readjusts many of the key market drivers. At least seven key trends are enabled as a result of these technologies [3]:

▶ The Internet is forcing companies to rethink strategic models and business models. The extended enterprise concept of electronically networking customers and suppliers is now a reality.

▶ New channels are changing market access and branding and causing disintermediation of traditional sales, information, and supply chain channels. For example, since companies can now build real time, intimate relationships with their customers, they are often cutting out the "middlemen" while improving service and reducing costs.

▶ The balance of power is shifting toward the customer. With the unlimited access to information afforded by the Internet, customers are much more demanding than their "non-wired" predecessors. True customer loyalty is harder to build, and cannot be relied upon.

▶ The face of competition is fundamentally changing. Not only are new competitors emerging, but traditional competitors are exploiting the Internet to become much more innovative and efficient.

► The pace of business change is increasing to "Internet speed." Planning horizons, information needs, and the expectations of customers and suppliers are now reflecting this new schedule.

► The Internet is pushing enterprises past their traditional boundaries. The new technologies have redefined relationships between customers and suppliers, and are challenging the existing internal boundaries between processes, functions, and business units.

► Knowledge is becoming a key asset and source of competitive advantage. Increased information about customers and their buying patterns is being used to great effect. We are becoming a knowledge-based economy.

All of these trends lead many organizations to believe that e-business represents the greatest opportunity (and greatest threat) that they now face. Responding to these challenges requires the support of advanced, innovative software solutions. Creating and evolving these solutions to meet these business needs provides the most important goal of IT departments today.

Today's Critical IT Issues

In response to these pressures, IT resources today are consumed by three basic kinds of activities:

► *Remediation and repair of existing systems.* Many existing IT resources have been consumed with remediation efforts involving issues such as Y2K. These tasks are aimed at upgrading existing systems to extend their useful life. These are tactical efforts aimed at addressing compelling short-term needs.

► *Leveraging existing assets to improve productivity and performance.* To supply new IT services in a cost-effective way, a great deal of effort is being placed on extracting value from existing systems, wrapping those pieces for access to new technologies, and assembling new applications. Building solutions from existing pieces will always be a key part of building cost-effective systems.

► *Supporting new business opportunities.* Strategic IT plans are being rewritten to comprehend the need to support e-business initiatives and make use of web-based technologies. In most organizations, many new projects in this area are now underway. These tasks represent the most important strategic development efforts taking place in most organizations.

As organizations take part in these activities, they face at least three critical issues [4].

Issue 1—Tying Together Many Disparate Services

How can users integrate a web-based front end into a legacy system back end—and then manage and evolve it?

Many organizations are faced with challenging software and hardware environments that have evolved over a number of years. Meeting new business needs means tying together existing systems with new web-based front ends. Many possible solutions can use this approach. For example, one approach is to use a data warehouse to collect data from many applications, and to make that information available via a web-based solution. We illustrate this with an example shown in Figure 3.1.

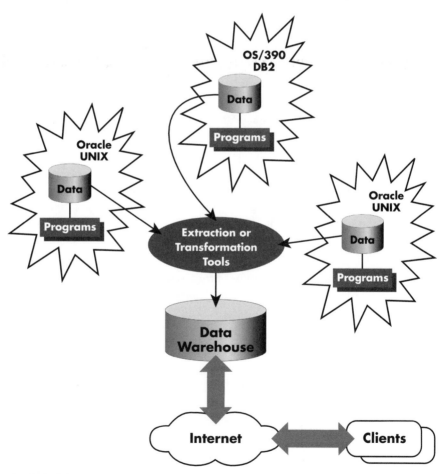

FIGURE 3.1. A simplified example of an e-commerce application.

Typical e-commerce applications require complex collections of new and existing technologies to be integrated to provide the complete solution. Customers interact with browsers across the Internet, but require access to a variety of back-end systems to carry out their business. This requires new business logic to be developed, transactions to be executed on the back-end systems, reformatting and translation of the data return, presentation of the data in meaningful ways to the user, and management of the user's interaction with all these systems across a single session. Making the task yet more complex is the fact that this system must deal with all of the scalability, security, and response time issues typical of any large-scale application.

This evolution to new systems using web-based architectures will introduce many complexities into the design life cycle. Most notably, the obvious approach is simply to add new browser-based interfaces to existing systems. This will bring existing functionality to the Web in a timely fashion, solving some part of the organization's needs to provide more open access to their information systems.

However, while this approach may be appropriate in some situations, it will be inadequate for others. For example, imagine a situation in which a back office order entry system is made available worldwide for direct customer access via the Internet. This may result in a huge increase in the use of that system, thousands of simultaneous requests for data, and a vastly different usage profile for the system. The original design of the system almost certainly was not based on meeting these needs. Simply providing a new user interface for the original system may not meet the required goals for quality, availability, and performance.

Issue 2—Visualizing and Managing Integration and Deployment

How can users substantially reduce the effort required to integrate the next bought, wrapped, or built application?

Many organizations have spent a great deal of time and effort over the past few years purchasing, installing, and deploying packaged applications. The most obvious examples of this are the range of Enterprise Resource Planning (ERP) packages from companies such as SAP, Baan, and PeopleSoft. These packages provide substantial functionality supporting common planning, tracking, and financial management for large corporations. By deploying them, an organization reduces the need for developing and maintaining these IT infrastructures themselves. The goal of these outsourcing efforts is to reduce internal IT costs by delegating the responsibility for large pieces of the organization's back-office function to these third-party vendors and their partners. The expectation is that this reduces maintenance costs and frees the IT staff to concentrate their efforts on value-added services for the organization.

In many cases these expectations have only partially been met. It is reported that many packaged applications are monolithic and unwieldy [5]. As a consequence, package-based solutions are frequently difficult to install, configure, and integrate with existing functionality. This has led to a number of costly failures in high profile projects using package applications [6].

Furthermore, it has also been found that while the cost of purchasing packaged software is less than the estimated cost of developing the functionality, a large hidden cost is involved in customizing the package to meet the organization's needs. In some published accounts the cost of customization can rise to over 80% of the total cost of a package replacement project. It appears that much of this effort is involved with understanding the organization's current business practices, aligning those business practices with the supported processes offered by the purchased package, and tailoring the package for maximum operational efficiency within the organizational context.

Issue 3—Managing the Infrastructure for Future Applications

How can users create an application services architecture that adapts quickly enough to keep up with the rapid evolution of web-based and distributed systems architectures?

With the rapid pace of change of web-based technologies, many organizations find themselves in a classic dilemma. Which technologies do they decide to adopt and when? If they wait too long for the market to decide on an obvious long-term technology direction, then they will lose customers and market share to their more advanced competitors. If they choose too soon they risk selecting a dead-end technology that will result in wasted effort, expensive maintenance, and delays while the systems are rewritten.

An approach taken by most organizations is to attempt to define a long-term strategy based on a set of core web technologies. This strategy offers a bold technical vision for their future purchasing decisions and recruitment practices. Furthermore, it provides the backbone for their future distributed systems deployment, and provides the scope within which other decisions on technology can be made. Unfortunately, defining this strategy is not easy. To be successful, software architects must select from among a myriad of technical choices, and must navigate the many twists and turns of the current web technology marketplace.

The Answer—Enterprise-Scale Solutions for the Internet Age

Addressing these issues requires a new approach to enterprise-scale application development aimed directly at meeting these needs. This approach must view application development from a new perspective, in terms of the needs of enterprise-scale systems developers in the Internet age. From this perspective, enterprise application development consists of three key activities:

▶ *Visualization.* Systems must be architected to meet business needs. Consequently, IT solutions are inherently business driven. Addressing these needs requires analysis of the business domain to understand the customer requirements, design of solutions based on that analysis, and visible traceability between those two aspects of a system. To do this requires technologies for visualization focused on helping an organization to understand the business in which they operate, design the elements of a solution, and refine each of these elements in sufficient detail to be implemented in an appropriate technology.

▶ *Componentization.* To be successful with enterprise application development in the Internet age requires a component-based approach. Components provide the conceptual metaphor required for the assembly of systems from a variety of existing assets. Design approaches must be driven by a component-based view of applications. Furthermore, new technologies assume a specific component model as the common infrastructure required for application assembly. As a result, there is no doubt that component-oriented approaches are beginning to dominate the software industry.

▶ *Utilization.* A deployed solution must be monitored, managed, and evolved over its lifetime. Tools supporting these activities are required to provide cost-effective support across a range of platform technologies. Furthermore, the use of component approaches supports redistribution of those components across different servers in the deployed system. This improves the flexibility of the system, allowing it to grow and evolve as the users' needs change.

These activities are driven by, and must respond to, the needs of a variety of web-based technologies. The assumption in enterprise-scale solutions in the Internet age is that the deployment platform consists of a web-based solution appropriate for the enterprise.

3.2   The Importance of the Middle Tiers

Enterprise-scale solutions are inherently large, complex, and distributed. To be effective they must be deployed to architectures that support these needs. Many choices face the designer in defining the architecture of distributed systems.

To understand these choices it is necessary to amplify the discussions of previous chapters, and explore two topics in further detail. First, it requires a deeper understanding of the migration of current design practices from developing systems based on client/server architectures to systems based on n-tier architectures. This in turn leads to the second topic—a broader examination of typical architectural styles for n-tier distributed systems.

From Client-Server to N-Tier Architectures

Because organizations operate in a decentralized fashion, or do business in many geographic regions, they typically require distributed computing support. Initially this was achieved through remote terminals connected over expensive proprietary lines to centralized mainframe computers. However, application systems in the 1980s began to make a move from mainframe-based to client/server architectures. While this move was implemented in many ways, the approach is characterized by data-intensive applications that were reengineered by separating remote data-intensive services from local desktop display functions. The functions that manipulated the data were initially executed on the (mainframe) server, but migrated to the desktop as the performance of desktop machines improved.

This client/server architecture is successful in two particular situations. The first is for data-intensive applications in which most of the business logic can be executed on the server manipulating the data that resides there. The processing takes place on the server, and the results of the processing transmitted to the client for presentation to the user. This leads to the notion of a "thin client" solution. The second is when there is a high bandwidth connection between clients and servers (such as a proprietary local area network). In this case large amounts of data can travel between clients and servers without significant impact on the performance of the system. This supports either a "thin client' or a "fat client" solution.

However, there are limitations with the client/server architecture in many kinds of common development situations. In particular, this approach breaks down where significant process-oriented business logic is required. The cause of the breakdown is the inability to adequately address the issue of where to execute this business logic. If it executes on the client, then a number of distribution issues must be addressed that inhibit performance and evolution of the system for large numbers of heterogeneous clients. If it executes on the server, it reduces flexibility, introduces a potential performance bottleneck, and too closely ties the business logic to the particular server technology used.

The answer is to introduce one or more intermediate tiers to manage and execute the business logic. These n-tier solutions introduce additional management challenges of the multitiers, but solve many issues with respect to performance, flexibility, and evolution of the systems. N-tier architectures are now the de facto way to architect robust, high-performance, enterprise-scale distributed systems.

The Role of the Middle Tiers in Web-Based Systems

The importance of the web as a deployment platform for distributed systems has introduced a number of challenges with respect to n-tier distributed systems. In particular, with the advent of the Internet and web technologies, system designers have had to reevaluate the applicability of n-tier architectures, and assess which technologies are appropriate at each tier. At the client tier, for example, end users of web-based systems have introduced two major changes in the architecture of deployed applications:

- ► Use of browser-style interfaces for data retrieval and update. As a consequence of the popularity of the web, browser interfaces are now a familiar and comfortable metaphor for accessing all types of data. This provides a common look-and-feel for all applications.
- ► Commonality of interfaces across heterogeneous client platforms. Today, it is common in any organization to have a large investment in a variety of desktop machines running different operating systems and support software. Application solutions should be able to execute on any of these without requiring custom changes for each desktop configuration.

Furthermore, the performance characteristic of the Internet as a distributed infrastructure for web-based applications encourages a thin client style of architecture for most forms of data-intensive applications.[2] The result of these requirements is the web-based systems architecture in which the web server

---

[2] This is not necessarily true for intranet-based applications, where a thin or thick client approach may be appropriate depending on the available local bandwidth for communications, and the required system performance characteristics.

plays the role of the middle tier. This initial attempt at producing a more appropriate architectural style for web-based systems concentrated on solving the problems of delivering interactive clients for a variety of web browser technologies. The information driving these clients remained in back-office applications and corporate databases. The business logic connecting the presentation aspects of the system to the back-office functions was embedded in the web server logic as part of the code written for the browser-based client, or alternatively grafted on to the back-office applications themselves. This architecture is illustrated in Figure 3.2.

A browser running on the client displays information by interpreting pages containing commands in HyperText Markup Language (HTML). A request from a browser uses the HyperText Transport Protocol (HTTP) to transmit the request, with a Universal Resource Locator (URL) identifying the web server to respond to the request, and the source of the action to be taken. The appropriate web server receives the request and acts upon it. In the simplest case, the URL simply identifies another page of HTML to be returned to the browser for display.

In web-based applications the request often requires some more complex processing to take place. Typically, this requires static text and formatting together with the execution of some business logic to create dynamic content for display. This dynamic content means that the information returned to the user is specialized for the request being made, to the identity of the user making the request, or uses information obtained from previous steps in the current user session. To create the dynamic content, interaction with external

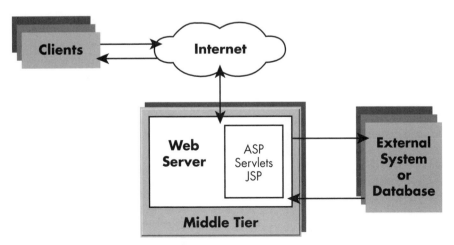

FIGURE 3.2. A web server application.

systems or databases may be required using calls to appropriate Application Programming Interfaces (APIs) or database interfaces. In each case, the web server programs are scripts containing a combination of business logic, presentation logic, data access logic, and integration logic. This business logic can be implemented in a number of ways, including Active Server Pages (ASPs), Java Servlets, and Java Server Pages (JSPs).

Many useful web-based applications have been developed using this kind of architecture. A number of the most successful sites on the Internet for conducting e-business have deployed some version of this architecture.[3] However, a number of limitations with this approach were apparent. This basic architecture for web-based systems has evolved in response to three major challenges:

► The business logic executing on the web server is complex to write, and to develop it requires a wide range of skills to be used. Not only must the developer of these applications be able to write the business logic, he or she must also be able to develop the access code that wraps the services supplied by existing systems, and design the rendering of the result for display as web pages to end users. Typically, each of these tasks requires a different specialized skill, rarely found in combination in the same person. As a result, organizations often have a team specializing in web graphics and user interaction to develop client aspects of a system, with separate teams focused on wrapping existing system functionality and data and developing new code.

The response to this limitation is to separate the user interface-focused processing from the application-focused processing. The former takes place on the web server, while the notion of an *Application Server* is introduced to manage the application-focused processing.

► There are many kinds of existing systems from which content for web-based applications may be required. These existing assets may consist of a wide range of databases, packaged applications, and previously developed systems. No single integration approach will be appropriate in all situations. While useful solutions can be produced, integrating with existing systems to create the dynamic content for the web-based applications can be a complex task often producing fragile, poorly structured systems.

The response to this limitation is the concept of *Enterprise Application Integration (EAI)*. This offers a standardized way to connect

---

[3] In reality, the architectures are more complex due to the need for security and replication of connections and data to handle large volumes of transactions.

various kinds of existing systems within a web-based application using common connectors and integration approaches.

► It is not a very efficient environment for agile development of applications supporting a stream of new business processes. As new business needs arise it must be possible to assemble applications from services provided from a number of existing systems in a more straightforward manner.

The response to this limitation is to consider each element in the system to be a *component* offering its services through well-defined interfaces. The application server supports a *component model* to allow components to be assembled by connecting the services through their interfaces to offer new business functionality.

We now examine each of these three elements of the solution— Application Servers, Enterprise Application Integration, and Components—in more detail.

3.3   THE APPLICATION SERVER

To simplify the development, management, and evolution of web-based systems, the middle tiers have now come to be viewed as logically consisting of two distinct pieces. As illustrated in Figure 3.3, these two pieces are the web server and the application server.[4]

As shown in Figure 3.3, one piece of the middle tier consists of the web server itself, responsible for receiving requests from the clients, parsing those requests, and generating the graphical user interface (GUI) for transmission back to the clients. Note, that while in theory the web server may be considered simply to be handling the user interface, there are in practice many additional tasks that it will perform. These include:

► Data validation prior to calling the application server to ensure that data fields in the forms are correctly formatted before submission;

► Data output formatting for display to the browser;

► Data input conversion to remove blank lines, spaces, upper and lower case characters, and so on;

---

[4] This is a logical distinction. They may be deployed on the same physical machine, distributed across many machines, etc. Furthermore, when physically deployed, both the web server and the application server hardware are typically replicated to improve performance, throughput, and availability.

► Session state management of the client conversation to allow users to move between pages of information and carry forward data relevant to their current task;

► Dynamic generation of displayed information based on requests from previous actions and tasks;

► Control flow of the application (page navigation) as the user moves from one page of information to another;

► Client and server error handling to allow graceful degradation of services, intelligent feedback, and easier restoration of previous stable states;

► Client formatting of all kinds of information, including text, graphics, photographs, video, sound, and so on.

While often dismissed as simply user interface design, this collection of tasks makes development of the web server piece of the applications complex to develop, and difficult to evolve.

The second piece of the middle tier is the application server. This part of the middle tier is where the business logic itself is executed. It is maintained independently from the web server to ensure that the presentation and user interaction aspects of the application are separated. This allows different teams to specialize on developing the business logic and developing the user interface aspects. It also allows for multiple presentations of the same business logic (for example, when there are different physical devices using the same application).

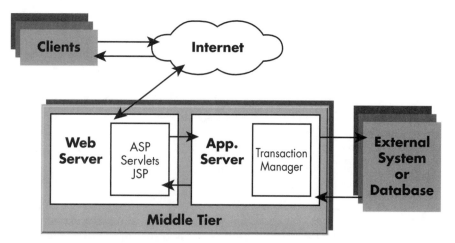

FIGURE 3.3.   The web server and application server in the middle tier.

Currently, there is much confusion about exactly what an application server is. Perhaps what we *can* agree on is that an application server is a standardized set of frameworks and servers on which to build enterprise-scale applications [7]. Because of the broadness of the definition, articles on application servers may discuss aspects of hardware, network connectivity, middleware technology, and software supporting the execution of applications on this platform.

An illustration of the capabilities of the application server is shown in Figure 3.4. This is a logical view of the application server's capabilities. Note that it is shown as the key enabling technology for tying back-end data-intensive applications to a variety of clients.

In Figure 3.4 we see that the application server can provide a wide range of support for enterprise-scale systems. In particular, the application server provides a core set of services for coordinating transactions, security, and data management. As a result, an important part of the application server is its ability to handle transactions and deal with asynchronous communication across the pieces of a distributed system. It achieves this with either application server-specific technologies, via integration with existing transaction processing, or message-oriented middleware solutions.

The business logic of the application must be written to be deployed within an application server. To allow this, an application server provides a description of its available services, defines the interfaces to those services, provides deployment capabilities for installing the software on the application server, and recommends a programming model for designing and implement-

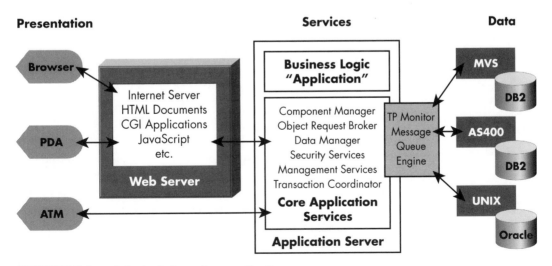

FIGURE 3.4.   A logical view of an application server.

ing applications for that server. Recent advances in the market for enterprise-scale solutions have led to standardization on these in the form of component models. A component model describes how to design and build applications as sets of interacting components for deployment to an application server supporting that component model. A number of competing component model standards exist, principally Microsoft's Component Object Model (COM+) and Sun's Enterprise JavaBeans (EJB). These are briefly described later in this chapter, and in much more detail later in this book.

Different kinds of application server technology supporting these standards are now available from a variety of vendors [8]. Each solution has its own advantages and limitations. For example, in some cases they favor a particular kind of middleware and offer a rich set of services targeting that particular middleware. In other cases, they are aimed specifically at Internet-based applications, and provide robust web server capabilities for supporting e-commerce applications. As a result, the choice of application server technology is a critical one for most organizations, with many competing needs to be weighed.

3.4   ENTERPRISE APPLICATION INTEGRATION

The application server is simply one piece of the solution to a much broader problem facing many organizations. In solving their IT problems, many organizations find that now their IT infrastructure consists of a puzzling collection of packaged applications, deployed mainframe systems, plus a variety of homegrown corporate and departmental utilities. Although they've solved many of their near-term IT needs, they are also finding that they face a growing problem with a key corporate IT need: connecting these solutions for a consistent view of their IT assets. One answer is to combine these isolated solutions to provide increased productivity and business intelligence to corporations. The broad term Enterprise Application Integration (EAI) covers the various aspects of this approach.

Consequently, if you open any magazine on application development, it's likely that you will see at least one article on EAI. However, as with most new approaches, the concept of EAI is a mixture of existing technologies and new perspectives, wrapped up with a large dose of marketing hype. It is important to look at a number of broad aspects of the EAI approach and their impact on enterprise-scale solutions as a whole.

Application Integration ... the New View of Development

Arguably, there is as much new code being written today as there ever has been. Yet looking at current magazines and journals it would be difficult to reach this conclusion. This is because there is a subtle perceptual change of an IT organization's role. Rather than "a developer of systems," today's IT organization is viewed as an "information solutions provider" in support of core business functions. These solutions provide critical business value to the corporation [9].

Seen this way, the IT organization takes a different perspective on how it provides solutions. Certainly, there is application development to be carried out. However, in offering solutions, many IT organizations look to outsource solutions via packaged applications, or try to wrap parts of existing systems and make those services available for use in new ways. This reuse of existing assets leads to an integration-centric view of application provisioning. The IT organization must find ways to deliver business value with approaches that allow them to:

▶ Tie packaged applications and legacy systems together;
▶ Deliver new services to internal users by leveraging existing systems;
▶ Connect customer-oriented front ends to back-office systems;
▶ Integrate supply-chain systems through common Internet portals.

As a result, many IT organizations see EAI as a critical aspect of their role—integrating existing and newly acquired services to provide enterprise-scale solutions.

EAI Through Connectors

Building new applications that integrate with existing systems has always been a key development challenge. To help with this, most large systems and packages provide Application Programming Interfaces (APIs) to expose their services and data to third-party access. Typically, new applications make calls through these APIs to access and retrieve data from the existing systems.

The additional challenge facing EAI is that many different APIs exist for a variety of existing systems and packages. In the past, organizations that were building integrated systems were required to develop and maintain that integration infrastructure themselves. They faced the challenge of keeping the infrastructure up-to-date as each of the constituent systems and packages evolved. This is a costly and error-prone task.

What is required is a consistent way to connect a variety of existing systems and packages. To assist with this, a number of EAI connector solutions have been developed. Initially, these connectors provided an intermediate proprietary representation, a set of translators into this intermediate representation from many of the common packages (e.g., the ERP packages from SAP, Baan, and PeopleSoft), and a toolkit for developing custom translators for other packages and systems. Use of these connectors helps to greatly reduce the effort required to integrate a collection of systems.

Proprietary connector-based solutions are now available from a number of vendors, and are used quite extensively in assembling new systems making use of existing services. However, the proprietary nature of the solutions does introduce a significant limitation to their use. To address this, many of the EAI connector vendors are moving towards adopting a standard connector approach based on the eXtensible Markup Language (XML). XML is a standard intermediate language for transmission of information in human-readable form to and from the existing systems. This approach has advantages because:

▶ XML-based approaches match very well with web-based technologies;
▶ Many organizations have started to develop XML skills;
▶ A range of tools supporting development, deployment, and management of XML are available or in development.

In addition, many package vendors are moving toward the use of XML as the standard technology for import and export of data from their packages. This should reduce the effort and improve the consistency of EAI solutions using a connector approach.

A Broader View of EAI

It is important to recognize that there are many aspects in providing EAI solutions. Unfortunately, many of the existing articles and products have focused only on connector-based solutions for enterprise resource planning (ERP) packages, such as those offered by SAP, Baan, PeopleSoft, and others. This is one of many misconceptions about EAI.

In fact, we can see that there are a number of approaches to application integration, with connectors being just one of them. As illustrated in Figure 3.5, we can distinguish four distinct approaches to application integration [10].

Integration

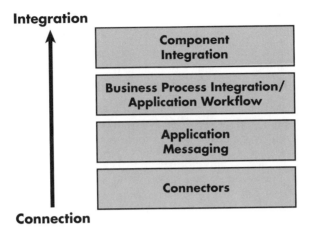

Connection

FIGURE 3.5.   Application integration approaches.

As shown in Figure 3.5, the four most common approaches to application integration are:

► *Connectors* providing gateway software to link web-based applications to services accessed through specific APIs. Connector technologies take the simplest approach to integration by providing mapping and translation mechanisms to allow different systems and packages to communicate and share data. A common way to achieve this is to use an exchange notation such as XML, together with agreed data definitions for the information exchanged.

► *Application Messaging Services* providing message-based communication among applications. A range of message-oriented middleware (MOM) products is available. They allow asynchronous communication among disparate systems based on management of queues. Each system connects to a queue and obtains items as and when it requires them. Products such as IBM's MQSeries and Microsoft's MSMQ have been successfully used for building distributed applications requiring coordination of services from multiple sources.

► *Business Process Integration and Workflow Services* providing additional capabilities to messaging services for message brokering, intelligent message routing, and message translation. As a result, developers can architect distributed systems by concentrating on modeling the workflow among users in a business process. These are mapped into underlying messages and message protocols as required. Efforts such as those employed by the Workflow Management Coalition (WfMC) are aimed at improving products supporting this style of application development.

▶ *Component Integration* providing interface-based integration of services via a component model. Component infrastructure technologies can be viewed as integration platforms for systems constructed from many pieces from a variety of sources. Component models such as Microsoft's COM+ and Sun's EJB define conventions for allowing these pieces to interact to produce a scalable, robust, component-based solution.

Each of these technological approaches can be used for connecting together systems and packages from various sources. These technologies have their roots in much earlier techniques for developing integrated systems, explored in domains such as application tool integration [11].

If we take this broader view of EAI, it leads us to the following conclusions [12]:

▶ *EAI is not just about connectors and adapters.* These are a short-term necessity to transfer data between packages and other applications. While they provide an important part of many EIA solutions, they are only a part of the overall goal of architecting a robust solution from a variety of assets across the organization.

▶ *EAI is more than a new name for middleware.* Middleware solutions provide the underlying "plumbing" required for any solution, but they are not enough to solve the entire integration problem.

▶ *EAI is more than just integrating packaged applications.* Most corporations require integration of a variety of existing systems, not just connectors to packaged applications. This area has proved to be a popular starting point for EAI, but it is by no means the only place to begin or end an EAI effort.

▶ *EAI solutions are not best assembled from miscellaneous "best of breed" solutions.* The solutions used for EAI must offer an integrated set of services covering all aspects of the EAI problem. A robust, well-integrated set of tools is needed. It is tempting to believe that each piece of the system can be independently acquired and later integrated to form a complete, coordinated solution. This is rarely the case.

▶ *EAI is more than simply a data synchronization problem.* Supporting data exchange across applications is important to EAI. But the real need is in integrating business processes to create efficient value-added services to the corporation. This inevitably requires data sharing and data transfer to be successful. However, the needs for data sharing must be derived from the business needs for the system to be successful.

▶ *EAI solutions are not simply plug-ins that provide "plug-and-play" integration.* Many vendors try to minimize the difficulties combining packages and systems with simple technology solutions. Combining large applications in new ways is a complex task requiring a well-suited set of skills, techniques, and tools. These EAI products help by producing a solid base of tools for creating a solution. However, that solution must be designed and implemented to solve a true business requirement.

▶ *EAI is an architected solution, not a tactical Band-Aid™.* Any EAI solution must be viewed as a strategic asset, not a short-term fix. This requires that EAI solutions be well planned, based on the corporation's business goals, and architected for their long-term maintenance and evolution.

We conclude that true EAI needs architected solutions allowing the combination of many different kinds of existing system assets with newly developed code. These systems must be deployable to today's distributed infrastructure platforms, and managed and maintained as important business solutions for the long-term benefit of the corporation.

3.5   COMPONENTS AND COMPONENT MODELS

Current trends are moving more enterprise-scale solutions toward the use of the Internet as a cost-effective infrastructure for distribution of these applications. With this goal in mind, development techniques for enterprise-scale solutions in the Internet age must support:

▶ Services that are designed and implemented in pieces by teams of developers;

▶ Deployment of these pieces across a range of machines;

▶ Integration of functionality derived from many sources, including purchased packages and previously developed systems;

▶ Targeting n-tier architectures involving web servers and applications servers.

Supporting these needs is the goal of components and component-based approaches to providing software solutions. Component-based approaches address two main concerns. The first is how to design and assemble solutions as a collection of interacting pieces. To do this requires techniques for describing the overall system architecture, for carving that into appropriate constituent pieces, and allowing each piece to be designed and provisioned in a way that facilitates its assembly with the other pieces.

Second, a standard set of services is required to handle the problem of accessing pieces of a distributed application when the location of each piece cannot be determined until runtime. To allow this, there must be standard services for naming, locating, and accessing these pieces. Additionally, to assemble the pieces into a complete application requires a standard way to identify which operations a given module will support, and a robust way to pass messages between the pieces to invoke those operations.

Thus, enterprise-scale solutions in the Internet age must be component-based. Consequently, products and services supporting web-based solutions must be based on a component standard.

As a result, when organizations start to provision distributed web-based solutions, they tend to move to components and to an n-tiered model that places business logic in components that reside on the middle tiers. Over the past few years this approach has been widely adopted by end-user organizations. It is supported by key standards from Microsoft through its COM+ initiative [13], Sun through its Enterprise JavaBeans (EJB) specification [14], and the Object Management Group (OMG) with its efforts to standardize a language and technology-neutral open server component model [15].

However, a component-based approach is more than simply deploying components to the middle tiers of an n-tier architecture. The application server is a platform for hosting distributed systems and integrating different kinds of assets across the corporation. To make use of this, distributed systems platforms require:

▶ A way to see the conceptual and physical architecture of the solution as a set of interacting pieces;
▶ A design approach supporting distributed systems provisioning that focuses on how the system should be partitioned for the greatest flexibility;
▶ A direct mapping from the system design into the underlying implementation technologies, supported by the application server.

The way to achieve this is to design with components to create solutions as sets of logical pieces, interacting via their defined interfaces, and to provision with components to create physical packages of system behavior for deployment to an infrastructure supporting a well-defined component model.

Designing with Components

Component approaches concentrate design efforts on defining interfaces to pieces of a system, and describing an application as the collaborations that occur among those interfaces. The interface is the focal point for all analysis and design activities. Implementers of a component can design and build the component in any appropriate technology as long as it supports the operations of the interface and is compatible with the component execution environment. Similarly, users of another component can define their use of that component by reference only to its interfaces. This provides a measure of independence between component developers, and improves the flexibility of the system as the components are upgraded and replaced.

As a result, the components can be provisioned using a variety of technologies, including wrapping some existing code or data, using the application programming interface (API) of a purchased package, or writing new purpose-built logic into an application development tool. As long as the behavior defined by the interface is supported, a client for that component does not need to be aware of the way in which that behavior has been implemented internally.

Solutions are designed as collections of collaborating components. However, there are different abstract levels on which this component design may be considered. At a conceptual level, a system may be considered to be a number of logical pieces supporting each major functional area of the system. However, at an implementation level, each logical component of the system may be supported by one or more physical components. These may have been developed in a variety of technologies. Finally, these physical components will be deployed to a set of computers in a distributed network. Many variations of their deployment are possible based on system requirements such as performance and availability.

In Figure 3.6 we illustrate the kinds of component architecture diagrams important in understanding how a distributed system is designed and deployed. The figure shows that different kinds of component architecture are needed, including conceptual, implementation, and deployment architectures. This concept of component architecture will be examined in detail in later chapters.

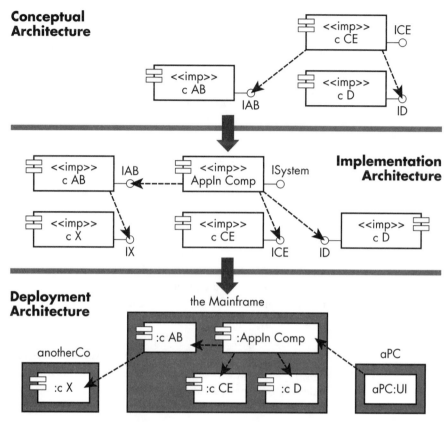

FIGURE 3.6.   Example of component architecture diagrams.

Implementing for Components

As highlighted earlier in this chapter, many organizations building distributed web-based applications develop solutions targeting an N-Tier architecture consisting of clients, web server, and potentially multiple levels of application servers and back-office systems. Consequently, the applications targeting these architectures are developed in pieces, and must be deployed and managed as a set of interacting services executing on these different tiers. Components and component technologies provide the enabling approaches for developing these applications in a robust, repeatable way based on industry standards.

It has been found that a key element for bringing together these pieces is the application server. Much of the logic necessary to tie together the various pieces is embedded in the components executing on the application server. As a result, the application server is essentially an integration infrastructure in which components can be executed. Because of the importance of components to web-based applications, many of the available application server technologies have become specialized toward supporting one of the many component standards that have been developed.

The component model defines a set of standards for designing, assembling, and deploying applications from pieces. It describes how each component must make its services available to others, how to connect one component to another, which common utility services can be assumed to be provided by the infrastructure supporting the component model, how new components announce their availability to others, and so on. In short, by supporting a particular component model the application server is providing a programming approach for developers to use that application server.

Three particular component models currently dominate the market: COM+, CORBA, and Java/EJB. These are summarized in Table 3.1, adapted from [4].

TABLE 3.1   *A Comparison of COM+, CORBA, and EJB from an EAI Perspective*

Standard	Maturity	Scalability	Pace of Innovation	ISV Mind Share	IT Mind Share	Summary
COM+	MTS is several years old	Departmental, enterprise in some cases	Fast, based on product needs	Leader	Emerging leader	Increasing popularity based on Windows domination
CORBA	Mature specs; immature service implementations	Enterprise in most cases	Slower, based on consensus	Laggard	Fading leader	Looking to tie in with Java and EJB direction
Java/EJB	Immature; lots of current activity	Departmental now, but aimed at the enterprise	Fast, based on rapid Java adoption and catch-up to Microsoft	Emerging leader	Emerging leader	Client-side Java now, giving way to server-side Java

Microsoft's dominance on the desktop is based on its Windows operating systems: Windows 95, Windows 98, and Windows NT. With its latest releases, Microsoft is positioning Windows 2000 as an application server platform based on its support for COM+, a combination of the COM object model, the Microsoft Transaction Server (MTS) for transaction management, and a programming model placed around these supported by events, asynchronous messaging, dynamic load balancing, and life-cycle management services. It offers a comprehensive approach to enterprise-scale application development targeting the Microsoft platforms.

The Object Management Group (OMG) has been developing standards for distributed systems for a number of years. It has been most successful with its Common Object Request Broker (CORBA) standard, and a number of implementations of that standard. This has been available for a number of years, supported by a growing number of services and tools. It is now about to release a component model for CORBA, heavily influenced by the Java/EJB standard. Products based on the OMG standards have been successful in their focus on supporting integration of heterogeneous platforms to create enterprise-scale systems.

Sun has had a great deal of success with its Java programming language, and the many services defined for building distributed systems for the Internet using Java. As part of the standardization of Java, Sun recently released the first version of its server-side standard for Java, Enterprise Java Beans (EJB). More than 50 companies have already announced that they will support the EJB specification by offering application servers supporting the EJB standard. This provides one of the final pieces for a complete end-to-end story for the use of Java as an enterprise application development language. With its promise of application portability across many application servers, many organizations are investigating EJB-based solutions as key technology for developing future web-based enterprise-scale systems.

3.6   Summary

Today's rapidly changing business environment requires innovative software solutions to help organizations be more competitive, achieve higher levels of service, and expand into new markets. Web-based technologies provide the platform on which these systems can be developed and delivered. The architectures of these systems will be N-tiered and require new approaches to design and deployment to take advantage of these infrastructures and their services.

However, many organizations are struggling to take advantage of these technologies. They are discovering that making effective use of web-based technologies requires appropriate methods and tools for describing new business practices, architecting solutions from a variety of existing and new pieces, and assembling existing systems and packages into robust, enterprise-scale applications.

Components and component-based approaches are aimed at providing a way to design, assemble, and deploy solutions that meet these needs. Supported by appropriate design techniques and infrastructure technologies, components offer the ideal approach to building enterprise-scale applications in the Internet age. The next part of the book explores components and component-based approaches, and how they can be the driving forces behind the current and future enterprise-scale solutions.

COMPONENTS AND COMPONENT-BASED APPROACHES

Component-Based Development Fundamentals

Components and component-based approaches are the driving force for the e-business revolution. They are the way enterprise-scale solutions for the Internet age will be developed. In a recent report [1], Gartner Group predicted that by 2003 up to 70% of all new software-intensive solutions will be constructed with "building blocks" such as prebuilt components and templates. Similarly, in its 1999 survey of worldwide markets and trends [2], International Data Corporation (IDC) estimated that by 2003 the worldwide market for component construction and assembly tools will be in excess of $8 billion, with an additional $2 billion spent on acquiring components. As a result, it is clear that over the next few years enterprise-scale solutions in the Internet age will undergo fundamental changes in both capability and focus.

Consequently, it is essential to understand the concepts and ideas that underlie the design and implementation of component-based solutions. Furthermore, this insight must be coupled with knowledge of many of the practical issues to be addressed in making a component approach succeed in the context of today's tool and infrastructure capabilities. This part of the book addresses the concepts critical to components and component approaches. The next part of the book deals with practical issues of the application of these concepts, and the technologies required to make it successful.

4.1   INTRODUCTION

Complex situations in any walk of life are typically addressed by applying a number of key concepts. These are represented in approaches such as abstraction, decomposition, iteration, and refinement. They are the intellectual tools on which we rely to deal with difficult problems in a controlled, manageable way.

Critical among them is the technique of decomposition—dividing a larger problem into smaller, manageable units, each of which can then be tackled separately. This technique is at the heart of a number of approaches to software engineering. The approaches may be called structured design, modular programming, or object-orientation, and the units they produce called modules, packages, or components. However, in every case the main principle involved is to consider a larger system to be composed from well-defined, reusable units of functionality, introduce ways of managing this decomposition of a system into pieces, and enable its subsequent reconstruction into a cohesive system.

While the concepts are well understood, most organizations struggle to apply these concepts to the provisioning of enterprise-scale solutions in the Internet age. However, driven by the challenges faced by software engineers today, many organizations are beginning to reassess their approach to the design, implementation, and evolution of software. This stems from growing pressure to assemble solutions quickly from existing systems, make greater use of third-party solutions, and develop reusable services for greater flexibility.

Consequently, renewed attention is being given to reuse-oriented, component-based approaches. This in turn is leading to new component-based strategies being defined, supported by appropriate tools and techniques. The collective name for these new approaches is *Component-Based Development* (CBD) or *Component-Based Software Engineering* (CBSE). For developers and users of software-intensive systems, CBD is viewed as a way to reduce development costs, improve productivity, and provide controlled system upgrade in the face of rapid technology evolution.

In this chapter we examine the renewed interest in reuse-oriented approaches, and define the goals and objectives for any application development approach able to meet the needs of today's software development organizations. Armed with this knowledge, we examine the major principles of CBD, and the characteristics that make CBD so essential to software developers and tool producers alike. We then consider the major elements of any CBD approach, and highlight the main concepts behind them.

4.2   THE GOALS OF COMPONENT APPROACHES

Recently there has been renewed interest in the notion of software development through the planned integration of preexisting pieces of software. This is most often called component-based development (CBD), component-based software engineering (CBSE), or simply componentware, and the pieces called components.

There are many ongoing debates and disagreements concerning what exactly are and are not components [3]. Some authors like to emphasize components as conceptually coherent packages of useful behavior. Others concentrate on components as physical, deployable units of software that execute within some well-defined environment [4]. Regardless of these differences, the basic approach of CBD is to build systems from well-defined, independently produced pieces. However, the interesting aspects of CBD concern how this approach is realized to allow components to be developed as appropriate cohesive units of functionality, and to facilitate the design and assembly of systems from a mix of newly and previously developed components.

The goal of building systems from well-defined pieces is nothing new. The interest in CBD is based on a long history of work in modular systems, structured design, and most recently in object-oriented systems [5]–[9]. These were aimed at encouraging large systems to be developed and maintained more easily using a "divide and conquer" approach. CBD extends these ideas, emphasizing the design of solutions in terms of pieces of functionality provisioned as components, accessible to others only through well-defined interfaces, outsourcing of the implementation of many pieces of the application solution, and focusing on controlled assembly of components using interface-based design techniques.

Most importantly, these concepts have been supported by a range of products implementing open standards that offer an infrastructure of services for the creation, assembly, and execution of components. Consequently, the application development process has been reengineered such that software construction is achieved largely through a component selection, evaluation, and assembly process. The components are acquired from a diverse set of sources, and used together with locally developed software to construct a complete application [10].

4.3   WHY COMPONENT-BASED DEVELOPMENT?

Part 1 of this book described many of the challenges facing software developers today to provision enterprise-scale solutions. By reviewing and distilling the challenges discussed in the previous chapters, we obtain the following goals and objectives for enterprise-scale solutions in the Internet age:

▶ *Contain complexity.* In any complex situation there are a few basic techniques that can be used to understand and manage that complexity. These are the techniques of abstraction, decomposition, and incremental development. Any solution to application development must provide ways to support these techniques.

▶ *Reduce delivery time.* The ability to deliver solutions in a timely manner is an essential aspect of any software development project. With the increased rate of change of technology, this aspect is even more critical. This need for reduced delivery time for software-intensive systems is often referred to as working at "Internet speed."

▶ *Improve consistency.* Most software-intensive systems share significant characteristics with others previously developed, in production, or yet to be produced. It must be possible to take advantage of this commonality to improve consistency and reduce development expense.

▶ *Make use of best-in-class.* In a number of areas there are well developed solutions offering robust, best-in-class functionality and performance. Taking advantage of these solutions as part of a larger development effort is essential.

▶ *Increase productivity.* The shortage of software development skills is causing a major backlog for systems users. Any new approaches must improve the productivity of skilled employees to allow them to produce quality results at a faster rate.

▶ *Improve quality.* As the economic and human impact of failure of software-intensive systems increases, greater attention must be turned to the quality of the deployed systems. A goal must be to support the building of systems correctly the first time, without extensive (and expensive) testing and rewriting.

▶ *Increase visibility into project progress.* Managing large software projects is a high-risk undertaking. To help this, greater visibility must be possible throughout the software life cycle. This requires an incremental approach to development, delivery, and testing of software artifacts.

▶ *Support parallel and distributed development.* Distributed development teams require approaches that encourage and enable parallel development of systems. This requires specific attention be given to manage complexity due to the need to partition and resynchronize results.

▶ *Reduce maintenance costs.* The majority of software costs occur after initial deployment. To reduce maintenance costs it must be possible to more easily identify the need for change, scope the impact of any proposed change, and implement that change with predictable impact on the rest of the system.

This list represents a daunting set of challenges for any approach. Yet it is components and component-based approaches that offer the most promising attempt to meet the challenges head-on, and provide the basis of a new set of techniques supporting the next generation of software-intensive solutions.

4.4   WHAT IS A COMPONENT?

The key to understanding CBD is to gain a deeper appreciation of what is meant by a component, and how components form the basic building blocks of a solution. The definition of what it means to be a component is the basis for much of what can be achieved using CBD, and in particular provides the distinguishing characteristics between CBD and other reuse-oriented efforts of the past.

For CBD, a component is much more than a subroutine in a modular programming approach, an object or class in an object-oriented system, or a package in a system model. In CBD the notion of a component both subsumes and expands on those ideas. A component is used as the basis for design, implementation, and maintenance of component-based systems. For now we will assume a rather broad, general notion of a component, and define it as:

> *An independently deliverable piece of functionality providing access to its services through interfaces.*

This definition, while informal, stresses a number of important aspects of a component. First, it defines a component as a deliverable unit. Hence, it has characteristics of an executable package of software. Second, it says a component provides some useful functionality that has been collected together to satisfy some need. It has been designed to offer that functionality based on some design criteria. Third, a component offers services through interfaces. To use the component requires making requests through those interfaces, not by accessing the internal implementation details of the component.

Of course, this definition is rather informal and provides little more than an intuitive understanding of components and their characteristics. It is in line with other definitions of a component [11, 12], and is sufficient to allow us to begin a more detailed investigation into components and their use. However, it is not sufficient for in-depth analysis of component approaches when comparing different design and implementation approaches. Consequently, a more formal definition of a component is provided later in this book.

To gain greater insight into components and component-based approaches, it is necessary to explore a number of topics in some detail. In particular, it is necessary to look at components and their use of object-oriented concepts, and view components from the perspective of distributed systems design. Based on such an understanding, the main component elements can then be highlighted.

Components and Objects[1]

In discussions on components and component-based approaches there is much debate about components in relation to the concept of objects and object-oriented approaches. Examining the relationship between objects and components provides an excellent starting point for understanding component approaches [13, 14].

For over 30 years there have been attempts to improve the design of programming languages to create a closer, more natural connection between the business-oriented concepts in which problems are expressed, and the technology-oriented concepts in which solutions are described as a set of programming language statements. In the past decade these attempts have led to a set of principles for software structure and behavior that have come to be called object-oriented programming languages (OOPLs).

There are many variations in OOPLs. However, as illustrated in Figure 4.1, there are a number of concepts that have come to characterize an OOPL [15].

---

[1] This discussion is based on John Daniel's excellent short paper on objects and component [13].

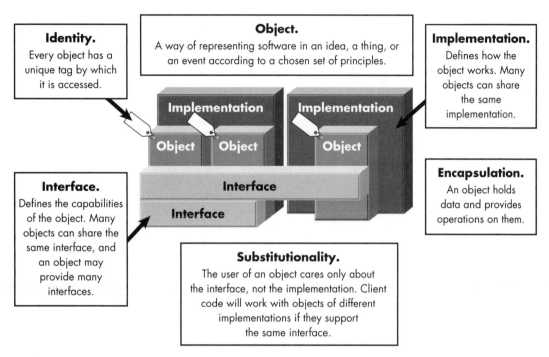

Identity.
Every object has a unique tag by which it is accessed.

Object.
A way of representing software in an idea, a thing, or an event according to a chosen set of principles.

Implementation.
Defines how the object works. Many objects can share the same implementation.

Encapsulation.
An object holds data and provides operations on them.

Interface.
Defines the capabilities of the object. Many objects can share the same interface, and an object may provide many interfaces.

Substitutionality.
The user of an object cares only about the interface, not the implementation. Client code will work with objects of different implementations if they support the same interface.

FIGURE 4.1. Basic concepts of object-oriented approaches.

The commonly identified principles of object orientation are:

▶ *Objects:* A software object is a way of representing software in an idea, a thing, or an event according to a chosen set of principles; these five principles are the following:

▶ *Encapsulation:* A software object provides a set of services and manipulates data within the object. The details of the internal operation and data structures are not revealed to clients of the object.

▶ *Identity:* Every object has a fixed, unique "tag" by which it can be accessed by other parts of the software. This tag, often called an object identifier, provides a way to uniquely distinguish that object from others with the same behavior.

▶ *Implementation:* An implementation defines how an object works. It defines the structure of data held by the object and holds the code of the operations. It is possible for an implementation to be shared by many objects.

▶ *Interface:* An interface is a declaration of the services made available by the object. It represents a contract between an object and any potential clients. The client code can rely only on what is defined in the interface.

Many objects may provide the same interface, and each object can provide many interfaces.

▶ *Substitutability:* Because a client of the object relies on the interface and not the implementation, it is often possible to substitute other object implementations at runtime. This concept allows late or dynamic binding between objects, a powerful feature for many interactive systems.

For the past decade object-oriented principles have been applied to other fields, notably databases and design methods. More recently, they have been used as the basis for a number of advances in distributed computing as an approach to support the integration of the various pieces of a distributed application.

Based on this analysis, a component can be seen as a convenient way to package object implementations, and to make them available for assembly into a larger software system. As illustrated in Figure 4.2, a component is from this perspective a collection of one or more object implementations within the context of a component model. This component model defines a set of rules that must be followed by the component to make those object implementations accessible to others. Furthermore, it describes a set of standard services that can be assumed by components and assemblers of component-based systems (e.g., for naming of components and their operations, security of access to those operations, transaction management, and so on).

Organizations can define their own component models based on the needs of their customers and the tools they use to create and manipulate components (e.g., Sterling Software's proprietary CS/3.0 standard for components

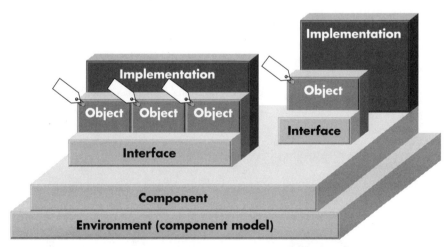

FIGURE 4.2.　The relationship between components and objects.

developed using the COOL:Gen product). Alternatively, a number of more widely used component model standards are now available, notably the Enterprise JavaBeans (EJB) standards from Sun Microsystems, and the COM+ standard from Microsoft.

In summary, we see that in comparing components to objects, a component is distinguished by three main characteristics:

► A component acts as a unit of deployment based on a component model defining the rules for components conforming to that model.
► A component provides a packaging of one or more object implementations.
► A component is a unit of assembly for designing and constructing a system from a number of independently created pieces of functionality, each potentially created using an OOPL or some other technology.

Components and Distributed Systems

The 1980s saw the arrival of cheap, powerful hardware coupled with increasingly sophisticated and pervasive network technologies. The result was a move toward greater decentralization of computer infrastructures in most organizations. As those organizations built complex networks of distributed systems, there was a growing need for development languages and approaches that supported these kinds of infrastructures.

A wide range of approaches to application systems development emerged. One way to classify these approaches is based on the programming level that must be used to create distributed systems, and the abstract level of transparency that this supported. This is illustrated in Figure 4.3.

Initial approaches to building distributed systems were aimed at providing some level of hardware transparency for developers of distributed systems. This was based on technologies such as remote procedure calls (RPC) and use of message-oriented middleware (MOM). These allow interprocess communication across machines independent of the programming languages used at each end.

However, using RPCs still required developers to implement many services uniquely for each application. Other than some high-performance real-time systems, this expense is unnecessary. As a result, a technique was required to define the services made available at each end of the RPC to improve the usability of these approaches. To allow this, the concepts of object-orientation were introduced as described above. By applying these concepts, application developers were able to treat remote processes as a set of

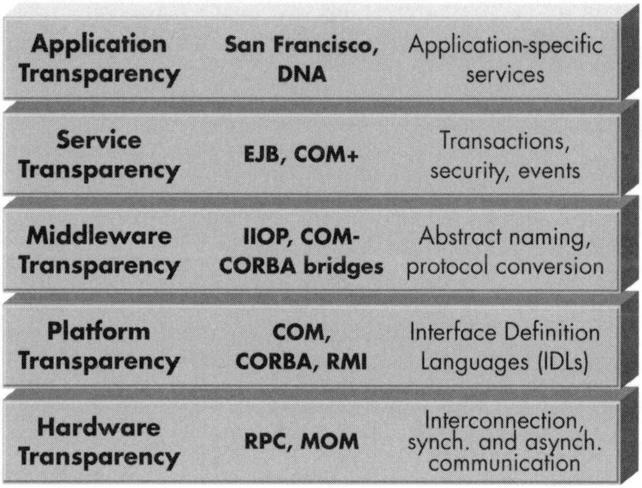

Application Transparency	**San Francisco, DNA**	Application-specific services
Service Transparency	**EJB, COM+**	Transactions, security, events
Middleware Transparency	**IIOP, COM-CORBA bridges**	Abstract naming, protocol conversion
Platform Transparency	**COM, CORBA, RMI**	Interface Definition Languages (IDLs)
Hardware Transparency	**RPC, MOM**	Interconnection, synch. and asynch. communication

FIGURE 4.3.   Different levels of transparency for distributed systems.

software objects. The independent service providers are now implemented as components. They are structured to offer those services through interfaces, encapsulating the implementation details that lie behind them. These service providers have unique identifiers, and can be substituted for others supporting the same interfaces. Such distributed object technologies are in widespread use today. They include Microsoft's Distributed Component Object Model (DCOM) and the Object Management Group's Common Object Request Broker Architecture (CORBA).

This approach resulted in the concept of an Interface Definition Language (IDL). This provides a programming language a neutral way to describe the services at each end of a distributed interaction. It provides a large measure of platform independence to distributed systems developers. The services are typically constructed as components defined by their interfaces. This provides remote access to these capabilities without the need to understand many of the details of how those services are implemented. Many distributed computing technologies use this approach.

However, many implementations supporting an IDL were not transportable across multiple infrastructures from different vendors. Each middleware technology supported the IDL in its own way, often with unique value-added services. To provide a middleware transparency for applications, bridging technologies and protocols have been devised (e.g., the Internet Inter-Orb Protocol (IIOP)). These allow components greater independence of middleware on which they are implemented.

Of course, what most people want is to assemble solutions composed of multiple components—independently deliverable pieces of system functionality. These components interact to implement some set of business transactions. Ideally, developers would like to describe the services offered by components, and implement them independently of how those services will be combined later on. Then, when assembled into applications for deployment to a particular infrastructure, the services can be assigned appropriate characteristics in terms of transactional behavior, persistent data management, security, and so on. This level of service transparency requires the services to be implemented independently of the characteristics of the execution environment.

Application servers based on the COM+ and EJB specifications support this approach. These standards define the behavior a component implementor can rely upon from the "container" in which it executes. When being deployed to a container, the application assembler is able to describe the particular execution semantics required. These can change from one container to another without impact on the component's internal logic, providing a great deal of flexibility for upgrade of component-based solutions.

Finally, it is possible in many domains to imagine common sets of services that would frequently be found in many applications within that domain. For example, in areas such as banking and financial management it is possible to construct a common list of services for managing accounts, transfer of funds between accounts, and so on. This is the goal of application transparency. Groups of experts in an industry domain have attempted to define common services in the form of a library, or an interacting framework of components and services. As a result, application designers and implementers in that domain can use a pre-populated set of components when designing new application behavior. This increases the productivity of developers, and improves the consistency of the applications being produced.

In summary, from the perspective of distributed systems, components provide a key abstraction for the design and development of flexible solutions. They enable designers to focus on business level concerns independently of the lower-level component implementation details. They represent the latest ideas of over two decades of distributed systems thinking.

Elements of a Component

As a result of these analyses, the elements of a component can now be discussed. Building on object-oriented concepts and distributed systems thinking, components and component-based approaches share a number of characteristics familiar to today's systems designers and engineers. However, a number of additional characteristics must also be highlighted. These are shown in Figure 4.4.

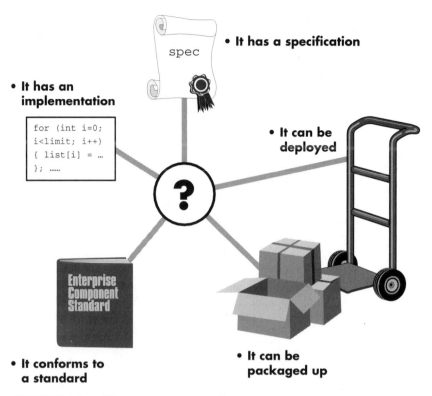

• **It has a specification**

spec

• **It has an implementation**

```
for (int i=0;
i<limit; i++)
{ list[i] = …
}; ……
```

• **It can be deployed**

?

Enterprise
Component
Standard

• **It conforms to a standard**

• **It can be packaged up**

FIGURE 4.4.   What is a component?

As illustrated in Figure 4.4, there are five major elements of a component:

▶ *A specification.* Building on the interface concept, a component requires an abstract description of the services it offers to act as the contract between clients and suppliers of the services. The component specification typically defines more than simply a list of available operations. It describes the expected behavior of the component for specific situations, constrains the allowable states of the component, and guides the clients in appropriate interactions with the component. In some cases these descriptions may be in some formal notation. Most often they are informally defined.

▶ *One or more implementations.* The component must be supported by one or more implementations. These must conform to the specification. However, the specification will allow a number of degrees of freedom on the internal operation of the component. In these cases the implementer may choose any implementation approach deemed to be suitable. The only constraint is on meeting the behavior defined in the specification. In many cases this flexibility includes the choice of programming language used to develop the component implementation. In fact, this behavior may simply be some existing system or packaged application wrapped in such a way that its behavior conforms to the specification defined within the context of the constraining component standard.

► *A constraining component standard.* Software components exist within a defined environment, or *component model.* A component model is a set of services that support the software, plus a set of rules that must be obeyed by the component in order for it to take advantage of the services. Established component models include Microsoft's COM+, Sun's Java Beans and Enterprise Java Beans (EJB), and the OMG's emerging CORBA component standard. Each of these component models address issues such as how a component makes its services available to others, how components are named, and how new components and their services are discovered at run-time. Additionally, those component models concerned with enterprise-scale systems provide additional capabilities such as standard approaches to transaction management, persistence, and security.

► *A packaging approach.* Components can be grouped in different ways to provide a replaceable set of services. This grouping is called a package. Typically, it is these packages that are bought and sold when acquiring components from third-party sources. They represent units of functionality that must be installed on a system. To make this package usable, some sort of registration of the package within the component model is expected. In a Microsoft environment, for example, this is through a special catalog of installed components called the registry.

► *A deployment approach.* Once the packaged components are installed in an operational environment, they will be deployed. This occurs by creating an executable instance of a component and allowing interactions with it to occur. Note that many instances of the component can be deployed. Each one is unique and executes within its own process. For example, it is possible to have two unique instances of an executing component on the same machine handling different kinds of user requests.

4.5   HOW ARE APPLICATIONS ASSEMBLED USING CBD?

Having described the basic component concepts, we now consider how these concepts are embodied in supporting a component-oriented approach to application assembly. In particular, we identify the key elements on which any CBD approach is based.

While much of the technology infrastructure for component-oriented approaches is in place, of equal importance to its success are the methods for developing component-oriented applications. Faced with the wealth of technology, software developers must be able to answer the key question of how to effectively design solutions targeting that technology. The software industry is only just beginning to offer guidance in this regard.

Fortunately, the latest wave of software development methods are beginning to rise to the challenge of supporting the development of distributed, web-based systems involving the reuse of legacy systems and packaged applications. A number of organizations have begun to publicize their methods and best practices for developing enterprise-scale systems from components. The three most prominent of these are:

> ▶ *Rational's Unified Process.* This is a broad process framework for software development covering the complete software life cycle. In architecting the solution, a component-based approach is encouraged, heavily influenced by the constraints of the Unified Modeling Language (UML) notation [16].
> ▶ *The Select Perspective Method.* A general component design approach is supported, targeted at the Select Component Manager. General component design principles target UML as the component design notation [17].
> ▶ *Sterling Software's Enterprise-CBD Approach.* Influenced by the Catalysis approach to component development, Sterling Software's approach encourages a strong separation of component specification from implementation using an extended form of UML [18]. This allows technology-neutral specifications to be developed and then refined into implementations in a number of different implementation technologies.

These approaches differ in many details. However, the abstract method that they encourage for component-based design is fundamentally the same. As illustrated in Figure 4.5, three key elements provide the focus of these methods: a diverse set of component stored in a component library, an inter-

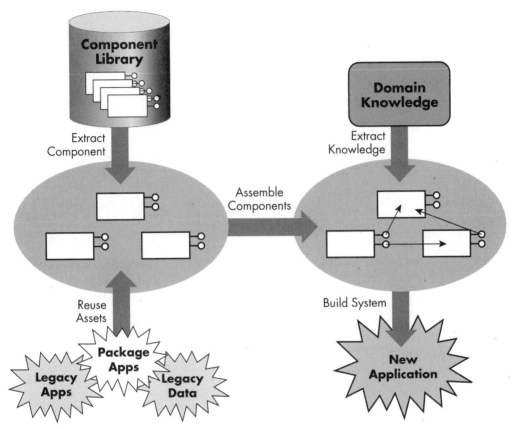

FIGURE 4.5. Elements of a component-oriented software process.

face-focused design approach, and application assembly based on a component architecture.

Sources of Components

A component has been informally defined as an independently deliverable
piece of functionality providing access to its services through interfaces. This
definition is important as much for what it doesn't say as for what it does say;
it does not place any requirements on how the components are implemented.
Hence, valid components could include packaged applications, wrapped legacy code and data, previously developed components from an earlier project,
and components developed specifically to meet current business needs.

The diverse origin for components has led to a wealth of techniques for
obtaining components from third parties, developing them in a variety of tech-

nologies, and extracting them from existing assets. In particular, many CBD approaches focus on wrapping techniques to allow access to purchased packages (e.g., Enterprise Resource Planning (ERP) systems) and to mine existing legacy systems to extract useful functionality that can be wrapped as a component for future use. This approach leads to a view of CBD as the basis for enterprise application integration (EAI). Many vendors providing technologies for combining existing systems take a component view of the applications being assembled, and introduce specific integration technologies to tie the systems together. Often this is focused on the data flows in and out of the packages, and consists of transformers between the packages offering a broker-based approach.

The sources of the components may be diverse and widespread, yet assembling solutions from these components is possible due to the following:

▶ Use of a component model as a standard to which all components can conform regardless of their heritage;

▶ A component management approach, supported by appropriate tools, for the storage, indexing, searching, and retrieval of components as required;

▶ A design approach that allows solutions to be architected from components by considering their abstract functionality, and ignoring peculiarities of their implementation for a later date.

This final aspect, a design approach targeting appropriate component architectures, is a key element to the success of component approaches in general. In particular, it is the motivation for interface-based design approaches.

Interface-Focused Design

Interfaces are the mechanism by which components describe what they do, and provide access to their services. The interface description captures everything on which the potential client of that component can rely since the implementation is completely hidden. As a consequence, the expressiveness and completeness with which the interfaces are described is a primary consideration in any component-based approach to software.

Furthermore, during the early stages of analysis and design, the focus is on understanding the roles and responsibilities within the domain of interest as a basis for the interfaces of the implemented system. This gives rise to a new form of design method: *interface-based design*. Focusing on interfaces as the key design abstraction leads to much more flexible designs [19, 20]. Designers are encouraged to consider system behavior more abstractly, define independent suppliers of services, describe collaborations among services to enact scenarios, and reuse common design patterns in addressing familiar situations. This results in more natural designs for systems with a greater independence from implementation choices.

Such thinking is an essential part of new application provisioning approaches in the Internet age. To target rapidly evolving distributed computing technologies requires an approach to design that can evolve as the technology changes. Familiar, rigid approaches to design are unsuitable. Interface-based design approaches represent a significant step forward in reducing the cost of maintenance of future systems.[2]

Applications and Component Architecture

Interfaces and interface-based design provide the techniques necessary for a component assembly view of software-intensive solutions. Component assembly concerns how an application is designed and built from components. In a component-based world, an application consists of a set of components working together to meet the broader business needs. How this is achieved is often referred to as the component architecture—the components and their interactions. These interactions result in a set of dependencies among components that form an essential part of a software solution. Describing, analyzing, and visualizing these dependencies become critical tasks in the development of a component-based application.

Typically, a candidate component architecture is proposed relatively early in a project. This consists of a number of known pieces of existing systems to be reused, familiar patterns of system interactions, and constraints based on imposed project and organizational standards. Consequently, at least two levels of component architecture become important.

The first is a logical component architecture. This describes the abstract design of the system in terms of the major packages of functionality it will offer, descriptions of each collection of services in terms of its interfaces, and how those packages interact to meet common user scenarios. This is often called the component specification architecture. It represents a blueprint of the design of the system. Analysis of this architecture is essential to ensure that the system offers appropriate functionality, and can easily be modified as the functional requirements for the system evolve.

---

[2] Detailed examples of interface-based design approaches are provided later in this book.

The second is a physical component architecture. This describes the physical design of the system in terms of selected technical infrastructure products, distributed hardware and its topology, and the network and communication protocols that tie them together. This forms part of the component implementation architecture. This architecture is used to understand many of the system's non-functional attributes such as performance, throughput, and availability of services.

4.6   WHAT IS THE CURRENT PRACTICE IN CBD?

A number of organizations are practicing component-based approaches today using a variety of technologies. While many component approaches are limited to client desktop applications (via ActiveX controls, visual Java Beans, and so on), there are others that are beginning to address larger-scale applications with significant business functionality. There are a number of very valuable lessons being learned by these pioneers of component approaches. Originally, many of these lessons were related to the vagaries and incompatibilities of specific component technologies. More recently, a number of published accounts discuss a much broader range of critical success factors for component approaches in areas such as organizational readiness, costs of component development, and management of deployed component-based applications.

Much can be learned from these existing users of components. There are four main ways that a great deal of useful information can be obtained: special interest groups, vendor-led user groups, specialist component service providers, and published experience reports and advice.

Special Interest Groups

As component-based approaches begin to gain in popularity, a number of special interest groups have been formed which concentrate in this area. These groups tend to offer broad-based advice and experience covering a range of technologies. While a number of these groups exist, one particular group worthy of attention is the CBD integration forum, CBDi Forum, formerly part of Butler Group and now an independent concern (see *http://www.CBDiForum.com* for more details).

The CBDi Forum provides a source of information and best practice on management issues surrounding delivery of enterprise-level business software applications. The CBDi Forum provides vendor-independent information which is based on practical user experience. The resources of the Forum are organized to allow users of component technology to learn from independent, unbiased sources, and to avoid costly mistakes.

A particular initiative of interest is the CBDi Forum's attempts to define a set of *Universal Component Concepts* (UCC). The UCC initiative aims to deliver a set of generally applicable concepts covering the basics of component-based development. It is envisaged that the set of concepts will provide clarity and lead to a better general understanding in the area of components and component-based approaches. The initiative, for example, will aim to clear up common misunderstandings between objects and components. In addition, the initiative aims to identify the generic process framework needed for component-based development.

As a result, the CBDi Forum tries to provide insight on architecture, process, and technology issues. Forum members include development managers, architects, strategists, project managers, analysts, and developers covering all types of technology and business environments.

Vendor-Led User Groups

With the availability of a range of tools supporting component-based approaches, many vendors are organizing user groups to share best practices in the use of those technologies. In many cases, these user groups offer the opportunity for those organizations new to component-based approaches to learn from the practical experience of others based on previous knowledge of the use of a specific technology solution.

All major component technology providers offer user groups of one sort or another. To illustrate the most advanced groups in this area, we briefly consider the Sterling Software Component-Based Development Advisory Board (CAB) (see *http://www.cool.sterling.com/cbd* for more details).

The Sterling Software CAB was formed in 1994 and today consists of more than 90 member companies and is growing rapidly. The CAB is a voluntary, self-run group whose primary objective is to facilitate the sharing of information regarding component-based development. The CAB provides a forum to network—to ask others for their opinions, to learn about different approaches to CBD, and to influence Sterling Software's direction in regards to its component technologies. Information is exchanged via monthly teleconference calls, worldwide biannual meetings, and a dedicated web site which delivers meeting notes, best practices, and a library of research materials.

Specialist Component Service Providers

As component approaches have become more popular, a number of specialist component service providers have emerged to support those interested in taking this approach. These services are an invaluable "jump-start" for organizations using a CBD approach. There appear to be four major roles assumed by these organizations:

► *Component developers.* A number of organizations specialize in developing components for a particular component infrastructure technology. Their primary business is the sale, distribution, and support of these components. Examine the Web sites and literature of the major component infrastructure vendors and supporters to obtain lists of component providers for a specific technology. For example, the OMG maintain a product and services guide for buyers of CORBA-based products at its web site (*http://www.omg.org*).

► *Component brokers.* The growth and variety of component providers has led to some organizations specializing as component brokers. Essentially, they offer a single point of contact for a variety of components from many vendors targeting many domains and multiple component infrastructure technologies. One of the best known of these component brokers is Component Source. Third-party component providers become members of Component Source and make their products available on the Component Source web site (*http://www.componentsource.com*).

► *Component educators.* Interest in component technologies and component-oriented design practices have also stimulated the education market to offer a number of appropriate courses, tutorials, and certification examinations. Most often, these are focused on a particular component technology or development approach, and are associated with a vendor in support of that technology. However, a number of independent organizations are now offering courses in general component concepts and their application. A web search will result in many organizations specializing in different kinds of customers.

► *Component-based consultants.* One of the best ways of getting started with component-based approaches is with the help and guidance of experienced consultants who have developed similar projects in the past. Their mentoring and advice can be essential to the success of the first component-based projects that an organization attempts. Mentoring services are very diverse in nature and frequently span broad technical and business areas. The most common use of a mentor is in situations where a client is moving from one technology to another. The mentor typically advises the client's strategist, planners, designers, and developers on matters requiring architecture, costing, estimating, business judgements, case histories, human resources, access to technical information and actual hands-on instruction, and on occasion, production of the actual results. Again, these consulting services are usually tied to a specific component technology and can be found by accessing the technology vendor's web site.

Experience Reports and Advice

The amount of available literature on components and component-oriented approaches is continuing to grow. There are now books describing the details of every kind of component technology, and frequent technical articles in software-focused magazines and journals.

However, perhaps the best source of advice on the practical application of component technology appears in a number of specialist magazines and conference targeting component-based approaches to software engineering. Two of the most influential are the monthly magazines *Component Strategies* and *Distributed Computing*. Both of these magazines specifically target the development of large-scale distributed systems using component technologies. Every edition contains success stories, experience reports, and practical advice on the application of component technologies.

Equally important are a number of conference series aimed at educating organization on component-based approaches. While many conferences target specific technologies or approaches, the most significant conference series aimed at a broad set of component technologies is the SIGS-sponsored Component Development conference series (see *http://www.componentdevelopment.com* for more details). Specific examples of the application of a range of component-oriented approaches are presented at these conferences.

4.7	SUMMARY

Component-based development of software is an important development approach for software solutions which must be rapidly assembled, take advantage of the latest web-based technologies, and be amenable to change as both the technology and user's needs evolve. One of the key challenges facing software engineers is to make CBD an efficient and effective practice which does not succumb to the shortcomings of previous reuse-based efforts of the 1970s and 1980s.

Fortunately, the past few years has seen a number of major advances in both our understanding of reuse issues and the technology support available to realize those advances. These are embodied in the rapidly growing field of component-based software engineering. This approach encourages a new way of application development that focuses on the following:

▶ Separation of component specification from component implementation to enable technology-independent application design;
▶ Use of more rigorous descriptions of component behaviors via methods that encourage interface-level design;
▶ Flexible component technologies leveraging existing tools and standards.

This chapter has identified the key concepts underlying a component-based approach to software engineering. These have been explored in the context of improving our understanding of CBD, assessing the current state of CBD technology, and improving an organization's software practices to enhance the effectiveness and viability of large-scale software development through the reuse of components. This will help to lead organizations toward an interface-based approach to application development and design that encourages the creation of systems that are more easily distributed, repartitioned, and reused. These attributes are essential to improve the future effectiveness of organizations in their development and use of large-scale software systems.

Component-based Development Insights

The previous chapter provided an overview of the fundamentals of CBD. In particular, it provided a brief introduction to the main CBD concepts, and highlighted the key elements of any CBD approach. This chapter takes the discussion one step further to provide deeper insights into many of those concepts, and describes in more detail the basic activities involved in a CBD approach.

Armed with the basic concepts provided in the previous chapter, there are three main areas on which to concentrate to obtain greater insight into CBD and its importance for driving future enterprise-scale solutions in the Internet age:

- ► A Deeper Understanding of Components.
- ► The Importance of Component Specifications.
- ► Elements of a Component Design Approach.

This chapter begins by considering how the key goal of delivering independent services can be achieved. It then addresses in detail the three essential areas highlighted above.

5.1   INTRODUCTION

Before we examine component concepts in more detail, we first examine two main questions that are precursors to any discussion of component-based approaches. The first question concerns what it means to provide reusable services, and the second asks how we are able to allow independent delivery of these services [1].

Provision of Reusable Services

Providing reusable services implies that a component offers capabilities that many other components may wish to access. To enable this, a fundamental tenet of CBD is that a component has a specification that describes what a component does, and how it behaves when its services are used. Given knowledge solely of the specification, any potential user, or client, of those services can focus on its part of the overall solution without concern for how those services are actually rendered. Useful components exhibit varying degrees of completeness and precision in their specifications, but any CBD approach must offer guidance on how to use the component specification to its greatest effect.

The services will be rendered by a programmer or designer who provides an implementation for a component expressed in terms of code and data which will be guaranteed to meet the specification. In general, the implementation may be written in a different programming language or executed on a different technology platform from the language and platform used by the client program. One component may be replaced by another in an application, as long as both purport to implement the same specification. The split between specification and implementation is an essential aspect of CBD and is the key to effective encapsulation, as illustrated in Figure 5.1.

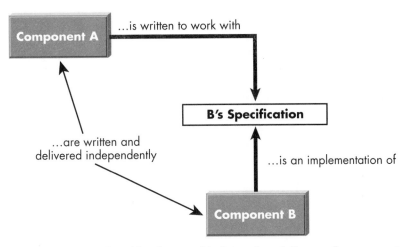

FIGURE 5.1.   Specifications and independent delivery of components.

Independent Delivery of Services

The other important element of component-based approaches is independent delivery. This refers to the issue of context awareness of components. Independently deliverable components are typically unaware of the contexts in which they may be used. This stresses the notion that components are expected to collaborate with one another to accomplish a solution, not interfere with one another. In particular, components cannot be developed with embedded dependencies on one another, or based on a shared external resource being present. One consequence of this is that two software components cannot share a common data structure directly. For example, two or more software components could not access the same columns in a relational database table. They may do so if, for example, a third component took the responsibility for updating the same column, unbeknownst to the first two components.

This does not mean that components have no dependencies on one another. A spell-checking component may require the services of a dictionary manager component. Both components are always needed, but perhaps an appropriate dictionary manager can be acquired from several sources, and delivered independently. As discussed later, the solution to this lies in the creation of appropriate component interfaces produced following a component-oriented modeling approach.

5.2   A DEEPER UNDERSTANDING OF COMPONENTS[1]

In the previous chapter we provided a general, intuitive understanding of what is meant by a component: it is a useful fragment of a software system that can be assembled with other fragments to form larger pieces or complete solutions. Such a definition highlights the emphasis placed by component-based approaches on the partitioning of an application into pieces, and on assembly as a primary means of application construction.

However, to be able to compare and contrast specific component technologies and approaches, a much more precise analysis of component characteristics is required. For this discussion, we develop a high-level conceptual model of component concepts capturing many important aspects of a component. A much more detailed analysis, including a complete metamodel of component concepts, is available elsewhere [4].

For this analysis we consider three particular perspectives that reveal many of the most interesting characteristics of components:

► *Packaging perspective.* A component as the unit of packaging, distribution, or delivery.
► *Service perspective.* A component as the provider of services.
► *Integrity perspective.* A component as a data integrity or encapsulation boundary.

These perspectives are abstracted from a number of concrete uses of components in a range of component technologies. In each of these technologies, it is possible to consider their approach as primarily rooted in one of these perspectives.

Packaging Perspective

From a packaging perspective, a component is considered an organizational concept aimed at identifying a set of elements that can be reused as a unit. The emphasis here is on *reuse*. This is a very broad definition and covers any reusable application development artifact including documents, source code files, object modules, link libraries, databases, and so on.

This is the perspective assumed in the Unified Modeling Language (UML) specification [5]. It defines a component as:

---

[1] This section is derived from the excellent short paper by John Cheesman discussing a number of different component perspectives [2, 3].

*"A physical, replaceable part of a system that packages implemen-
tation and provides the realization of a set of interfaces."*

It is useful to distinguish a number of different kinds of artifacts that
could be considered a component. UML, for example, identifies a number of
specializations (or stereotypes) of a component such as executable, document,
file, library, and table. From this packaging perspective, each of these can be
considered a particular kind of component.

Some people also find it useful to consider a special kind of packaging
component focused on the physical packaging of an executable component. This
is valuable, for example, when a component is an executable file or a Dynamic
Link Library (DLL). In these cases, there is often specific information needed
about the physical characteristics of the component required for determining
where and how that component executes. This is a specialization of a packaging
component we shall refer to as a component server, as illustrated in Figure 5.2.
This shows a *Component Server* as a specialization of a *Packaging Component*.

The packaging of a component (executable) into servers will generally
be based on the deployment or distribution requirements of that component.
For example, a large enterprise-level component that manages one or more
disparate databases may be partitioned into a number of DLLs, which can be
allocated to specific nodes in an enterprise network. At the opposite end of the
spectrum, simple desktop-based components can be bundled into a single
library or executable to simplify delivery.

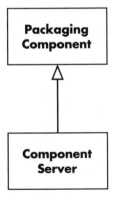

FIGURE 5.2.   Packaging component and component server.

Service Perspective

The service perspective considers a component to be a software entity that offers services (operations or functions) to its consumers. The emphasis here is on components as *service providers*. Designing and implementing an application involves understanding how a collection of components collaborate by making calls to each other's services.

This perspective highlights the importance of a contract between the provider and the consumer of a set of services. Services are grouped into coherent, contractual units called *interfaces*. An interface is a set of operations that a consuming component can call upon to access the services of another component. The interface can be compared to a contract because it describes everything that a potential consumer of that component's services can rely upon, and is the only way for a potential customer of those services to gain access to them [6].

This is the perspective taken in the *Component Description Model* (Cde), part of the *Open Information Model* (OIM) supplied with the Microsoft Repository [7]. The Cde offers a services-oriented component definition:

> *"A component is a software package which offers services through interfaces."*

The service perspective of a component is a "logical" notion of a component because how a developer decides to partition the functionality required into meaningful service components is essentially a design decision. With respect to the earlier description of the "physical" packaging perspective of a component, a many-to-many relationship may exist between a service component and a component server. For example, we may decide that a set of services for managing the maintenance of a list of customers forms the "logical" service component we will call "Customer Management." In a particular implementation, this may be realized as many "physical" component servers via a set of related DLLs. This is illustrated in Figure 5.3. *Both Service Component and Component Server are specializations of Packaging Component.*

By focusing on the notion of a contract, the service perspective introduces an important distinction between the specification of a component (*what* it does) and its implementation and executable forms (*how* it does it). This distinction is fundamental to the management of dependencies between components and begins to address the important requirement to be able to *replace* a component with minimal impact on the consumer, often referred to as "plug-and-play."

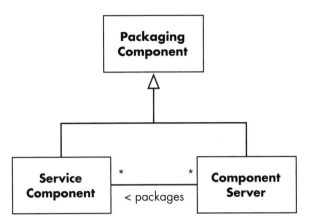

FIGURE 5.3. The packaging and service perspectives.

This distinction between specification and implementation is important. Consumers of a component should only be dependent on the specification of that component. Any dependency on its implementation (whether through direct knowledge or due to unspecified assumptions that happen to be support-ed) will mean that the application is likely to fail when the component is upgraded or replaced.

Integrity Perspective

To allow components to be installed and upgraded in self-contained units requires a view of components as consistent, replaceable units. Although the service perspective allows dependencies between components to be managed, it does not identify the component replacement boundary. This is a further per-spective on components emphasizing that a component can provide an inde-pendent, replaceable unit of behavior. We can refer to this as an *independent* component.

The *integrity perspective* defines a component as an implementation encapsulation boundary. It is the set of software that collectively maintains the integrity of the data it manages, and, therefore, is independent of the imple-mentation of other components. This criterion is a necessary condition for *component replacement*.

An integrity perspective is the approach supported by a number of differ-ent reuse-oriented technologies. Sterling Software's CS/3.0 standard, for example, supports the reuse of business functionality across applications built using the COOL:Gen tool [8]. It defines a component as follows:

"A component is an independently deliverable package of software operations that can be used to build applications or larger components."

This emphasis on independence is important because service components do not necessarily have implementation independence. Typically, they share data or have some other dependency on another component. As a result, collections of service components may be part of one independent, replaceable component. An independent component and all its subcomponents form a single implementation encapsulation boundary and therefore can be replaced as a single unit. Subcomponents are still components in that they offer services through interfaces, but they do not designate an encapsulation boundary. This is illustrated in Figure 5.4.

In Figure 5.4, we illustrate the relationships between the three perspectives on components and enrich this simplified conceptual model by introducing interfaces, component specifications, and model elements. Each of these perspectives builds on the other. The service perspective, for example, is a specialization of the packaging perspective.

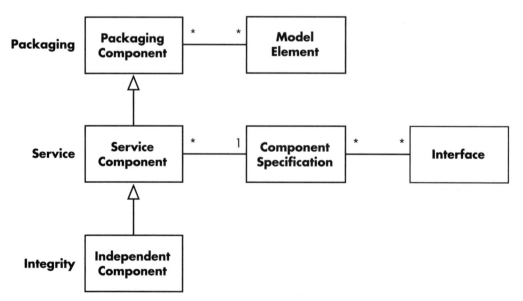

FIGURE 5.4.   Three component perspectives.

An Illustrative Example: Microsoft Excel

To illustrate these different perspectives, consider a familiar component-based application, Microsoft Excel. The packaged item is `excel.exe`. This is a single "physical" component server and contains a number of "logical" service components such as *Application*, *Chart*, and *Sheet*. Each of these is an independent component providing an encapsulation boundary. As a result, each of them could potentially be individually replaced. An alternative implementation of the Sheet component, for example, could be implemented which could interoperate correctly with the Application component, without having any implementation knowledge of the Application component.

Within each component, there are a number of subcomponents. The Sheet component contains the *Range* and *Cell* components, for example. But Sheet, Range, and Cell share implementation and data knowledge and are therefore not independently replaceable; they can only be replaced as a unit.

Table 5.1 provides an illustrative categorization of a variety of existing software development artifacts into one of the preceding perspectives. The categorization is illustrative rather than definitive. That is because the categorization for a particular item relies on assumptions about that particular item. Class libraries, for example, have been placed in the packaging column because they do not separate specification from implementation, and reuse (through implementation inheritance) usually makes use of implementation knowledge. Frameworks have been placed in the integrity column on the assumption that they are binary modules that make calls to application-specific extension code, and their implementation logic is not exposed.

TABLE 5.1   *A Sample Component Categorization*

PACKAGING	SERVICE	INTEGRITY
files, documents, directories	database services	databases
source code files	operating system services	operating systems
class libraries	function libraries	frameworks
templates, tables	system utilities	ActiveX controls
executables, DLLs	individual API functions	some COM classes
	COM classes	Java Applets
		applications
		complete APIs

5.3   THE IMPORTANCE OF COMPONENT SPECIFCATION

From the earlier discussion of components, the importance of describing component behavior in some meaningful way is seen to be essential. The main dilemma that arises is how to describe this behavior in a way that is sufficiently precise, yet easy and intuitive for software engineers to develop and understand. To achieve this, both the implementation and the specification may be described in source code or text. The usual form of component behavior description may consist of some or all of the following:

- ► a list of operation names and signatures defining the input and output parameters for each operation;
- ► an informal textual description of the component's functionality, intended usage scenarios, and history of development;
- ► an informal description of the component's operating context (e.g., hardware platforms and operating system), expected versions of installed software, and known limitations or deficiencies;
- ► performance and availability data for typical execution of the component.

However, to improve our ability to find and assemble components into complete solutions, more detailed and rigorous descriptions of component behavior are necessary. In this section we consider the elements of a component description that would facilitate more rigorous approaches to selection, comparison, and analysis of components.

The Role of Interfaces

A component specification often includes a set of services that naturally group into meaningful clusters. These clusters of service specifications are known as *interfaces*. An interface summarizes how a client should interact with a component, but still hides underlying implementation details. An interface provides the information a client can depend on, permitting the designer of the client to be unaware of any implementation—unaware potentially whether an implementation even yet exists.

In fact, although interfaces can be described from the point of view of component specifications, an interface may exist separately from any component that implements it. This is because an interface succinctly summarizes a parcel of behavior and responsibilities for some situation—behavior and responsibilities any component in that situation must uphold.

As an example, suppose a useful parcel of behavior is defined concerning the management of a set of names and addresses. This is defined by operations such as "add a new address" for a person, "how long" has a person been at an address, and "where" was a person living three years ago. Let's call this bundle of behavior the interface IAddressManagement.

Furthermore, suppose two software companies, Xsoft and Ysoft, separately decide to build components that offer address management capabilities for sale to application builders, so each has an implementation of IAddressManagement. Meanwhile, an application builder writing a personal information management application realizes that she needs address management capabilities. Scanning a catalog of interfaces, she finds one that looks right and, by writing her code in terms of the IAddressManagement interface, finds she has a choice of whether to buy from Xsoft or Ysoft. She decides to buy from Ysoft because it is less expensive.

But another application builder who is building a customer information system for a client also realizes that he needs an address management capability. Looking in an interface catalog, he finds IAddressManagement and has the choice of discussing purchase from Xsoft or Ysoft. He notices that although Xsoft's address management component is more expensive than that from Ysoft, it also supports IAdvancedAddressManagement. On consulting the interface definition, he finds that this would suit some other aspect of his application so he decides to buy from Xsoft instead. This example is illustrated in Figure 5.5.

This example illustrates a number of important points with respect to CBD. First, interfaces are the primary means for potential clients of a component to make decisions on whether a particular component is suitable. Hence, interfaces must be precisely and unambiguously defined, easy to search for, and stored in some readily accessible form.

Second, a component may offer multiple interfaces. Clients of a component may make use of one or more of these interfaces as appropriate.

Third, well-defined interfaces encourage competition among component implementers, allowing potential users of a component to choose among them on the basis of non-functional attributes such as cost, quality of service, reliability, etc.

However, this scenario is based on a very important premise: the description of the interface must be sufficiently rich to allow meaningful analysis of the component's suitability and limitations without the need to examine the component implementation. Achieving this goal is a difficult task. In general, it requires the component to be described by one or more models

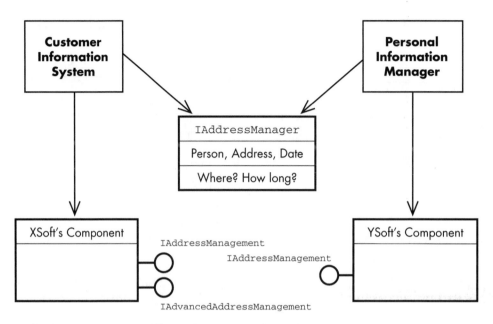

FIGURE 5.5.   Using different implementations of address management.

of its behavior. The models must capture the essential behavior of the component in a precise, unambiguous way. However, they must also be sufficiently abstract to allow multiple competing implementations to be developed that conform to that behavior.

The Importance of Models

Both the implementation and specification of a component may be described in more helpful, abstract forms in terms of models of what they do. Implementations are usually described in terms of models. This has been the strength of many application development tools for the past decade. Often source code and other design artifacts are partially, and occasionally completely, generated from the abstract, easier-to-understand implementation models.

But great value exists in having models of specifications too. Most efforts to describe specifications take the form of interface descriptions in source code or text form. However, models of these, which enable higher level abstraction, are also possible. Advantages of doing this include:

- ▶ models of interfaces can supply semantics of behavior;
- ▶ interfaces with models are easier to inspect to see whether they might be useful collections of behavior;

▶ components whose interfaces have model information can be self-describing;

▶ the impact of using someone else's interface is easier to gauge if that interface has a semantic model.

From this discussion we see that two particular kinds of models are of critical interest: *domain* models and *specification* models.

A domain model represents objects within the domain of interest and the relationships among them. A domain model sets the context for what solutions will be trying to accomplish. Its focus may vary considerably. For example, a domain model may be a business process, either one that exists, or a desirable target (e.g., an order fulfillment process for a large organization). In such cases the domain model might also include process models, workflow models, and details of collaborations in the process. A domain model could be a small, complex part of one process (e.g., to gain a detailed understanding of the rules for credit checking during order fulfillment), or it could be some part of an engineering application (e.g., the objects in the domain of a just-in-time stock control system that interact with the order fulfillment process).

A specification model is a detailed description of a set of objects or an interface that completely specifies the behavior of that set, or that interface, in all possible circumstances of relevance to the domain. Note that in this context the notion of a "set of objects" is an important one. It allows collections of objects with similar behavior to be modeled by a single object type, more often abbreviated to type. Types are the essence of detailed object modeling. In essence, the type of an object provides a boilerplate with which to describe individual objects. The external view of the type is the set of operations and the signatures (i.e., the parameters to the operations) the type is prepared to make available. The type also defines the way an object's state is modeled. But implementation details of the operations or ways in which the state can be implemented are not part of the definition of the type. The type only provides a specification of the object's behavior—it is independent of any possible implementation.

If the operation signatures are said to describe what will happen when an operation supported by an object is called, then the specification model provides the explanation of what the operations mean—the semantics of interaction. These semantics must be precise and unambiguous to enable correct service selection, yet sufficiently rigorous to ensure precise and predictable outcomes during interaction. In particular, since all clients of a component rely on the interface definition, the behavior of the object over time must also be defined.

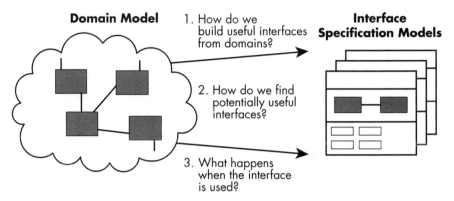

FIGURE 5.6.   The central questions of object modeling for CBD.

Figure 5.6 illustrates the central questions that underlie the relationship between domain and specification models.

These questions are essential in supporting the search, assembly, and upgrade approach of CBD. Of course, in practice, both domain and specification models are comprised of several different kinds of diagrams that view aspects of the domains and specifications from different perspectives. Whichever notations are used, a number of issues should be noted:

► Useful interfaces are built by understanding what behavior is required by individual objects that participate in key activities in the domain. Object types and collaborations are used to describe consistent behavior within the domain. Common, reusable behavior to be implemented by one or more components can be published as interfaces.

► Specification models of interfaces that have already been defined, and perhaps have component implementations, can be matched against objects and collaborations in the domain model, allowing a greater chance of finding a close match than by simply browsing application programming interfaces (APIs).

► When an interface is used in a domain model, an accurate mapping can take place between the terms in the interface specification model and those in the domain model. The protocol for interacting with the interface can be specified in the domain model more precisely.

Collaborations and Roles

To be effective, a component specification is responsible for describing the behavior of a component during all its interactions [9]. In addition to interactions among components, interactions among objects in the domain must also be examined. A type specification must capture with it the semantics of all possible interactions. A description of an interaction is called a collaboration. Collaborations may be complex, involving many parties and an agreed sequence of actions among them. During this sequence the same participant may play different roles, and at times different participants may play the same role.

The role a type plays in a domain model collaboration can help select those aspects of behavior in a model that must be supported in an application system. Hence, interfaces are those roles and types for which we expect there to be an implementation. During application and component design, an interface will represent the role a component plays in an application model collaboration. This provides the important link between behavior driven object modeling, and application design from components.

As an illustration, consider an example from real life. Moving to a new house is an example of a collaboration in which various parties are involved—realtors, attorneys, banks, local authorities, and individuals. Individuals often have two roles, as both vendors and purchasers. Various actions must take place in sequence, such as having the property surveyed before a loan can be secured. There are even actions that must take place simultaneously, such as exchanging contracts for the property.

As well as playing different roles in a collaboration, such as an individual property owner being both a vendor and purchaser, different participants may play the same role (e.g., there may be multiple vendors and purchasers in a chain of property transactions enacted simultaneously).

Figure 5.7 shows a model of the "Move House" collaboration. It depicts the objects and the roles they are playing, and shows that knowledge of an object is built up by accumulating the responsibilities players take on as participants in different collaborations. However, at this point, the collaboration is not sufficiently detailed to clearly understand the responsibilities of all the participants. For example, if our task was to construct an information system to support the activities involved in moving to a new house, we do not yet have sufficient detail to describe the interfaces required, and thereby to describe the software components to be reused or built.

The collaborations are further refined to describe more clearly the actions of which it is comprised, as shown in the lower half of Figure 5.7. The refinement indicates which of the participants are now involved in the lower level actions, and whether these actions should be carried out sequentially, in parallel, or are conditional on some event. The diagram shows, for example, that the joint action Arrange Finance involves a Bank, a Surveyor, and the

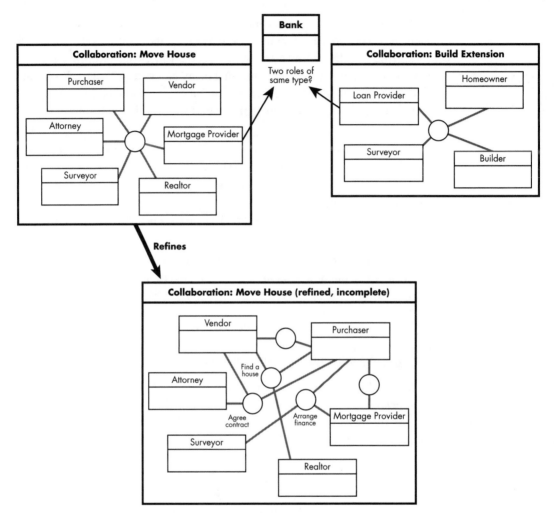

FIGURE 5.7. "Move House" scenario: Collaborations are refined to identify roles and actions.

Purchaser. In practice, further refinements would be needed to be able to ascribe individual actions to the roles responsible for them. This results in a protocol involving localized actions for the roles, and describes their actions, sequence, and dependencies on actions of others in the collaboration. The actions may then be grouped into interfaces, which provide a set of actions we want to name as a separate entity.

A good way to help refine collaborations down to the protocol between localized actions is by using scenarios. A scenario is an example of the collaboration taking place, showing how the individual participants work together to achieve the objective of the collaboration. Scenarios therefore involve typical objects, not types, and are a good way of checking who does what in a collaboration. By using a variety of scenarios, most or all aspects of a collaboration can be examined, illustrating behavior in typical and unusual situations.

Sometimes collaboration descriptions are called use cases, especially when describing key events and actions in high-level business processes. Expressing these high-level processes and interactions with customers using scenario analysis is then referred to as use case modeling. Many object modeling methods endorse use case modeling, but often fail to emphasize the significance of collaboration refinement, protocols, interfaces, and localized actions. As discussed, these are critical elements of behavior driven models.

5.4   THE ELEMENTS OF A COMPONENT-BASED APPROACH

Having discussed the key role played by interfaces, and the importance of models in describing a component's behavior, we can now turn our attention to the elements of a practical component-based approach to application development. The basic approach of CBD is the move toward applications assembled from components that have been developed as independent services communicating over a common infrastructure making use of common services. From this description we can identify four essential elements of CBD that must be defined:

► Application assembly from components;
► Provision of independent services;
► A common component infrastructure;
► Use of standard services.

The component development and application assembly process is governed by CBD-oriented methods. These result in components providing independent sets of services. The services provided by a component are described in a specification, and any number of component implementations conform to this specification. The components communicate via a component infrastructure. This provides the coordination and synchronization between the components.

Application Assembly from Components

The discussion above highlights the key part played by interfaces, and the importance of role and responsibility modeling in obtaining well-scoped interfaces. How do these ideas fit into an overall development approach appropriate for assembling enterprise-scale solutions from components?

The basis of component-oriented approaches is that application developers change the way in which they think about building systems. Traditional approaches to software development are based on phases such as specification, design, implementation, testing, and deployment. In contrast, a CBD approach concentrates on architecting a solution, scoping and identifying components, selecting existing components, wrapping and integrating components, and testing and deploying the final solution. Consequently, the move toward CBD requires existing software analysis and design approaches to be reconsidered. In particular, any method supporting CBD is required to exhibit at least the following four key principles:

- ▶ *A clear separation of component specification from its design and implementation.* This allows component behavior to be described independently of its implementation, and supports the possibility of multiple alternate component implementations for the same specification.
- ▶ *An interface-focused design approach.* The goal of the CBD method must be the definition of encapsulated behavior accessible through well-defined interfaces. Interfaces provide a contract between providers and consumers of services allowing greater independence across components.
- ▶ *Formally recorded component semantics.* Informal descriptions of component behavior can be provided by way of operation signatures and informal text. However, details of operation semantics require formal, verifiable descriptions using pre-conditions and post-conditions attached to each operation. Without this, component behavior is ambiguous and open to misinterpretation by its potential users.
- ▶ *A rigorously recorded refinement process.* Stages in the specification and design process must be recorded to maintain a design record of a component's evolution. Justification for each refinement must also be captured. Use of a component by a third party requires this level of information to assure its quality and to understand aspects of the designer's rationale.

To illustrate these principles, we consider an approach to component modeling inspired by Catalysis, a "next generation methodology for modeling and constructing open systems from components and frameworks" developed by Desmond D'Souza and Alan Cameron Wills [9]. Many variations of this approach exist. However, the illustration provided here is sufficient to gain insight to a number of key elements of these approaches.

There are seven key ideas that characterize a Catalysis-inspired approach to component modeling and embody the principles described above [10].

Describe the Static Aspects of the Domain

A user describes the static structure of the elements of interest within a domain as a set of related types in a type model. The structural relationships among types represent the static constraints that exist among elements of the domain.

For each type in a domain the user describes its features (attributes and operations) in detail. Particularly important are the pre- and post-conditions that define the semantics of each operation by describing the state that must exist before the operation can take place, and the state that will result having executed the operation. Informal definitions of the pre- and post-condition can be given. However, more valuable are pre- and post-conditions in some formal, verifiable notation supported by a component modeling tool (e.g., in the Object Constraint Language (OCL) [11]).

Describe the Dynamic Aspects of the Domain

Interactions among types are modeled as collaborations. Changes of state in a domain occur through interactions among behavior bearing types in that domain. These interactions are represented as collaborations in which types play roles in which they initiate or respond to requests to carry out actions.

A collaboration diagram records the interactions among types in the domain as a sequence of messages (operation invocations). A type responds to a message by invoking the named operation with the given parameters and performing the state change defined in the pre- and post-conditions of that operation.

Allow Multiple Views of the Domain

At any time the user may wish to focus attention on some set of types or interactions in a domain. To do this, a user must be able to create views focused only on those elements that are of interest for some specific purpose.

Track Each Important Step in the Design Process

As a user progresses with their modeling there will be important stages in which they will wish to record the current model. This can be used for backup purposes should the user wish to return to that point in the modeling, and as an historical record of design rationale of how the final model evolved.

Modeling progression within a domain is recorded through the concept of model conformance. A conformance is a relationship between two descriptions of the same thing (types, collaborations, etc.). A conformance is accompanied by a mapping that justifies the conformance claim. Several types of conformance exist: a component implementation conforms to the specification; a class that implements a set of behavior conforms to a type that specifies the behavior; a set of fine-grained actions conform to a more abstract single joint action.

Support Reuse of Previously Modeled (Parts of) Domains

Typically, modeling is carried out by groups of users over an extended period of time. To support this, tools and techniques must allow discrete parts of a domain to be modeled, and allow those parts to be combined in semantically meaningful ways. Domains can be considered to act as scoping boundaries for describing behavior. A user can import one domain into another, or can decompose one larger domain into a number of smaller domains. This supports both top-down and bottom-up development methods.

Package Appropriate Behavior as Interfaces of a Component

Having modeled the static and dynamic aspects of a domain, the user must decide how that behavior should be packaged in terms of implementable units which may be developed independently, shared across projects, and executed on different machines.

This packaging takes place by describing which interfaces will be packaged within a single component specification. Each behavior-bearing type is an interface offering a set of operations. The user selectively decides on the grouping of those interfaces into components specifications. Each component specification is an identification of the interfaces it supports.

Check for Completeness and Consistency

A user may perform component modeling purely as an intellectual exercise to provide greater understanding of some area of their business. However, more typically a user performs that modeling as the step toward one of two goals.

The first goal is to create a component specification that can serve as a definition of the requirements for some externally acquirable or acquired implementation. In this case, the user will not implement the component themselves, but will rely on the component specification as a complete and unambiguous contract to be met by an external provider of that implementation.

The second goal is to create a component specification as a preparatory step before producing an implementation satisfying that behavior. In this case, the user will either directly implement each of the operations offered by the component in some programming language, or will develop models describing the implementation details of those operations from which code can be automatically generated for some target platform. In either case, the component specification is the basis on which the implementation is created.

In a component modeling approach there must be a number of consistency and completeness checks that the user can execute to ensure that the component specification is suitable for either of these goals.

Provision of Independent Services

Components are independent pieces of functionality providing services to other potential client components. As a consequence of maintaining this independence it is necessary to support:

► Design-time independence of components to allow applications to be described as collaborating sets of service providers;
► Execution-time independence of components to enable components to find out about each other's existence during execution and make use of newly discovered services.

At design time, provision of independent services requires interactions among components to be defined based on an abstract description of each component's functionality. One of the major drawbacks of previous approaches to software reuse is that detailed knowledge of the implementation of a reusable item was needed to find, integrate, or upgrade the reused piece. As a result, each of these tasks depended on the implementation, making it difficult for the implementation to be changed without major impact on those tasks. In a component-based development approach, a specification of what a component does is separated from how the component is implemented. As a result, the dependencies can now be between component specifications, allowing implementations to be used or replaced with predictable impact on the system.

There are many advantages to this separation of a component's specification from its implementation. For example, this separation is the means through which controlled changes to an evolving system can occur. Through this separation, component implementations can be upgraded without impact to users of the services offered by that component. Hence, a component can readily adapt to new operating requirements to implement improved algorithms, or to take advantage of new platform capabilities.

At execution time, some measure of independence between components is also required. This independence is maintained through mechanisms that allow late binding of clients to providers of services. A potential client of a component's services typically queries the component to obtain information about the services it currently provides, and then binds to those services to make use of them. This approach accommodates changes to component services with minimum impact on its current or future clients.

A Common Component Infrastructure

It must be possible to specify and build components independently of each other, yet still be possible to assemble them to form a single, integrated application. How is this achieved? The answer lies in a shared component infrastructure employed by all components within the application. The infrastructure accepts the responsibility for providing the necessary coordination and communication among assembled components.

There are two distinct aspects to a component infrastructure. The first aspect is a set of agreements, standards, obligations, and responsibilities that must be accepted by any component wishing to make use of the component infrastructure. This is often called the Component Model, or in the case of object-based systems it is often called the Component Object Model.

The second aspect is a set of mechanisms that implement the coordination and synchronization necessary to allow components to communicate. These mechanisms naturally make use of particular technologies (e.g., languages, communications protocols, and operating system services), and are therefore tied to specific target platforms.

Component Models

For any CBD approach, the technology supporting that approach is based on a particular perspective defining what it means to be a component, and how components find out about and make use of each other's services. This perspective is embodied in a set of rules that must be followed by any component wishing to be considered a component within that approach. These rules are necessary to enable a single component infrastructure to provide communication and synchronization services among the independently-developed components. These rules form the basis of the component model that guides component implementers and application assemblers in the design, implementation, and use of components.

In general, there are two approaches used in component models to encode these rules. The first approach uses separate component specifications describing the services offered by the component independent of the component implementation. The second relies on specific patterns of component implementation to enable information about the component's services to be inferred. A particular component model may use either, or both, of these techniques.

The first approach, using separate component specifications, is the clearest and most visible way to define a component according to a particular component model. The specification typically consists of:

▶ A set of operation signatures providing the name of each service provided by the component, together with typed input and output parameters.
▶ A description of the semantics associated with each service provided by the component. This may be as simple as a textual annotation containing free-form text describing the operation, or as complex as a formal definition of behavior in terms of pre-conditions and post-conditions.

Some additional conventions may be used with this approach to encourage a common naming strategy for component specifications, or to validate consistency and completeness of the semantic definitions of component behavior.

One or more implementations of the component must be available, each one conforming to the component specification. These may be closely tied to the specification through the use of a common language or syntax, or may be completely separate and able to be stored, maintained, and managed as a separate artifact. Provided this conformance between specification and implementation is maintained, users of a component can rely solely on its specification. System integrators making use of components require no access to the component implementation, allowing the implementation to be more easily upgraded or replaced.

The second approach is to encode the component model in the component implementations themselves. This approach may be less flexible than the first approach, but it avoids the overhead of designing, managing, and maintaining separate component specifications.

To implement this approach there are generally some rules or "patterns" that dictate how components should be implemented for this component model. To produce a component conforming to that component model, the user may need to do no more than ensure these patterns are followed when implementing the functionality. Typically, this is no more onerous than following standard naming conventions for operations, inheriting behavior from specific predefined classes, using a particular exception handling scheme, or implementing some well-known interfaces.

Using this approach, the system integrator is able to expect the existence of certain behavior as part of the implementation of every component conforming to this component model. As a result, the system integrator can take advantage of that behavior during execution. Furthermore, the component infrastructure is able to keep track of components because it knows how to extract information about aspects of the services provided by the components.

Component Infrastructure Mechanisms

The role of the component infrastructure mechanism is to support one or more component models. Specifically, it is responsible for providing the underlying implementation that enables component interaction for components conforming to the component models it supports. To do this, the component infrastructure mechanism must support a number of functions, including the ability to allow users to register new components, keep track of the services offered by existing components, and implement intercomponent requests for services.

In particular, the component infrastructure mechanism is responsible for implementing the detailed communication and synchronization behavior expected when one component implementation makes use of a service offered by another component implementation. A significant amount of low-level interaction between processes may be required to achieve this. The component infrastructure mechanism masks much of this complexity from the user.

The task of a component infrastructure mechanism is made more difficult due to the various distribution schemes that may exist for components. Often, a component on one machine wishes to access services provided by a component on a remote machine. The component infrastructure mechanism not only makes this possible, but in many cases it also makes the location of the components largely transparent between the requester and provider of services. As a result, at design time and implementation time, neither the component nor system integrator need be concerned with the location of the component whose services it uses.

In general, as defined by Roger Sessions, there are four categories of component interactions that a component infrastructure mechanism must deal with:[2]

---

[2] For further details refer to the ObjectWatch Newsletter at *http://www.objectwatch.com.*

▶ *In-process local components.* Some components cannot run independently, but rely on additional services made available by a container in which it executes. The container provides common services for such things as user interface display and persistent data management. Web browsers and programming environments are typical containers used by some component infrastructure mechanisms.

▶ *Stand-alone local components.* Often, a stand-alone application can be wrapped to look like a component, and in that way allow other components to access some of its functionality. Such a component can execute on its own without the need for external services. Common desktop applications are the most frequent target of this approach.

▶ *Stand-alone remote components.* Stand-alone applications on a remote machine may also be wrapped for access by a component. The component infrastructure mechanisms must manage all the necessary network communication to achieve this.

▶ *In-process remote components.* Often, components on a remote machine can act as a server to multiple components on a variety of client machines. The server component requires a container in which to execute that is specific to the machine on which it is executing. Database and transaction server components are most often accessed this way.

Use of Common Services

The ability to reuse pieces of functionality is a major motivating factor in component-based solutions. Consequently, it makes sense to try to look for opportunities to build collections of components that can be reused from one system to the next. In fact, there are many services found to be required by all or many applications. Rather than have each application develop them independently, it makes sense to attempt to standardize those services across families of applications. The way in which these common services are defined, implemented, and made available can vary to quite a large degree. The reason for this variance lies in the source of the commonality across the applications, and the kinds of services that must be shared.

Providing common services relies on a number of important factors. In particular, those wishing to share the services must agree on the details of those services. This means that agreements must be made on the syntax (what it is called), the semantics (what it does), and the implementation (how it is invoked). For different kinds of services, there are specific challenges to making the agreements necessary for each of these.

In general, there are four distinct categories of common services that can be defined depending on the utility of the service. These categories relate to the kinds of services they provide in terms of the business function they perform and the degree of commonality they seek to provide.

Business Domain-Specific Components

Within any business domain there are services which are commonly found across applications supporting that business. As a result, any organization offering a suite of applications for that domain is likely to make use of those common services. In a business domain such as banking or insurance, examples of common services in this category may include calculating a person's credit rating, obtaining a list of recent transactions, or validating an account number. Each of these services may be considered essential to many applications in that business domain, and for which there would be considerable benefit in carrying it out in a single, consistent way.

However, while there is commonality, these services likely implement algorithms specific to an organization operating in that business domain. Hence, these services may be considered to provide significant competitive advantage to that organization over its competitors. Therefore, while these services may be shared across the organization, in most cases they will unlikely share the implementation of these services with other organizations. For example, in the case of validating an account number, the implementation of this service may not only be specific to a single organization, it may also embed information with security and confidentiality implications. As a result, each organization will likely provide its own catalog of business domain-specific components.

Generic Business Domain Components

However, there are generic business domain components that can be shared by different organizations within that business domain. These components implement functionality specific to the business domain, but not considered to provide competitive advantage to an organization in the way the component is defined and implemented. On the contrary, there may be reasons for sharing such components in an effort to improve integration and coordination across organizations.

The generic business components most often defined arise as a result of partnerships among organizations within a particular business domain. These partnerships may be motivated by business needs (such as a strategic alliance among partners on a large project), by standards bodies (such as an IEEE committee), or by technical considerations (such as a vendor assisting its product users to share their results). An example of the latter class is the Sterling Software CBD Advisory Board. They have defined generic business components in a number of business domains such as banking and insurance. Typical components in these domains include those for currency conversion, customer information management, and financial report writing.

Business Infrastructure Components

There are some capabilities that can be found as part of the business infra-structure of applications in many business domains. These are services that may form the building blocks of other, business domain-specific services. These services can be distinguished from the technical infrastructure services in that the services provided are specifically targeted at business activities. Examples of these services include those for trading, persistent data manage-ment, and authentication.

An interesting subclass of these services is those designed specifically to support electronic commerce over the Internet. These services allow validation and verification of communicated information, access to electronic forms of payment, and real-time tracking of ordering information.

Often, these services can be obtained from a third-party vendor special-izing in component provisioning for a particular component infrastructure technology. For example, The Theory Center offers a range of e-business com-ponents for application servers supporting the EJB standard. They comprise a family of industry specific EJBs that provide 50 to 75 percent of the common e-business functions, and allow organizations to focus programming resources on their core competencies and unique competitive requirements. Many kinds of domain-specific e-business solutions can be implemented based on these components (see *http://www.theorycenter.com* for more details).

Technical Infrastructure Components

The component infrastructure acts as the "plumbing" that allows communica-tion among components. For components to communicate they must share an understanding of how to use the infrastructure. As described earlier, this could be as simple as a set of naming standards for operations, a standard place to put information about the components, and, in particular, a set of conventions about how to make use of other components using the infrastructure. However, in addition to this, the infrastructure must provide common services in a num-ber of areas to allow components using the infrastructure to do so effectively and efficiently. This may include services to:

► find out which components are currently connected to the infrastructure;
► make reference to other components through some meaningful naming scheme;
► guarantee once-only delivery of messages between components;
► manage transactions consisting of multiple interactions among components;
► allow secure communication between components.

Large parts of most large scale distributed systems built today are devoted to managing services such as naming, security, transactions, and event handling. By providing these common services as part of the component infrastructure this burden is removed from the application developer. As a result of using this infrastructure, users are free to concentrate on developing the application functionality of their business-level components without having to develop the complex code needed to support their robust, fault-tolerant distribution across a heterogeneous network of machines.

As a result, these low-level infrastructure services are frequently the responsibility of the vendor of the component infrastructure technology. For example, IONA is a vendor of CORBA-based infrastructure products. It also provides a rich set of services supporting developers using those products to create robust CORBA-based distributed systems. These services are one way IONA is able to distinguish its core infrastructure products from those of its competitors.

5.5   SUMMARY

In this chapter we have considered three of the key areas facing anyone interested in understanding more about CBD. These have led us to discuss in detail what is meant by a component, how interfaces are defined, and what it means to describe a component's behavior.

In closing, it is worth reiterating the relationship between CBD and object orientation. Object modeling is critical to the definition of component behavior in CBD. The essential points involved in defining component behavior can be summarized as:

► Establish what important objects there are in the domain, and what important interactions occur between them.
► Do this by studying collaborations, a context for understanding detailed interactions among objects playing different roles.

▶ Specify context-dependent behavior shared by many objects as a role, and general behavior as a type. Types and roles, being such similar concepts, are usually shown using the same notation.

▶ Selected roles and types considered important for implementation of behavior are refined, grouped, and published as interfaces. The interfaces may then be enrolled in interface catalogs.

▶ In building applications, interfaces are allocated to components, and the necessary implementations are acquired or developed.

As a result of this deeper understanding of components and CBD, further analysis of products and approaches can be undertaken to obtain insight into their strengths and weaknesses. In choosing among these technologies an organization's particular needs and capabilities can then be assessed with greater confidence.

APPLYING COMPONENT TECHNIQUES

CBD TECHNOLOGY AND STANDARDS

M any elements are essential to successfully practice CBD when building enterprise-scale solutions in the Internet age. As with all complex design and development projects, success can only be achieved with an appropriate amount of effort directed at this wide range of activities. As illustrated in Figure 6.1, people, technology, and processes each have an important role to play. Gaining an appropriate balance among these (often competing) elements is key to sustained success.

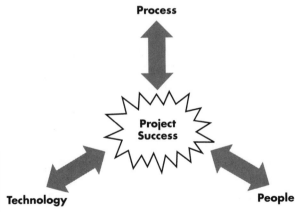

FIGURE 6.1. Dimensions of project success.

Typically, for new development approaches such as CBD much of the initial focus is centered on the technology issues—obtaining broad agreements on the desirable properties of the technology, gaining experience in its application, and encouraging a competitive marketplace of solutions based on a set of standards (whether de facto or de jure) across a range of vendors. However, it is often the remaining two aspects, process and people, that are seen as the dominant elements in taking a new approach "across the chasm" from early adopter experiences into mainstream use in a wide number of organizations [1]. It is there that many issues surrounding the cost-effective application of the technology within the constraints inherent in any large organization are addressed.

Consequently, a CBD project requires appropriate attention to be focused on:

▶ The technology used to design, architect, assemble, and manage a component-based system;
▶ The methods and techniques appropriate to a component approach to software for all roles within the project, and for management staff supporting the project;
▶ The education, training, and experience of individual software development staff, and the readiness of the organization as a whole to adopt a component-based approach.

This chapter examines the first of these elements: the technology. Subsequent chapters address the other two areas. In particular, in this chapter we discuss the major constituents of a technology base for CBD in terms of the common industry standards that currently prevail. However, while we mention a number of vendor-supplied products, we specifically do not look at these products in any detail. There are many papers and reports from analysts and technology commentators providing comparisons and analyses of specific component technologies.[1] Additionally, the vendors themselves provide a wide variety of detailed information at their web sites.

The remainder of the chapter is organized as follows. Section 1 provides an introduction to the main technical elements to be considered. Section 2 looks at the UML notation for describing CBD artifacts. Section 3 describes the Microsoft Repository and its use for storing and managing components. Section 4 considers the three component models that provide the basis for the vast majority of component infrastructure products. The chapter is concluded in Section 5 with a short summary.

---

[1] See Appendix A for a summary of useful resources.

6.1   INTRODUCTION

A wide range of technologies can be employed in developing and maintaining enterprise-scale systems using a CBD approach. These technologies cover many activities within the CBD life cycle. Rather than provide a long laundry list of different technologies that could be used, here we focus on those that appear to be common across many kinds of solutions.

To gain a deeper understanding of the key technologies, we consider three perspectives on CBD based on the stage in the development process that is the primary focus for attention. This is illustrated in Figure 6.2.

A number of technologies are necessary to support these perspectives. While there are many choices available for specific technology implementa-

Analysis and Design Time	**Implementation and Assembly Time**	**Deployment Time**
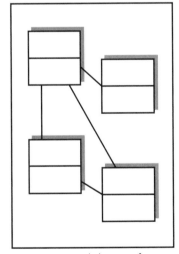	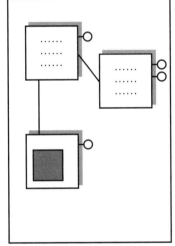	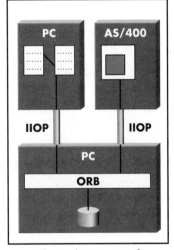
Conceptual design of a system's behavior in terms of services and interfaces	Packaging of components into deployable units conforming to a component model (standard)	Physical instances of components deployed in a specific target environment

FIGURE 6.2.   Three perspectives on CBD.

tions, the industry has come toward general agreement over the past few years on standard technology approaches in three key areas:

► *The notation used to describe the different aspects of components across the three perspectives.* In describing these different component perspectives there must be some commonly understood notation to capture the relevant semantics. The most widely used notation for this is the Unified Modeling Language (UML). Almost all component modeling tools make use of some elements of the UML notation.

► *A repository approach to the sharing and management of components.* To facilitate sharing there must be a well-defined place in which to store descriptions of the components and the component implementations themselves. Currently, the Microsoft Repository is the most widely supported component repository in use by many tool vendors.

► *The technical infrastructure in which to execute applications assembled from components and other applications.* The components execute within the context of a component infrastructure conforming to a component model. Three component models are popular: the OMG's Common Object Request Broker Architecture (CORBA), Microsoft's Component Object Model (COM), and Sun's Java Beans and Enterprise JavaBeans (EJB) specifications. Each is supported by a number of implementations and supporting technologies.

In the remainder of this chapter we discuss each of these three elements in more detail.

6.2   THE UNIFED MODELING LANGUAGE (UML)

Describing a software system at a higher abstract level than the programming language code is a critical approach to understanding any non-trivial system. As a result, wide ranges of notations and languages to be used during analysis and design have been developed during the past 20 years. Unfortunately, while there may be many agreements across these languages on basic modeling concepts, the details of the languages are often substantially different.

Consequently, by the mid-1990s the software industry was faced with a wide variety of modeling notations and languages, each with its supporters and critics. Software development organizations faced a number of inefficiencies in translating designs from one notation to another, retraining designers to use different notations, and in finding appropriate tool support for these notations. For many years there has been interest in defining a single, common notation for describing system designs. A number of efforts in this regard have been attempted. However, they have all failed for a variety of political, technical, and marketing reasons. The most recent attempt in this regard is the Unified Modeling Language (UML). In this chapter we discuss the background of UML, examine its basic characteristics, and comment on why UML has succeeded where others have failed.

What Is the UML?

The Unified Modeling Language (UML) is the latest in a long list of object-oriented analysis and design notations that have appeared in the last decade [2]–[4]. Its initial intent was to unify the approaches advocated by three of the key contributors to the software design field: Grady Booch, Jim Rumbaugh, and Ivar Jacobson. However, UML has now moved far beyond its original goal, and is likely to have a profound impact on the object-oriented analysis and design community at large. Three factors have contributed to providing UML with the potential to become the single, core notation for the next generation of analysis and design methods.

First, from a political perspective, UML is being developed by a consortium led by the three leaders in object-oriented analysis and design methods. The consortium includes a wide collection of object-oriented analysis experts cooperating with the three instigators to refine all aspects of the UML notation. As a result, it has wide appeal among software professionals, and its use has the respect and confidence of the majority of the software industry.

Second, from a marketing perspective, wide acceptance of this work is being sought by submitting the UML specification to a standardization process within the Object Management Group (OMG). This is a fast, efficient standardization process in comparison with more traditional routes such as IEEE and ISO. Furthermore, the OMG currently has over 900 member organizations, ensuring that its standards are well supported by appropriate tools and technologies. Hence, the UML is perceived as an open, widely supported standard representing the best thinking of a wide range of experts.

Third, from a technical perspective, an insightful decision was made early on to concentrate attention on a standard modeling *language*, not a standard modeling *method*. This distinction is important since widespread agreement on methods is much less likely than agreement on the notation and language used to describe the artifacts of a method. In fact, a single method for analysis and design is unrealistic given the wide variety of systems being produced. However, a single common notation allows users of different methods to communicate through the commonly described artifacts they produce, and for tools supporting those methods to be able to interchange artifacts using the common language.

Background to the UML

As illustrated in Figure 6.3, the initial goal of the UML was an attempt to consolidate a number of popular object-oriented analysis and design notations in use in the early 1990s [5]. The impetus for this was the move in 1994 of James Rumbaugh to work with Grady Booch at Rational Corporation. They began to merge the methods they had developed (OMT and Booch), and in 1995 they produced their first public description of their merged method, version 0.8 of the Unified Method documentation.

Later in 1995, Rational Corporation bought the company formed by Ivar Jacobson and he began to work on merging his method (OOSE) with 0.8 of the Unified Method. During 1996, these three methods gurus, now widely referred to as the "three amigos," began to concentrate on the notational aspects of the merged method and renamed their work the Unified Modeling Language (UML). The UML development team was also broadened at this point to include a number of other major players in the analysis and design

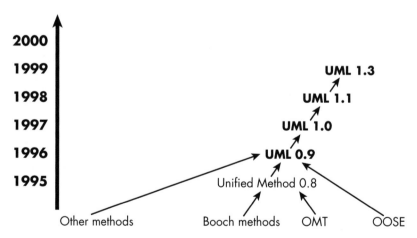

FIGURE 6.3. The evolution of UML.

world.[2] In particular, important contributors to UML and their primary interests included:

- ▶ Digital Equipment—relating UML to other OMG standards.
- ▶ Hewlett Packard—reusable frameworks and the use of patterns.
- ▶ i-Logix—definition and use of executable behavior.
- ▶ ICON Computing—precise behavioral modeling of component and framework-based systems.
- ▶ MCI Systemhouse—uses of modeling languages for distributed systems architectures.
- ▶ Microsoft—building component-based systems using ActiveX and COM.
- ▶ Oracle—modeling business processes and business models in UML.
- ▶ Sterling Software—type models and specifications, and business modeling.
- ▶ Unisys—formalizing relationships and constraints in the meta-model.

Also during 1996, a task force of the OMG was set up to look at standardization in the analysis and design area. In their usual manner, the OMG task force produced a request for proposals (RFP) to provide such a service. In January 1997, various organizations submitted proposals for an analysis and design methods standard to facilitate the interchange of models. The team released version 1.0 of the UML documentation as their proposal to the OMG.

Subsequently, the OMG persuaded the rival respondents to the RFP to join forces to define a single submission. Under the leadership of Rational, this led to the UML consortium expanding to include organizations such as IBM and Platinum. With the help of these organizations, updates to the specification were produced and in 1998 this resulted in the release of the UML 1.1 specification. Further additions are now in progress and have resulted in the UML 1.3 specification released in the summer of 1999. Work on future editions of the UML specification is continuing.

What is Defined by UML?

UML can be described at two distinct levels. For end users of UML, they see a specific notation in which their designs are described. This notation is discussed in detail in a *UML Notation Guide* [2]. On the other hand, tool imple-

---

[2] Note that in recent months a number of these organizations have been acquired, or have merged with others. For continuity, we refer here to the original organizations involved with the UML effort.

menters supporting the UML notation will work with a detailed description of the UML syntax and semantics. This has been defined using a meta-model described in the *UML Semantics* [3] document.

Most people use UML to specify, construct, visualize, or document a software-intensive system. While UML maintains a single, consistent model of a system, users may wish to focus on a variety of specific views of the underlying model expressed as graphical diagrams. UML supports the following views:

► *Use case diagram.* This captures system functionality from an end-user perspective. It is typically developed early in the development life cycle to specify the context of a system and to derive a set of user-focused requirements.

► *Class diagram.* This captures the essential vocabulary of a system. It is built and refined throughout the development life cycle, recording the names, properties, and relationships of the primary model elements in the system.

► *Behavior diagrams*:
  • *State diagram.* This captures event-based dynamic behavior of a system. Changes of state and model elements can be described and analyzed.
  • *Activity diagram.* This captures activity-oriented dynamic behavior within the system. This is useful for describing business workflows within a system.
  • *Sequence diagram.* This captures the time-related dynamic behavior of a system. It allows analysis of flow of control for typical scenarios of use.
  • *Collaboration diagram.* This captures message-oriented dynamic behavior of a system. It illustrates coordination of elements in the system in response to specified events.
  • *Package diagram.* This captures the decomposition of modeling elements into packages, and the dependencies among packages. These packages can be used to increase understanding of the main elements of the system, or as the basis of sharing between designers.

► *Implementation diagrams*:
  • *Component diagram.* This captures the physical structure of the implementation of a system. It is built as part of the architecture of a system to organize and manage the physical elements of the solution.
  • *Deployment diagram.* This captures the physical topology of the system's hardware. It is built as part of the architectural description

of a system to identify the features of the deployed system that impact such aspects as system integrity and performance.

These provide multiple perspectives of the system under analysis or development. The underlying model integrates these perspectives so that a self-consistent system can be analyzed and built. These diagrams, along with supporting documentation, are the primary artifacts the designer sees.

Supporting Component Modeling with UML

The UML notation is specifically designed to support a variety of analysis and design methods. In fact, large parts of a variety of existing object-oriented methods can be supported with the current UML notation. Additionally, a number of organizations are developing specific object-oriented methods that can directly take advantage of the constructs provided in UML.

In addition, component-based design was another key goal of the UML notation. From its earliest days, the UML notation was intended to support the design of distributed systems for deployment to a range of middleware products. To support this, an important aspect of UML is the ability to describe applications as sets of interacting components deployed on a collection of nodes. This component notation support can be used for a variety of component modeling approaches.

For any component modeling method chosen, UML has been developed within the context of object-oriented analysis methods, which exhibit three primary characteristics: use-case driven, architecture centric, and iterative and incremental.

Use-Case Driven

Many current object-oriented methods rely heavily on use case analysis as a primary means of requirements elicitation and as the basis for project management. A use case is a snapshot of one aspect of a system operation. It captures one typical example of a user interacting with the system to perform a task. By documenting a wide collection of use cases, the analyst builds up a complete external picture of the user's view of the system. As a consequence, the collection of use cases documents user-level requirements for what the system should do.

However, a good collection of use cases is not only important for understanding what users want, it also plays a role in dividing the operation of the system into meaningful pieces to be used as the basis for project planning, prototyping, and project tracking. As a result, use case analysis is frequently used as a primary technique in the early stages of any systems analysis effort.

While the basic concept of use cases is common across a variety of object-oriented methods, the exact view of how to use them is not. For example, there are differences of opinion concerning the most appropriate granularity for use cases when analyzing a system, the perspective from which use cases are documented, and the extent to which use cases are used to extract system-level behavior in addition to user-level behavior.

UML provides explicit support for use cases. Actors (i.e., participants in typical activities) can be linked to use cases to model specific roles being performed within a system. Use cases themselves can be linked through two specific kinds of relationships. A use case can be extended by another use case, typically to model unusual or errant behavior. Similarly, a use case can make use of another use case as a way to avoid repeatedly defining common behaviors across use cases. Eventually, a use case is realized in terms of models which it implements. A number of realizations for a single use case can be defined to record different design alternatives.

Architecture Centric

In designing a system, many of the system's inherent qualities are determined by the decisions made on what the major functional pieces of the system are, and how they interact. Capturing these decisions in a clear and precise way is critical to effective software development.

In object-oriented analysis methods, the focus of any description of the system is on identifying data abstractions and their behavior in response to particular events and stimuli. The design of the system is typically based on creating the most appropriate cohesive units of behavior that satisfy the functional requirements of the system.

The static aspects of a system design are modeled in UML using a class diagram. Class diagrams allow the main classes of a system to be documented, and in some ways resemble the familiar entity types of traditional analysis methods. In UML, a class is a very general modeling concept and can be used to represent high-level conceptual ideas during initial domain analysis, interfaces or roles during system specification and design, or functions in the code during implementation. In a class diagram a designer would use stereotyping, naming conventions, or annotations to distinguish which of these kinds of concepts a class represents.

However, the key to many object-oriented analysis methods is to capture, understand, and optimize the dynamic aspects of a system by modeling the changes in class instances over time, and the interactions among cohesive units. To capture and analyze the dynamic behavior of a system, a variety of modeling techniques are typically used in any object-oriented analysis method. In UML, support is provided for four kinds of diagrams, as follows:

► *State diagrams* model the states of each piece of a system and the transitions that occur between states over time in response to different stimuli. Using these diagrams, the typical life cycle of the system can be examined.

► *Activity diagrams* capture internally-generated sequences of events within a system. They are a restricted form of state diagram where external events and asynchronous behavior are ignored to concentrate on the internal processing that takes place within a system.

► *Sequence diagrams* explicitly model the message structure of a system, and the time-ordered sequence of messages sent and received in a system. As a result, they are useful for helping a designer to optimize the message traffic throughout a system.

► *Collaboration diagrams* allow the structure of interactions among pieces of a system to be easily visualized, independently of the sequence of events. Using this diagram, a more abstract view of the flow of data through the system is provided.

Iterative and Incremental

An attraction of many object-oriented analysis methods is that they encourage the rapid design and deployment of a system, facilitating an iterative and incremental approach to design. In fact, iterative design is the key to exploiting object-oriented analysis methods effectively.

Many of the diagrams discussed above encourage iterative and incremental design through appropriate encapsulation of design elements. Object-oriented analysis is fundamentally based on the ability to extend existing behaviors as represented in both static and dynamic views of a system.

However, incremental design also means that the ability to refine designs from high-level concepts to detailed implementation must be possible. Issues such as deployment to specific software modules, processors, and hardware devices cannot be ignored, and become key aspects of a system as its operational aspects are iteratively improved.

There are two kinds of diagrams in UML for modeling the refinement of a design to an implementation.

► Component diagrams model the mapping of logical elements of the design to implementation artifacts such as files, source code modules, and executables. Both interfaces and calling dependencies among components can be represented in this way.
► Deployment diagrams show the organization of the hardware and the binding of the software to physical devices. In effect, these diagrams capture the configuration of runtime processing elements and the software components, processes, and executables that reside on them.

Advanced UML Concepts

Two further aspects of UML are worthy of note, as they support advanced concepts considered essential to modern object-oriented approaches: patterns and stereotypes.

Patterns

In recent years the concept of a pattern has become an important part of many object-oriented analysis methods. A pattern is a way to document a known approach to solving a problem. The problem could be some aspect of analysis, design, or implementation. Patterns are smart, generic, well-proven, simple, reusable design solutions [6].

The patterns concept can be used in object-oriented analysis methods to teach those new to object-oriented approaches. A pattern presents a form of "model answer" for certain situations and allows the novice designer to build on established ways to approach common situations. A pattern can help a novice designer to concentrate on good object-oriented designs and learn by following an example.

In UML, patterns can be used to describe the key ideas in the system. In effect, they allow the designer to explain why the design is the way it is by reference to an established pattern. They are recorded as a form of template collaboration which contains placeholders that are later instantiated with specific model elements.

Stereotypes

UML has an extension mechanism that uses stereotypes. These can be used with any diagram to extend its meaning. For example, a number of predefined UML class stereotypes have been defined for modeling concepts such as events, exceptions, and interfaces.

The user is free to define additional stereotypes to capture modeling concepts of particular value within certain domains. In this way, UML is capable of being used as the basis of domain-specific modeling methods in areas such as telecommunications, real-time equipment monitoring, and system command and control.

6.3   THE MICROSOFT REPOSITORY

As the software industry moves toward assembly of applications from available components, one of the major issues to be faced is where and how to store components so that they can be shared and searched effectively and efficiently among a group of users. A component repository is designed to provide persistent storage of component specifications and implementations, and to facilitate many of the management functions required to keep track of components with and across organizations.

However, to share components effectively it is important to keep track of not only the executable component itself, but also the component specification that provides descriptive information about the component. Recording a component's specification as a separate, managed artifact is essential for obtaining many of the reuse advantages promised by CBD.

The Microsoft Repository is a database that stores and shares components, models, objects, and relationships together with their descriptive information [7]. It is intended to be used as the focal point for information sharing among software development tools and users by supporting reuse, tool interoperability, team development, data resource management, and dependency tracking.

Background

In any software project there are many different artifacts created throughout the requirements, design, implementation, and maintenance process. Keeping track of these artifacts and their relationships is a critical part of any software development environment. Most importantly, the move toward component-based development increases both the number and diversity of artifacts created and used. Hence, the need for managing the artifacts and their relationships increases further.

Furthermore, many different tools and tool suites are available supporting the design, implementation, and evolution of software components. One of the critical decisions facing any software project manager is to decide on the tools that will be chosen to support the project. In particular, the manager must ensure that the tools selected can work together cooperatively to share information about the artifacts being developed and used. Unfortunately, no widely-supported agreements exist among tool vendors regarding the sharing of information about the artifacts that they produce. Hence, assembling a collection of tools to support component-based development (or any other development approach) is too often costly, unpredictable, inefficient, and brittle.

Recognizing these needs, Microsoft and Sterling Software have worked together on the joint design of a repository specifically targeted at storing descriptive information about the structure of software systems and their associated artifacts for component-based development projects. The design that resulted from this effort, implemented by Microsoft as the Microsoft Repository, was previewed to software vendors and system integrators in October, 1996. The initial release of the repository, Microsoft Repository 1.0, was made available as part of the Microsoft Visual Modeler product, demonstrating the use of the repository for managing Visual Basic components.[3]

More than 20 tool vendors currently support (or have announced their intention to support) the Microsoft Repository, including most of the major Computer-Aided Software Engineering (CASE) tool vendors. As a result, the Microsoft Repository offers the promise of interoperability among these CASE tools, allowing components to be developed using one tool, their descriptions to be inspected using a different tool, and a selection of components to be selected and assembled by yet a third tool.

The Conceptual Design of the Repository

For two tools to share information about components (or any other kind of software artifact) agreements at two different levels must be made. At one level, they must share access to the same underlying storage engine. Typically, this occurs through a common application programming interface (API) provided by the storage engine and made available to the two tools. At another level, the two tools must agree on some common semantics of the information they store and retrieve from the storage engine. To do this, they will use a common information model describing the information they wish to share in the repository. When one tool stores information in the storage engine, another

---

[3] The initial release of the Microsoft Repository was bundled with a component modeling tool based on Rational Rose and Visual Basic 5.0. However, stand-alone versions of the repository are also available.

tool can retrieve that information using the storage engine's API, and can interpret the descriptive information it retrieves using the information model.

The Microsoft Repository directly supports both of these levels of agreement by providing:

- ▶ a storage engine that offers an object-based interface to an underlying relational database system.
- ▶ an extensible repository information modeling approach that allows existing kinds of information to be augmented, or for new kinds of information to be added.

To achieve this, the Microsoft Repository provides three key elements. First, to capture the semantics of shared information, the Microsoft repository uses an information model to describe objects and relationships of an application. The information model is extensible to application developers, allowing them to evolve an application design over time. Second, the Microsoft Repository provides a set of well-defined interfaces for manipulating the design information in the repository. An object becomes a repository object by exposing a set of Microsoft Repository interfaces. A developer uses these object interfaces to store properties and to store relationships to other objects. Repository objects are also COM objects, so they inherit all the characteristics of COM technologies. Third, a shared database spanning many application models is implemented that provides relationships between the models through links. The repository engine is a layer of functionality that is supported by either Microsoft SQL Server or Microsoft JET database system.

Information Models for CBD

Tools that use the Microsoft Repository must define the kinds of data that they will manipulate. The definitions of these kinds of data, called *types*, are stored in the repository by creating an appropriate tool information model. A tool information model is a representation of the data of interest to the tool. Because the information model is stored in the database, other tools can now use that information model to access the information in the repository.

As illustrated in Figure 6.4, the Microsoft Repository has defined a number of information models under the name of the *Open Information Model* (OIM). These information models form a logical hierarchy—the child model in the hierarchy extending the model elements defined in the parent. Most importantly, one of the models in the OIM describes (the static elements of) the UML. Use of this model allows many parts of UML diagrams to be stored in the Microsoft Repository via this information model.

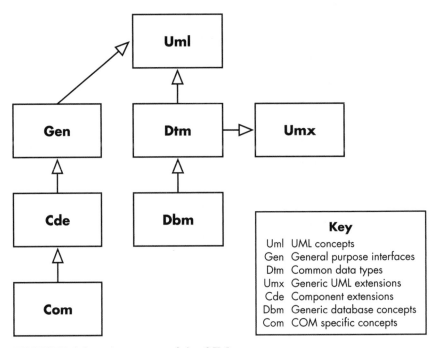

FIGURE 6.4. An extract of the OIM.

Furthermore, the UML information model in the OIM is extended with additional component concepts in the component description model (Cde). This model describes many important aspects of a component, including interfaces, component specification, component packaging, and component instances. As a result, component descriptions, component implementations, and instances can all be stored using these common definitions.

By inheriting and extending from the models in the OIM, a number of additional tool information models have been defined for different uses. For example, Visual Basic 5.0 includes the Microsoft Repository together with a tool information model called the Microsoft Development Objects (MDO) model. This model allows Visual Basic programmers to share data of interest to them via the Microsoft Repository.

6.4   COMPONENT INFRASTRUCTURE
TECHNOLOGY

To support a component-based approach, it is common to use some form of component infrastructure (sometimes also called "component-oriented middleware") to handle all of the complex details of component coordination [8]. Essentially, the component infrastructure provides a common set of component management services made available to all components interested in using that infrastructure. The component infrastructure imposes constraints on the design and implementation of the components. However, in return for abiding by these constraints, the component developer and application assembler is relieved from the burden of developing many complex services within their application.

To understand component infrastructures, it is necessary to understand the kinds of services the infrastructure can make available, and the different competing infrastructure implementations currently available.

Component Infrastructure Services

The use of a component infrastructure arises as a result of a simple premise: the services common to many components should be extracted and provided once in a consistent way to all components. This provides greater control and flexibility over those common services, and allows component developers to concentrate on the specification and implementation of business aspects of the component.

There are many kinds of services that the component infrastructure may offer. However, the component infrastructure is typically responsible for at least the following categories of services:

▶ *Packaging.* When developing a component it is necessary to provide some description of that component in a form that is understandable to the component infrastructure. At a minimum, the component infrastructure needs to know what services the component makes available, and the signatures of the methods which invoke those services. Requests for external component services must also be made in some standard form so that they can be recognized by the component infrastructure.

▶ *Distribution.* The distribution services are responsible for activating and deactivating component instances, and for managing the allocation of component instances to remote host processes on which they execute.

Once a client of a component service makes a request, the component infrastructure is responsible for routing that request to the appropriate component instance, which may involve activating a component instance to service the request. This provides location transparency between clients and servers of requests—the client does not need to know where the component instance servicing the request resides, and the component instance does not need to have knowledge of the origin of possible requests.

▶ *Security.* In distributed systems there must be services for authenticating the source of requests and responses to requests, and for privacy of connections when information is transmitted. The component infrastructure may provide various levels of privacy to ensure secure, trusted connections between components can take place.

▶ *Transaction Management.* As each component may manage its own persistent data, a single high level function may require many interactions among components affecting many individually managed pieces of data. As a result, partially completed functions have the potential for leaving this collection of data in an inconsistent state. Distributed transaction management is provided by the component infrastructure to manage and coordinate these complex component interactions.

▶ *Asynchronous Communication.* It is not always necessary or possible to communicate synchronously between components. Because components may be distributed across multiple host processes, there is always the possibility that some components will be unavailable to respond to requests. The component infrastructure supports asynchronous communication among components, typically through some form of queuing system for requests.

Component Infrastructure Implementations

In the world of component infrastructure technologies, a number of solutions are now in use. Currently, there are three dominant component infrastructure choices possible: The Object Management Group's (OMG's) Object Management Architecture, Microsoft's distributed computing architecture, and Sun's Java-based distributed component technology. In each of these there is a vision for building enterprise-scale component-based applications supported by a set of standards and products. Here, we briefly review the main elements of these approaches.

OMG's Object Management Architecture

The need for a widely agreed upon component infrastructure led to the formation of the Object Management Group (OMG), a consortium of over 900 companies attempting to come to agreement on an appropriate component model and services for building component-based distributed systems. The OMG is a large and complex organization, with many special interest groups, focus areas, and task forces. It attempts to provide standards for building component-oriented applications, and encourages those standards to be followed by vendors of component infrastructure products and developers of component-oriented applications. There are many OMG standards under development, a number of them currently being supported by products.

OMG's vision for component-oriented applications is defined in its Object Management Architecture (OMA) [9]. This consists of a specification of the underlying distributed architecture for component communication providing the packaging services and some of the distribution services. The remaining component infrastructure services are developed to make use of those services.

The main component infrastructure standard provided by OMG is the Common Object Request Broker Architecture (CORBA) [10]. This defines the basic distribution architecture for component-oriented applications. There are three major aspects of CORBA:

- ► The OMG's Interface Definition Language (IDL), which describes how business functionality is packaged for external access through interfaces.
- ► The CORBA component model describing how components can make requests of each others' services.
- ► The Internet Inter-ORB Protocol (IIOP), which allows different CORBA implementations to interoperate.

Together with the CORBA standard, a set of additional capabilities is defined in the CORBAServices standards [11]. A wide range of services has been defined, or is currently under investigation. However, the following services are those that are most often found in currently available implementations:

- ► Life cycle services, which control the creation and release of component instances.
- ► Naming services, which allow identification and sharing of component instances.
- ► Security services, which provide privacy of connection between a client and provider of services.

▶ Transaction services, which allow a user to control the start and completion of distributed transactions across components.

Recently, the OMG also released a request for proposals for a component model for CORBA [12]. This is intended to extend the CORBA model to allow CORBA components to be defined through extensions to the IDL. This would allow server-side components to be created and their relationships to be described. The proposal under consideration draws many of its design ideas from Sun's Enterprise JavaBeans (EJB) specification (discussed later). It is expected that this proposal will be accepted as an OMG standard early in 2000.

A number of implementations conforming to the various OMG standards are now available on a variety of platforms. For distributed applications executing across heterogeneous platforms, the OMG approach to component infrastructure has been shown to be a viable way to build component-based applications. There are a number of examples of successful component-based implementations in applications domains such as banking, telecommunications, and retail.

Microsoft's COM+

As can be expected, Microsoft, the largest software company in the world, has had a major influence in how people think about components and component-oriented approaches. As Microsoft shifts its focus from desktop applications to enterprise-scale commercial solutions, it has described its vision for the future of application development as a component-oriented approach building on Microsoft's existing dominant desktop technologies [13].

To enable sharing of functionality across desktop application, Microsoft developed the Component Object Model (COM) as the basis for interapplication communication [14]. Realizing the value of COM as a generic approach to component interoperation, Microsoft defined its strategy of component-based applications to consist of two parts. The first is its packaging and distribution services, Distributed COM (DCOM), providing intercomponent communication. The second is currently referred to as Microsoft's Distributed interNet Applications (DNA) architecture, providing the additional categories of component infrastructure services making use of DCOM. These ideas are collectively referred to as Microsoft COM+ [15].

The packaging and distribution services implemented in DCOM consist of three major aspects:

▶ The Microsoft Interface Definition Language (MIDL), which describes how business functionality is packaged for external access through interfaces.

► The COM component model describing how components can make requests of each other's services.

► The DCOM additions to COM providing support for location transparency of component access across a network.

Additional component infrastructure services are provided by Microsoft via two products, both making extensive use of the underlying packaging and distribution services:

► The Microsoft Transaction Service (MTS), which provides security and transaction management services.

► The Microsoft Message Queue (MSMQ), which provides support for asynchronous communication between components via message queues.

The Microsoft component infrastructure services offer significant functionality to builders of component-based applications for Windows platforms. For anyone building a distributed WindowsNT or Windows2000 solution, these services provide essential capabilities to greatly reduce the cost of assembling and maintaining component-based applications.

Many Windows-based applications make significant use of the COM+ technologies, including many of Microsoft's own desktop applications, such as the Microsoft Office Suite. Furthermore, a wide range of Microsoft-focused components are available from third-party software vendors (for example, there are well in excess of 100 COM components listed at ComponentSource. See *http://www.componentsource.com* for details.

Sun's Java-Based Distributed Component Environment

One of the most astonishing successes of the past few years has been the rapid adoption of Java as the language for developing client-side applications for the web [16, 17]. However, the impact of Java is likely to be much more than a programming language for animating web pages. Java is in a very advantageous position to become the backbone of a set of technologies for developing component-based, distributed systems. Part of this is a result of a number of properties of Java as a language for writing programs:

► Java was designed specifically to build network-based applications. The language includes support for distributed, multithreaded control of applications.

► Java's runtime environment allows pieces of Java applications to be changed while a Java-based application is executing. This supports various kinds of incremental evolution of applications.

► Java is an easier language to learn and use for component-based applications than its predecessors including C++. Many of the more complex aspects of memory management have been simplified in Java.

► Java includes constructs within the language supporting key component-based concepts such as separating component specification and implementation via the interface and class constructs.

However, Java is much more than a programming language. There are a number of Java technologies supporting the development of component-based, distributed systems. This is what allows us to consider Java as a component infrastructure technology [18].

More specifically, there are a number of Java technologies providing packaging and distribution services. These include [19]:

► JavaBeans, which is the client-side component model for Java. It is a set of standards for packaging Java-implemented services as components. By following this standard, tools can be built to inspect and control various properties of the component.

► Remote Method Invocation (RMI), which allows Java classes on one machine to access the services of classes on another machine.

► Java Naming and Directory Interface (JNDI), which manages the unique identification of Java classes in a distributed environment.

An additional set of technologies support the remaining component infrastructure services. These are necessary to allow Java to be used for the development of enterprise-scale distributed systems. These technologies are defined within the Enterprise JavaBeans standard. Enterprise JavaBeans (EJB) is a standard for server-side portability of Java applications [20]. It provides the definition of a minimum set of services that must be available on any server conforming to the specification. The services include: process and thread dispatching, and scheduling; resource management; naming and directory services; network transport services; security services; and transaction management services.

The goal of the Enterprise JavaBeans specification is to define a standard model for a Java application server that supports complete portability. Any vendor can use the model to implement support for Enterprise JavaBeans components. Systems such as transaction monitors, CORBA runtime systems, COM runtime systems, database systems, Web server systems, or other server-based runtime systems can be adapted to support portable Enterprise JavaBeans components. By early in 2000 all leading platform middleware vendors (except

Microsoft) will have delivered (or claimed) support for the EJB standard. It is considered the primary alternative to Microsoft's COM+ model.

As illustrated in Figure 6.5, the EJB specification describes a number of key aspects of a system. In particular, a user develops an Enterprise JavaBean implementing the business logic required. The user also defines a home interface for the bean defining how the EJB objects (i.e., instances of the EJB) are created and destroyed, and a remote interface for clients to access the bean's behavior. An EJB executes within an EJB container. Many EJB containers can operate within a given EJB server. The EJB server provides many of the basic services such as naming, transaction management, and security.

The EJB specification was made available early in 1999. However, by the end of 1999, over 25 vendors already offered EJB-compliant containers. These implement the component infrastructure services that any application developer can rely on when designing a component-based application in Java. The strong support for EJB from both Sun and IBM provides significant impetus to the case for EJB as an important player in the future of component infrastructure services.

Toward the end of 1999, Sun Microsystems announced a new initiative aimed at bringing together a number of existing Java initiatives to provide a standard platform on which to build distributed applications in Java. This initiative, known as the Java 2 Enterprise Edition (J2EE) standard, builds on the Java 2 standard, and adds most of the important programming interfaces in an

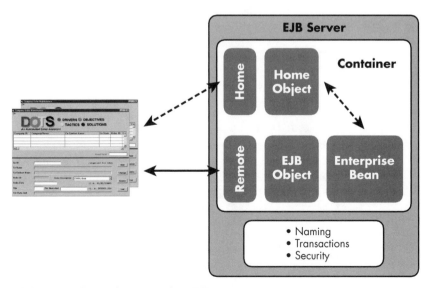

FIGURE 6.5.   Elements of an EJB server.

application server [21]. For example, J2EE includes the EJB specification for server-side components, together with the necessary application programming interfaces (APIs) required for building clients and connecting them to these server-side components (e.g., the Java Server Page (JSP) API for dynamically generating web pages, and the Java Naming and Directory Interface (JNDI) for locating and accessing distributed Java objects).

To fulfill the promise of making the development of component-based systems in Java easier, the J2EE augments this collection of standards and interfaces with [22]:

► A programming model for developing applications targeting the J2EE platform. This provides an outline approach to distributed application development, and highlights a number of key design heuristics for creating efficient, scalable solutions in Java.
► A compatibility test suite verifying J2EE platform implementations conform to the J2EE platform as defined by the collection of standards and APIs. This encourages portability of solutions across different vendor's implementations of the J2EE platform.
► A reference implementation that offers an operational definition of the J2EE platform. This demonstrates the capabilities of the J2EE platform, and supplies a base implementation for rapid prototyping of applications.

By collecting these elements together under a single umbrella, Sun aims to simplify the creation of distributed systems development for Java.

6.5   SUMMARY

Developing large-scale distributed systems is a complex, error-prone task. There are many technologies required as the basis for a complete solution to constructing enterprise-scale solutions using components. In this chapter we have examined the three key areas where some agreements over these technologies have emerged over the past few months: component modeling notation, component repository, and the component models guiding the component infrastructure. In each of these areas broadly similar approaches now exist. Consequently, they form the core of many current component-oriented tool suites, architectures, and strategies.

To use these technologies effectively requires methods and techniques tuned to the needs of distributed systems designers targeting component-based solutions. Our experiences and understanding are just beginning to reach the point where common approaches are beginning to emerge. In the next chapter we consider one key area that provides the focus for much of the current attention: component-oriented modeling approaches.

APPROACHES TO COMPONENT-ORIENTED MODELING

In the previous chapter we considered the core set of component technologies important for any enterprise-scale component solution. While the technology is a necessary element of any solution, on its own it is insufficient. A major part of any solution is the approach to be taken (i.e., the methods, techniques, processes, and heuristics) to apply the technology in context. These elements are essential for effective use of the technology.

In this regard, a number of questions must be addressed. In particular, how do we describe the behavior expected from each component, and arrive at an appropriate component architecture for an application? The answer lies in following the steps of a component-based modeling approach.

The goal of this chapter is to provide a high-level understanding of the major elements of component-based approaches to enterprise-scale solutions in the Internet age. Consequently, we describe the main steps and techniques of component-based modeling approaches, and compare component modeling techniques and their role in provisioning enterprise-scale solutions in the Internet age. More detailed studies of specific methods and approaches to component-based design are available elsewhere [1]–[4].

7.1   INTRODUCTION

Much of the required technology for supporting component-based applications is in place and gaining wide acceptance in the software community. Component-based applications can now be described and manipulated, and collections of implemented components can be assembled to provide a complete application. However, of equal importance to the success of CBD are the methods and best practices for developing component-based applications. These methods are required to help software engineers make the best use of the available technology. Faced with the wealth of technology, software developers must be able to answer the key question of how to effectively design solutions targeting that technology. The software industry only recently began to offer guidance in this regard.

Fortunately, the latest wave of software development approaches are beginning to rise to the challenge of supporting the development of distributed, web-based systems involving reuse of legacy systems and packaged applications. A number of organizations have begun to publicize their approaches and best practices for architecting enterprise-scale solutions from components. However, the range of support and the relationships among the different approaches, methods, and techniques can often make it very difficult to obtain a detailed comparison.

To help with this problem, it is useful to consider the different elements required of any development approach. These are illustrated in Figure 7.1.

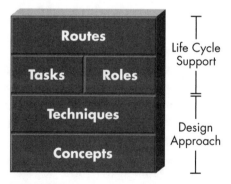

FIGURE 7.1.   Elements of a software development approach.

In Figure 7.1 we distinguish between five necessary elements of any software development approach:

▶ *Concepts.* A strong, unified set of concepts underlies any design approach. These concepts offer a vocabulary and a set of ideas that frame the way a solution is perceived and explored. In object-oriented approaches, for example, these are the often-quoted concepts of encapsulation, inheritance, and polymorphism. They are the key ideas that form the basis of any technologies embracing an object-oriented approach.

▶ *Techniques.* Built on these concepts are techniques for making use of the concepts in many different circumstances. For example, many OO approaches describe techniques for defining hierarchies of classes representing specialized behavior, and for analyzing end-user behavior via use cases. These techniques are used in combination as part of any useful design method.

▶ *Roles.* Within a development approach different people assume different roles in the process, and may apply techniques in different ways depending upon the role. For example, a technique such as interaction modeling can be used in one way by business analysts to examine how users in a domain collaborate to solve a problem, and in a different way by system architects to describe data and event synchronization among a set of subsystems.

▶ *Tasks.* In any software project people assume various roles and use the underlying techniques defined to carry out many tasks. For example, defining a candidate system architecture may be a task carried out by a system architect using techniques such as class modeling and interaction modeling. A development approach will consist of a large number of such tasks tied together by various constraints and dependencies.

▶ *Routes.* Collections of tasks form some recognizable path through the whole development process. Many paths could be defined by emphasizing some tasks, omitting others, and by relating the tasks in different ways. For example, early in the development life cycle a rapid application development route may emphasize domain analysis and delay internal system design tasks, while a waterfall approach may reverse the order of many of those tasks. Each is a valid way to relate a set of tasks in meeting a particular set of design goals.

In the recent wave of CBD development approaches, these five elements are normally considered to be the constituents of two kinds of support. The first is an overall software life cycle supporting acquisition, management, and deployment of components as the major elements of a solution. The second is a set of modeling and design ideas encouraging interface-focused concepts and techniques for architecting component-based systems. In this chapter we separately consider each of these ideas, looking first at examples of CBD life cycle approaches, and then at a number of interface-focused design methods.

7.2	THE CBD LIFE CYCLE

A broad development life cycle provides the framework within which a component-based approach is applied. This framework ties together the major activities that take an application from its inception in terms of business needs to its conclusion following retirement of the software after some period of deployment and maintenance. In many respects this framework of activities is not specific to a CBD approach. Rather, it emphasizes traditional best practices in terms of requirements management, design, implementation, and ongoing maintenance [5].

Consequently, many of the best practices used in traditional software development approaches are equally applicable to a CBD life cycle. For example, a CBD project is more likely to succeed by applying the ideas of incremental development and release, strong project management, and emphasizing the importance of testing and quality assurance. However, in some cases, the general software development life cycle has been specialized with the needs of a component-based solution in mind. We illustrate this by examining two prominent commercially supported CBD life cycle approaches: the Rational Unified Process, and Sterling Software's Enterprise CBD. These approaches offer routes throughout the software development process specifically targeted at component modeling and implementation techniques.

The Rational Unified Process

The Rational Unified Process (RUP) is a broad process framework for software development covering the complete software life cycle. It consists of a set of best practices covering business modeling, requirements management, analysis and design, implementation, testing, and deployment. These are supported by online tools and process guides describing each of these practices and their application [6].

The primary focus of the RUP is derived from earlier work by Ivar Jacobson on the Objectory process [7]. Hence, the RUP is driven by a use-case-centered view of developing system requirements. An additional perspective has expanded this by emphasizing a set of models highlighting the proposed system's structure and architecture. This is referred to as the "4+1" view of a system due to the fact that it offers four views of a system, each offering insight into different aspects of a system's behavior. The synthesis of these views leads to a robust central software architecture for the system.

As a result, the RUP provides a user-centered design approach concentrating on deriving flexible software architectures. The various perspectives are synchronized and refined by encouraging an iterative approach to development based on many of the techniques familiar from rapid application development, and exemplified in a number of spiral-based object-oriented approaches [8].

As illustrated in Figure 7.2, the key to the RUP is the separation of stages within a typical software project from the activities (called "process workflows" in RUP) that take place throughout the software life cycle. The highest level activities distinguished are requirements management, analysis, design, implementation, and testing. Unlike the waterfall process, RUP recognizes that there are many times when some aspect of all of these activities will be taking place at the same time. On the other hand, within each activity there are well-defined, sequenced stages of inception, elaboration, construction, and transition. While they occur in sequence, there may be many iterations of this set of stages before a project is completed.

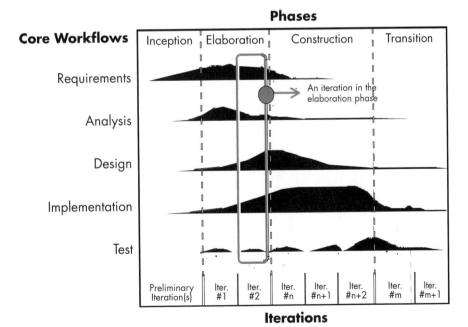

FIGURE 7.2.   Phases, iterations, and process workflows in the RUP.

On top of this framework of stages and activities, the RUP overlays three essential elements:

▶ *A set of modeling techniques and notations.* These are those defined in the Unified Modeling Language (UML). The role of each of the diagrams in the UML is defined in terms of the stages and activities it supports.

▶ *Tool support from various Rational tools.* The activities are mapped to the tool offerings from Rational in the area of requirements management, analysis and design, testing, and configuration management. To a lesser degree, the role of third-party tools for implementation is also defined.

▶ *Method guidance and support.* To encourage and support users in applying RUP, various techniques, heuristics, and best practices support the method. These are made available using online browser-based technology with predefined templates for different documentation, project management, and reporting tools.

The result of these ideas is that the RUP provides the overall framework for applying an object-oriented design approach within the context of Rational's tool offerings. It allows users to consider each of the tools in relation to its role within the development process as a whole, and to the other tools in the Rational product suite in particular.

It is worth emphasizing, however, that the RUP is not specifically targeted at component-based development per se. Rather, the RUP offers a general framework for object-oriented design and construction that can be used as the basis for many methods. Use of the UML as the basic modeling notation provides a great deal of flexibility in design approach, but specific support for key component modeling concepts is somewhat lacking, as we shall discuss later in this chapter.

Sterling Software's Enterprise-CBD Approach

Over the past few years there has been increasing use of Sterling Software's application development tools in component-oriented development projects [9]. Based on feedback from these customers, Sterling Software's Enterprise CBD (E-CBD) approach was developed [10]. It consists of a framework of phases and tasks for use with any enterprise-scale solution using components. It prescribes a detailed approach to component modeling resulting in a robust component architecture for the solution. Provisioning of the components can take place using a variety of technologies. However, the most detailed implementation path defined is based on Sterling Software's own proprietary component model, CS/3.0, for implementation in its COOL:Gen product [11].

The E-CBD approach defines a framework for describing a range of component-oriented development activities. It is intended to be used for a family of routes (i.e., collections of tasks and roles) defined by Sterling Software, its partners, and customers. This allows these routes to be optimized for different needs. However, regardless of the specific routes defined, the E-CBD approach is specifically targeted at creating three main artifacts specific to component-based approaches:

▶ A domain model to provide a business-focused view of the area of interest. The goal of the domain model is to record major events and dependencies as perceived by business users of a system. This may represent the current "as is" view of the domain or the desired "to be" view of that domain.

▶ A component specification architecture describing a proposed system in terms of its major functional elements and their interactions. This architecture offers a logical view of the system's behavior in terms of the primary roles supported by each piece of the system.

▶ A component implementation architecture to provide a visualization of the system as it is to be implemented. This will highlight the physical components of the system and their dependencies, and may include aspects of their proposed deployment to specific nodes on a network of machines.

Sterling Software and its partners have already defined a number of routes within the E-CBD framework. These are aimed at implementation of different kinds of systems, offering guidance and heuristics for appropriate component-based solutions for those systems. The primary CBD route defined, known as *RouteOne*, describes a detailed pathway through the software development life cycle of a component-oriented project for large-scale business systems typical of the insurance, banking, and telecommunications industries. This pathway offers a complete set of tasks and roles for an enterprise-scale project based on six basic phases. These are illustrated in Figure 7.3.

In each of the phases a set of tasks and roles are defined as examples. It is expected that customers would customize them to match their own specific needs. The actions associated with each of these tasks are explained in some detail based on a consistent set of underlying concepts provided by a Unified Component Model (UCM) [12]. This model is a synthesis of a range of component concepts found in the UML, Microsoft Repository, Java Beans and

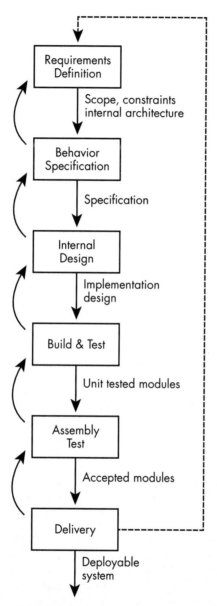

FIGURE 7.3.   The primary phases in RouteOne.

Enterprise JavaBeans, CS/3.0, and the Catalysis component modeling approach.

The primary tasks described for each phase of RouteOne include the following:

▶ *Requirements Definition*—capturing requirements, preparing a business type model, and defining a component architecture.

▶ *Behavior Specification*—building an "as is" context model, building a domain model, building a "to be" context model, specifying an interface, identifying and specifying a component, agreeing on application workflow, specifying user interface layout, deciding on a provisioning approach, and specifying additional software modules.

▶ *Internal Design*—identifying internal types, designing an event action, designing an operation implementation, refactoring the design, specifying an internal type, designing the persistent storage, and initiating nested threads.

▶ *Build and Unit Test*—writing the logic unit, generating and installing the persistent storage schema, designing the unit tests, running the unit tests, installing acquired components, and running integration tests.

▶ *Assembly Test*—designing the assembly tests, running the assembly tests, running the system tests, and running acceptance tests.

▶ *Delivery*—preparing component deliverables, publishing component deliverables, and deploying the application.

Since RouteOne is a generic task structure for CBD projects, it is applicable to both application development using components, and to the component provisioning process itself. As a result, the same idea of phases and tasks in RouteOne can be applied to teams carrying out these tasks concurrently. This approach supports the organizational structure frequently found in component-oriented development projects in which separate teams are responsible for the architecture of the solution and the provisioning of the components.

A suitable delivery mechanism is essential to provide the guidance and advice required to apply RouteOne in an easily accessible form. To achieve this, details of RouteOne are provided in the *Advisor*, an online encyclopedia of information bundled as part of a number of Sterling Software's CBD tools. The *Advisor* offers a wealth of details and examples on component approaches in general, E-CBD, and RouteOne, amounting to over 250 pages of text. In particular, a great deal of *Advisor* deals with practical aspects of component-based development essential for project success. This includes details of appropriate packaging strategies for model elements, version control and configuration management guidelines, and design heuristics aimed at high-performance distributed systems for a variety of target deployment technologies.

The *Advisor* employs a number of innovative techniques to aid the delivery of this large amount of information. In particular, it provides a "look-and-feel" based on web browser technology, extensive use of hyperlinks relating the information, and an Internet-based subscription service to obtain timely updates to material, additional examples, extended techniques, and so on.

Sterling Software's E-CBD approach is being applied in practice in over 90 organizations worldwide. These organizations form a customer advisory board (CAB) for the E-CBD approach, offering feedback to refine the approach, gathering best practices, and providing a community of expertise in the application of component techniques. This feedback is made available to others via ongoing updates to *Advisor*.

7.3   Interface-Focused Design Approaches

While the overall component-oriented software development framework is important, the real differences among software development approaches are evident when details of the design and assembly of component-based solutions are examined. Traditional design techniques are poorly suited to the requirements of component-based systems. They offer little in the way of techniques and guidance for defining and using interfaces as key design abstractions. By following such approaches, users are on their own to decide what makes a good interface, how to understand an application's qualities in terms of the interfaces and their dependencies, and how to architect large-scale systems from collections of components.

Many of the current object-oriented methods have recently begun to highlight interfaces as key design abstractions targeting languages such as Java, which include interfaces as first-class concepts in the programming language [13]. However, two approaches stand out as offering the most to say about interfaces-based design techniques and their use in building component-based systems: the Unified Modeling Language (UML) and Catalysis. Here, we examine the use of UML and Catalysis concepts as the basis for component-based development approaches.

A UML-Inspired Component Modeling Approach

The UML is a notation for describing software systems founded on an underlying set of concepts and techniques for developing software-intensive systems. As a result, UML designers have made some important choices with respect to modeling distributed systems as part of the notation. These choices have a direct consequence on the modeling approaches being encouraged and supported. With the strong support for UML in many organizations, it is essential to consider UML from the perspective of its view on components and component modeling. Here, we illustrate a UML-inspired approach to component modeling. Further details of the use of UML for modeling distributed systems are available elsewhere (e.g., [14, 15]).

The UML has a single, broad view of a component as a physical, material element of a system that can reside on a node (e.g., a file, a page of HTML, a relational table, an executable image, and so on). A component is defined as a physical and replaceable part of a system that conforms to and provides the realization of a set of interfaces.

While the UML supports these general concepts, there is no first class support for the concept of an interface in its notation. Rather, the logical description of the interface is modeled as a special kind of a class using the UML stereotyping mechanism. It can be shown in its full form as an interface description, or in its abbreviated form as a "lollipop" attached to the component realizing the services. These two representations are semantically equivalent. This is illustrated in Figure 7.4.

In Figure 7.4 we illustrate the UML approach to representing a component and its interfaces using the example of an account interface (Account) being implemented by one component (Account_impl) and used by another component (Customer_impl). In the UML, a component offers services defined by an interface. The component is said to "realize" that interface. On the other hand, a component may also use the services of another component via one of its interfaces. We say that the client component "depends" on the server component through that interface. Of course, there may be many real-

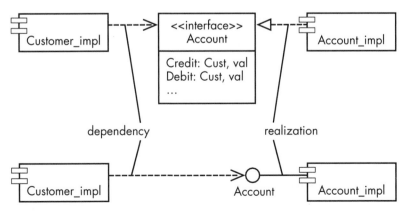

FIGURE 7.4.   An example of components and interfaces in UML.

izations of a single interface (each making different implementation decisions), or many users of a single interface.

Component Modeling in UML

While UML offers a notation to describe components, it does not prescribe a way to design component-based systems. Rather, it offers support for a set of techniques that can be used to derive an appropriate component-oriented solution. However, perhaps the best way to look at component modeling in the UML is to consider a simple example and the kind of modeling artifacts that would be produced while modeling components. For the purpose of illustration, consider a bank that would like to offer online bill payment service to its customers. A UML approach to component modeling is illustrated with some fragments of the design artifacts that could be produced in designing such a system.

We illustrate some of the UML's capabilities as they would typically be used in a CBD project. To reiterate, the UML does not propose any specific component modeling approach. Here, we follow a set of steps typical of anyone using a UML-inspired approach to solve a business need by defining a set of components prior to implementation. In particular, no attempt is made to cover use of all the diagrams and modeling techniques supported by the UML. That is provided in the many books on UML modeling readily available.

Use Case Diagram

The first step is often to understand the scope of the system to be implemented. In UML a use case diagram defines how objects outside of a system (called *actors*) interact with the system's intended functions (called *use cases*). Figure 7.5 shows a sample use case diagram for an online bill payment system. The customer and the check printing system are actors that interact with the system. Several use cases are illustrated here, each one depicted by an ellipse labeled with the name of the use case. For example, the customer can log into the system, get an account balance, show suppliers, and schedule payments.

Typically, the analyst chooses use cases covering the major functionality of the system and refines them to sufficient detail to gain a reasonable understanding of the use of the system. Notice that some factoring of the use cases is possible to allow repeated tasks to be reused via the <<include>> stereotype, or specialized using the <<extends>> stereotype. At this stage, key tasks performed by the analyst include understanding which use cases need to defined, deciding on the detail in which to explain them, and discovering their relationships.

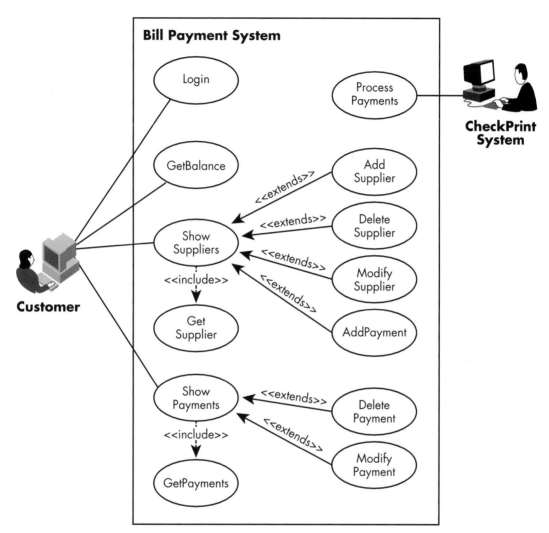

FIGURE 7.5. An example of use cases in UML.

Sequence Diagram

In UML a sequence diagram shows interactions among objects to effect a desired operation or result. Details of individual use cases from use case diagrams are often shown using sequence diagrams. Figure 7.6 shows a sequence diagram detailing the *GetMerchants* use case. Objects participating in this use case are shown in the horizontal dimension and the messages exchanged among these objects are shown in the vertical dimension. Time is assumed to proceed down the page.

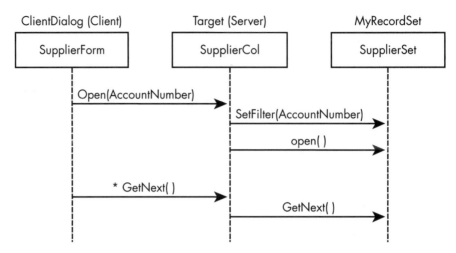

FIGURE 7.6.   An example of a sequence diagram in UML.

A sequence diagram is one of two kinds of interaction diagrams available in the UML. The same information can also be shown on a UML collaboration diagram. In UML a collaboration diagram is an interaction diagram that emphasizes structural organization of objects that send and receive messages, as opposed to UML sequence diagrams emphasizing the sequence of the interactions that occur.

Class Diagram

Having defined use cases and described their interactions in detail via sequence diagrams (or collaboration diagrams), a set of interfaces can be defined supporting the required behavior. This is the interface-based design stage that characterizes a component modeling approach. The UML provides flexible notation support, and hence provides no advice on the difficult task of deciding which are the most appropriate interfaces, how to manage interface dependencies, which interfaces to assign to each component, and so on. Such advice is provided by design approaches that use the UML notation to capture the designs (e.g., [13]).

The results of these aspects of component modeling are captured in the UML via a class diagram. This shows the static structure of the system via its interfaces, classes, their internal structure, and their relationships with each other. As there is no first class notion of interface, the UML stereotyping mechanism is used to mark those classes with the stereotype <<interface>>. Figure 7.7 shows a class diagram containing an interface called "Account" and

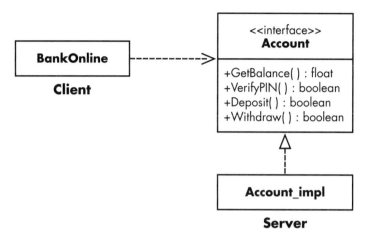

FIGURE 7.7. An example of a class diagram in UML.

its member functions. The Account interface is implemented by the class "Account_impl" and is used by the class "BankOnline."

As discussed earlier, sometimes an interface is shown using a "lollipop" style of notation—a small circle attached by a solid line to the class which it implements. For completeness, Figure 7.8 shows this alternative notation.

Implementation classes would now be designed to describe how the functionality offered by the interfaces would be provided. Detailed design of this implementation may require any of the other diagramming techniques of the UML depending on the complexity and nature of the functionality to be implemented. Eventually, the completed (implementation level) class diagram can be used to generate the skeleton of the implementation in a programming language such as C++ or Java. The developer now codes the business logic implementing the defined functionality.

FIGURE 7.8. An example of an interface-style class diagram in UML.

Component Diagram

Finally, we can begin to look at components and their relationships. In the UML the component diagram is used to show the organization and dependencies among a set of components. These components are physical elements of a system, including elements such as source code, binary code, or executable files. Components package the interfaces and classes shown on class diagrams. Component diagrams are used to visualize the static aspects of these physical components and their relationships. As the UML has a physical orientation to components, the component diagram is most often used to model source code as a collection of related files, dependencies among executables that form a complete application, or physical data stores.

Figure 7.9 shows a fragment of a component diagram for an online bill payment system. It consists of three separate executable components and their dependencies.

While we have described component diagrams from a forward engineering perspective, more commonly they are used early on when reverse engineering an existing system. The source code, binaries, and executables can be visualized as components in component diagrams that will in turn be refined into classes, sequence diagrams, and so on.

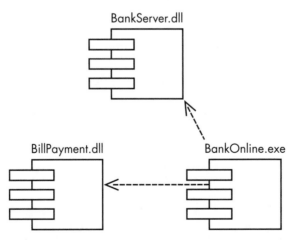

FIGURE 7.9.   An example of a component diagram in UML.

Deployment Diagram

As a final step, the deployment of the physical components to execute on particular nodes in the system is considered. In the UML the deployment diagram defines the physical architecture of the system. In this simplified example, we may decide that the BankOnline component resides on the customer's machine and the remaining components reside on the bank's servers. This could be represented in a deployment diagram, as illustrated in Figure 7.10. We would then assign appropriate components to each of the nodes of the deployment diagram to show their distributed runtime deployment.

Summary

UML provides a useful set of constructs for describing many aspects of components as physical, deployable elements of a system. UML supports a number of component modeling concepts natively, while allowing other aspects to be supported through the UML extension mechanisms of stereotypes and tagged values.

Consequently, the UML is appropriate for many kinds of component modeling. In particular, the UML is appropriate for object modelers who wish to package object-oriented implementations described as classes into deployable items in a distributed system. It is also appropriate for reverse engineering

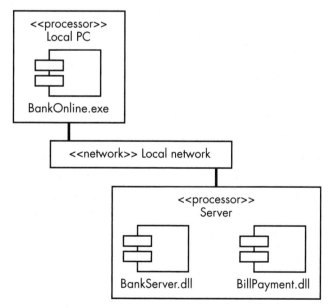

FIGURE 7.10.   An example of a deployment diagram in UML.

of existing object-oriented implementations to obtain some measure of visualization of the underlying structure of the system as a set of related components.

A Catalysis-Inspired Component Modeling Approach

There are a number of limitations in the current UML for enterprise-scale
component modeling, particularly for non object-oriented component implementations, or when the choice of implementation technology has yet to be
made. These include the following:

► To model interfaces, component specifications, and other key component
   concepts, the user is required to make use of extension mechanisms in
   the UML such as stereotypes and naming conventions. As a result, these
   are not supported as first class concepts in UML tools, and may be inter-
   preted differently by individuals or organizations.
► It is difficult to describe the dynamic behavior defining how multiple
   components collaborate to fulfill a specific required behavior. A combination of use cases and sequence diagrams (or UML collaboration diagrams) must be used to describe the object-level interactions among
   classes.
► Interface descriptions must be described in some detail to allow the component producer and consumer to work independently. UML does not
   support the definition of interface behavior at the required level of precision. It has no concept of interface type model, and cannot support
   named pre- and post-condition pairs.
► UML provides no specific support for any component modeling method.
   This provides a great deal of flexibility, but results in no guidance or verification of good component modeling design principles. More specifically, the majority of developers with an implementation-focused view
   of components, and the UML, does not encourage or support a component-based architecture during the specification and design of a system.

To address these concerns, a number of additional approaches to component modeling are being promoted. These involve extensions (or conventions)
in the use of UML, together with a set of design principles to encourage good
component design. For example, extensions to the UML have been defined in
the Catalysis method [3] and are the basis of a number of component modeling tools supporting those extensions. Such an approach has the advantage of
providing purpose-built component modeling support, a specific notion of type
collaboration to describe interactions among interfaces; allows rigorously
defined behavior of interface operations via named pre- and post-condition

pairs; and facilitates visualization of component relationships via specification-level component architecture diagrams.

Hence, two UML-based component approaches are commonly practiced and seem likely to remain in use in the software industry. The first is rooted in object-oriented analysis and design and provides the greatest flexibility to those wishing to work within the object-oriented paradigm for analysis, design, and implementation. Tools based strictly on support of the UML notation provide excellent support to those wishing to take this approach.

The second focuses on component modeling as the driving force within development and concentrates on allowing component architecture visualization and component specification in a technology-neutral way. This is most appropriate for enterprise-scale solutions in which implementation decisions are yet to be made, or when non-object-oriented implementation technology will be used for significant portions of the system. This is supported in the Catalysis approach, a set of concepts and techniques for component modeling utilizing the UML notation.

Here, we describe some of the basic goals and characteristics of a Catalysis-inspired approach to component modeling. In particular, we highlight only a few of the capabilities of the Catalysis approach in support of the specification, design, and implementation of enterprise-scale distributed systems. Many more examples are provided in [3], and at *http://www.catalysis.org*.

The Goals of Catalysis

A component-based development approach has a significant impact on the ways in which software is designed, developed, and evolved. The impact is profound, affecting every aspect of the software life cycle. Given this impact, the question arises as to which analysis and design method to use to guide a CBD project. Taking full advantage of CBD requires new analysis and design methods that are much more closely aligned with CBD principles. The characteristics of such a method would include at least the following:

- ► Systems can be modeled as collections of interacting components.
- ► System behavior can be analyzed in terms of component interfaces.
- ► Component specifications can be described independently of the component's implementations.
- ► A precise, formal notation is available for describing component specifications, sufficient for rigorous analysis of those specifications against a user's needs.
- ► Patterns of component interactions can be explicitly modeled, and subsequently reused across system designs.

► A rigorous, repeatable refinement process is followed to relate an abstract description of a system's behavior to a more detailed one.

► Modeling concepts are mapped directly to concrete representations in UML.

► Familiar, best-practice modeling concepts from current object-oriented and structured methods are incorporated wherever possible.

Supporting these characteristics is the goal of the Catalysis method, a "next generation methodology for modeling and constructing open systems from components and frameworks" [3].

The Basic Constructs of a Catalysis-Inspired Approach

The aim of a Catalysis-inspired approach is to capture the behavior of some domain of interest in a precise way, yet at the appropriate level of abstraction. For gaining an initial understanding of a business domain, this may be at a high level, concentrating on describing user-perceived interactions within the domain. In contrast, when beginning implementation of a system, a much more detailed, technology-focused view of the behavior is required.

Furthermore, a Catalysis-inspired approach recognizes that these different levels of abstraction are often related. They typically provide alternative views of the same behavior. As a result, it must be possible to relate elements of these abstract views to each other in clear, unambiguous ways.

While the details of Catalysis may be somewhat complex, the approach itself is based on a small number of underlying concepts. The four main concepts it depends upon are types, conformance, collaborations, and frameworks:

► *Types.* Objects of interest in a domain are described by their behavior. Interesting collections of the behavior describe a role that object can play when requested. This behavior can be expressed as a type. A type defines the externally visible behavior of an object in a particular role. Unlike the concept of a class, a type does not describe an implementation. Rather, it defines the behavior that any implementation must provide. This behavior is described in terms of the state of any correct implementation and how that state is permitted to change. The state may be as simple as a list of attributes, but more often is itself a set of related types forming that type's type model. Changes to the state are described as operations affecting the attributes or type model.

As illustrated in Figure 7.11, some objects may play the role of order maintenance, and support the behavior defined. This role provides an interface, a grouping of behavior, supported by an object. Hence, that behavior can

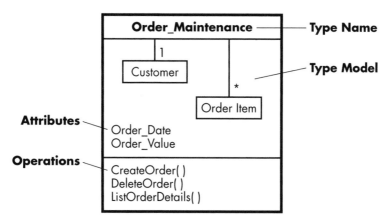

FIGURE 7.11.   An interface type.

be viewed as a behavior-bearing type offering services via a set of operations. The interface's type model constrains the vocabulary to be used in describing each operation's behavior. For example, by reference to the type model, it is possible to describe the behavior of `DeleteOrder` when the order requested is for an amount greater than some threshold value, or for customers with many orders placed.

> ► *Conformance.* Conformance is a relationship between two descriptions of the same thing. One description is considered more abstract than the other, more concrete description. This notion is used in different ways to provide traceability among artifacts. For example, a specific component implementation can be said to conform to a specific component specification, or a set of classes can be said to conform to a particular type (e.g., they implement the behavior defined by the type).
> ► *Collaborations.* A collaboration describes how a group of objects interact. Different kinds of interaction need to be explored to understand the dynamic behavior of a system. In a collaboration, typed objects are said to perform specific roles with respect to the other types. It is these roles that help us to identify the collection of behavior that corresponds to a particular interface.

As illustrated in Figure 7.12, a collaboration defines the actions that relate one or more types. In this case, the Customer type is involved in an interaction with the `TrackingSystem` type via the action `CheckDelivery`. `CheckDelivery` is an example of a joint action. That is, it relates behavior among types without assigning ownership for that action. In a later refinement of this behavior, that action may be assigned to a type (e.g.,

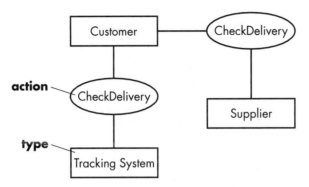

FIGURE 7.12.   Collaborating types.

the Customer may specifically call an operation provided by the TrackingSystem to check the status of a delivery).

▶ *Frameworks*. Recurring patterns of structure and behavior can be described as a framework. A framework contains placeholders as generic items that can later be replaced with specific items of relevance to the context within which it is applied. This specialization of a framework allows common structure and behavior to be reused from one situation to the next. This is a mechanism for allowing recurring patterns of behavior to be factored into reusable elements of a design.

These four concepts form the cornerstone of component modeling in Catalysis. From a very high-level perspective, Catalysis supports the modeling of a system by using type models to capture the externally visible behavior of sets of objects. Refinements from abstract to more detailed descriptions of a system are recorded by capturing conformance between types. The interactions among types are modeled as collaborations. This captures a set of actions involving multiple, typed objects playing defined roles with respect to each other. Recurring patterns of structure or behavior are captured using frameworks. Placeholders can be used in a framework to make it more generic, and to widen its applicability.

A variety of design methods can be defined using analysis techniques based on these concepts. We now describe a simplified component modeling approach based on these Catalysis concepts.

Component Modeling in a Catalysis-Inspired Approach

To describe the behavior expected from each component and arrive at an appropriate component architecture for an enterprise-scale solution, we follow a component-based modeling approach. Broadly speaking, this consists of describing the behavior within the domain of interest, and packaging that behavior into meaningful pieces that together form the application of interest.

As shown in Figure 7.13, translating the business need to a business solution requires three key steps: understanding the context, defining the architecture, and provisioning the solution. These may occur in any order. In fact, it is typical that as a new development project starts many aspects of the provisioned solution are already fixed (e.g., use of legacy code, a technical infrastructure, and various existing practices).

Here we illustrate the basic steps in modeling a component-based application using extracts from a familiar, simplified customer order management example.

UNDERSTAND THE CONTEXT. Two aspects of the domain of interest must be described: the static and dynamic behavior. These may be in the form of a high-level description of some of the primary business types in a domain, or may be a more detailed domain model. In a UML-inspired approach, much of this could be modeled via a combination of class modeling, use case modeling, and sequence (or collaboration) modeling. In a Catalysis-inspired

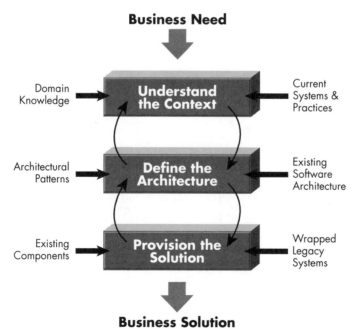

FIGURE 7.13. Elements of a component-based development approach.

approach, a user describes the static behavior of interest within a domain as a set of related types within a type model, an abstraction of the UML class concept. The structural relationships among types represent the static constraints that exist among elements of the domain.

This is illustrated in Figure 7.14 where the boxes represent types and the line paths represent static type relationships. Unlike the traditional use of class diagrams for describing the design of a single implementation, the model captures constraints that must be true in any conforming implementation.

The dynamic behavior in a domain can be modeled in Catalysis as interactions among types, recorded as type collaborations (an abstraction of the UML [class] collaboration concept). Changes of state in a domain occur through interactions among behavior-bearing types in that domain. These interactions are represented as collaborations in which types play roles to initiate or respond to requests to carry out actions. This is illustrated in Figure 7.15 where the boxes represent roles, and the ellipses represent joint actions among identified roles.

For each type in a domain the user continues by describing its features (attributes and operations) in detail. Particularly important are the pre- and post-conditions that define the semantics of each operation by describing the state that must exist before the operation can take place, and the state that will result having executed the operation. Informal definitions of the pre- and post-conditions can be given. However, more valuable are pre- and post-conditions in some formal, verifiable notation supported by a component modeling tool.

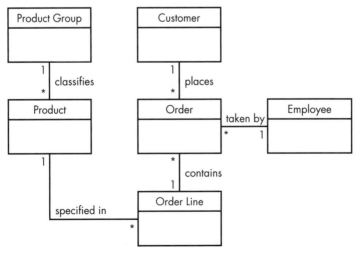

FIGURE 7.14.   An example of a type model.

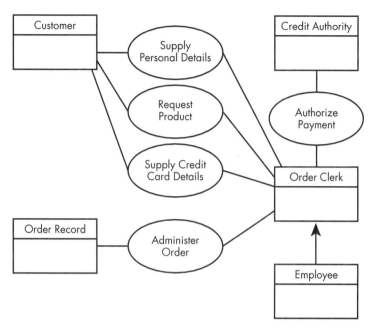

FIGURE 7.15.   An example of a domain model.

In a Catalysis approach, an interface type model is used to define the concepts and constraints referenced by the pre- and post-conditions, and any interface-wide constraints.

DEFINE THE ARCHITECTURE.   Having modeled the static and dynamic aspects of a domain, the user must decide how that behavior should be packaged in terms of implementable units which may be developed independently, shared across projects, and executed on different machines.

In particular, it is likely that a number of the interfaces will be realized by implementations that come from existing legacy systems, packages, or third-party components. Hence, to a large extent, this packaging decision may have already been carried out, or may require writing of wrappers to present that functionality via the specified interfaces. In any case, the models developed while understanding the context act as a definition of the required behavior.

In general, the behavior defined is grouped into meaningful units that can be implemented as replaceable units. Each unit is a component supporting one or more interfaces. This collection of interfaces specifies the component's behavior. The user selectively decides on the grouping of those interfaces into component specifications based on many criteria (e.g., a basic functional partitioning of the system, available packages and legacy systems, organizational constraints, proposed deployment and performance requirements for the system, and so on). This requires the skills and experience of distributed systems designers.

Now we are able to view the defined functionality in terms of a set of components. These components have dependencies based on the previously modeled interactions among their constituent interfaces. The collection of components and their dependencies can be viewed as a component specification architecture for the application. A component specification architecture identifies all the constraints guiding the implementation of the system. This is in contrast to the UML form of component dependency diagram that shows physical dependencies among components such as executables, libraries, tables, and files.

A component specification diagram is illustrated in Figure 7.16 where the boxes denote component specifications with attached interfaces shown as "lollipops." Line arrows between boxes or lollipops indicate dependencies.

Note that in practice modeling the component specification architecture is most often an ongoing parallel activity to modeling the domain. An initial, first-cut component architecture can be produced based on a high-level domain model and knowledge of existing components or legacy code to be used as part of the implementation. This can then be successfully refined as the individual interfaces and component specifications are identified in more detail, and a deeper understanding of the behavior within the domain is obtained.

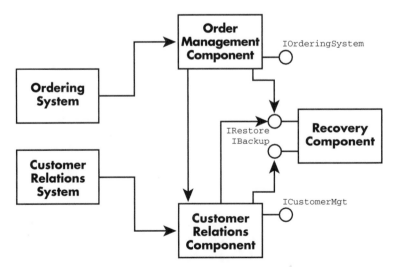

FIGURE 7.16.   An example of a component specification architecture.

This approach is consistent with the typical approach used by many designers following a component-based approach. Their role is one of negotiation and compromise between the specified behavior of a new set of services and available solutions. Reusing existing functionality is essential to provision a new solution quickly and efficiently.

PROVISION THE SOLUTION. The final system will be implemented through detailed design and implementation of each of the constituent components, together with their assembly into an overall system as dictated by the component specification architecture. This will require additional design of the implementation details of each component. Typically, this is itself a complex design task, requiring many of the same techniques employed to create a component specification architecture. In this case, it will result in a component implementation architecture describing the physical components and their realization in a particular target technology.

There are many potential choices for implementation technologies. Sometimes the choice of implementation technology has already been made (for example, when reusing existing components or wrapping legacy code). Other times the implementers are free to choose an implementation technology which matches their domain needs and skills.

Additionally, the implementation choice is governed by the particular component technology infrastructure to be used. In most cases, the choice of component infrastructure technology is made at a corporate or departmental level. In any case, the components to be implemented must all be designed and coded using techniques appropriate to the technology. For example, if Microsoft's COM+ has been chosen, then the implementation languages and tools will be those supported by Microsoft: typically, Visual Basic, Java, or C++ via the Microsoft Visual tools. For this technology there are well known approaches to create high-performance, robust solutions, specialized knowledge and skills to use the technology efficiently, and collections of third-party components off the shelf.

Having developed the component implementation architecture, the components may be provisioned independently by different teams of developers. Dependencies among components are well known, and the sharing among components is defined by the specified interfaces. From the component models and component specification architecture it is possible to generate the interface description language code used by the component infrastructure technology (for example, the OMG's Interface Definition Language [IDL]). A number of commercial products supporting the UML are able to generate IDL from appropriate UML models. The component implementers would then be responsible for making the design decisions and implementing the described functionality, or creating the appropriate wrapper to access an existing package or system.

As implementation proceeds, much more is learned about the application being developed, the needs of the users, and the architecture of the required system. Frequently while developing the component implementations and assembling the final application it will be required to change the component specifications or component dependencies accordingly. To be effective, these changes must be documented within the component specifications and component architecture diagrams, maintaining this tight relationship between understanding the context, defining the architecture, and provisioning the solution. To achieve this with current tools and technologies is far from automatic, and often requires a great deal of discipline on behalf of the developers.

Summary

To overcome some of the shortcomings of the UML, a number of additional concepts can be defined to support component modeling and design. The Catalysis method defines a behavioral approach to component modeling that allows the behavior within a domain to be more accurately described and then partitioned into appropriate components offering access to behavior through well-defined interfaces.

Building on these concepts, a Catalysis-inspired modeling approach can use these ideas to produce a component specification architecture representing the system to be developed as a logical set of functional units. This provides a comprehensive framework for provisioning the individual components from existing system functionality, packaged applications, or through new development activities. In the case of a new development of a component, this itself may use Catalysis concepts in designing the component to create a component implementation architecture describing the solution to be realized.

7.4   SUMMARY

Component-based development of software is an important development approach for software systems which must be rapidly assembled, take advantage of the latest web-based technologies, and be amenable to change as both the technology and application needs evolve. One of the key challenges facing software engineers in the Internet age is to make CBD an efficient and effective practice which does not succumb to the shortcomings of previous reuse-based efforts of the 1970s and 1980s.

The keys to this include:

▶ Separation of component specification from component implementation to enable technology-independent application design;

▶ Use of more rigorous descriptions of component behaviors via methods that encourage interface-level design;

▶ Flexible tool architectures for CBD leveraging existing tool technologies and standards.

This chapter has explored these issues in the context of CBD approaches that will enhance the effectiveness and viability of large-scale software development through the sharing of components—independently deliverable software packages offering services through their interfaces. The result is an interface-based approach to application development and design that encourages the creation of systems that are more easily distributed, repartitioned, and reused.

AN ILLUSTRATION OF A COMPONENT-BASED METHOD

To illustrate component-based approaches to software-intensive solutions, we describe a simplified example of a project that involves modeling and implementation of a new component-based application. Although many aspects have been simplified for presentation here, we attempt to highlight a number of key aspects of component-based approaches discussed in previous chapters of this book. Most notably:

▶ A behavioral approach to modeling that is characteristic of component-based techniques;

▶ The specification of interfaces as well-defined contracts between implementers of behavior and consumers of that behavior;

▶ The packaging of interfaces into components representing deployable units of functionality;

▶ The important role played by a component architecture in describing how different services relate in providing a complete solution.

The goal here, however, is not to provide a complete, in-depth example. A more complete component modeling example is provided in Appendix B. Furthermore, examples of component design and implementation for specific technologies can be found in a number of books and papers (e.g., [1]–[3]). Rather, this chapter illustrates primary considerations inherent to many component-based approaches.

8.1   INTRODUCTION

Many of the ideas presented thus far can be made more concrete with the help of an illustrative example. Of course, it must be emphasized that the description below is intended to illustrate component-based approaches. There are many possible permutations to this approach to suit different needs and contexts. For now we simply provide sufficient detail to highlight some key concepts. For full details of various component-based approaches, the reader is referred to the many available books and papers specific to each approach.

For ease of presentation, we organize this illustration around the three phases of a component-based development approach described previously in Figure 7.13. Notably,

- ▶ Understand the context;
- ▶ Architect the solution;
- ▶ Provision the solution.

Within these phases we describe a general component-based modeling approach that could be supported by many commercial methods and tools.

Having taken a component-based design approach, many alternatives exist for provisioning the solution. Each of these solutions has advantages and disadvantages. For this illustration we will consider deployment to a typical web-based infrastructure consisting of Java applets running in a web browser, with business logic developed as an Enterprise JavaBean (EJB) to be deployed to an application server supporting the EJB standard. As with many large-scale applications, we will assume the application needs to interface to existing functionality and data previously deployed to a mainframe system.

Of course, deployment to any particular target technology requires a number of detailed steps to be followed specific to the technology in use. These are dealt with in detail in the documentation provided with each vendors' products, and are not repeated here.

An outline of the main steps in the design process and the tools used to support them are illustrated in Figure 8.1. For this example the Sterling Software product COOL:Spex is used for understanding the context and specifying the components. This is a purpose-built component modeling and architecture tool supporting a Catalysis-inspired approach to CBD. For provisioning the solution a combination of Sterling Software's COOL:Joe and BEA/Symantec Visual Café are used. COOL:Joe is a Java-based development and assembly tool targeting EJB. Visual Café is used for client development in Java.

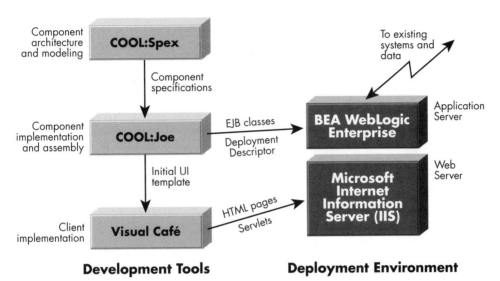

Development Tools   **Deployment Environment**

FIGURE 8.1. An overview of the development tools and deployment environment.

In this example we consider the operation of a small savings bank with a number of branches located in several cities.[1] The bank is interested in expanding its operations to provide web-based access for customers to their account information. We shall consider part of the design for upgrading the software-intensive systems that will be required to support this goal.

8.2   UNDERSTAND THE CONTEXT

For this example we consider three activities to be primary in understanding the context:

▶ *Requirements definition* to obtain a clear statement of initial requirements;
▶ *Use case modeling* to identify current users and their activities;
▶ *Business type modeling* to create a representation of the main business roles and relationships in the domain of interest.

---

[1] This example is based on John Dodd's paper describing an approach to CBD for use with Sterling Software's tools [4].

Requirements Definition

As with every software project, the early stages are taken up with attempting to obtain a collection of high-level statements that summarize the sponsor's requirements. Often these will be provided by the sponsor based on previous analysis and research. Other times this information must be extracted and confirmed based on meetings with management, employees, and customers.

For this illustration we shall assume that a statement of requirements has been provided for the project. These requirements cover a wide range of needs. Many involve the functional expectations for the system's operation and management, while others describe the quality and performance metrics for operation of the system, and define specific technical criteria restricting the solution's characteristics to ensure it is maintainable within the context of a wide range of existing systems. Other requirements may focus on effective management of the development project itself, such as the reporting criteria for the project, key milestones and dates, etc.

Typically, the requirements are documented in some textual form, perhaps supported by tools for assisting with the traceability of those requirements into design artifacts, implementation, and test scripts. More frequently, as in this illustration, the requirements are recorded in a textual document, and traceability is managed manually and recorded in a spreadsheet.

Once agreed upon, these requirements form the basis of future development. Ideally, they are testable statements used to build test cases and as acceptance criteria. At the very least, the project team is usually required during system acceptance testing to give some written or verbal mapping between these requirements statements and the implemented system.

Requirements rarely remain static throughout the life of a project, however. Over time, the needs of the users of the system evolve, and more appropriate solutions are defined due to a greater understanding of their needs. The initial requirements definition is used as the basis for further negotiation on the system's scope and functionality.

Use Case Modeling

Over the past few years it has been found that a great deal can be learned about the context for a future system by considering typical examples of its proposed use. This idea has been formalized with the concept of a use case. A use case is a description of a user's interaction with a computer system. A use case can be expressed as a goal (e.g., "withdrawing money from one account and depositing it in another") or as an interaction (e.g., "initiating a transaction to transfer money between two accounts"). In either situation, use cases are a well established technique for documenting the current or desired behavior of a system from a user's perspective.

Some of the issues associated with use case modeling stem from deciding which interactions are valuable to model as use cases, understanding the relationships and dependencies among defined use cases, and documenting use cases at an appropriate granularity. For component-based approaches, the answers to these questions arise from a number of sources. These include:

▶ Extracting typical services from the statements of requirements. Sometimes these are explicitly described (e.g., "The system shall allow a teller to list the last five transactions for any customer" results in an obvious use case to allow a teller to list customer transactions). However, more often they are implicitly inferred from the external behavior required of the system (e.g., "Checks for amounts in excess of $10,000 must be countersigned by a supervisor" implies there are different situations to be described for cashing checks of different values).

▶ Examining the results of a previous business process improvement excercise, or business process reengineering (BPR) project. Described processes and activities are often suitable candidates for use cases. Typically, a direct mapping exists from individual workflows in a BPR model to a first-cut set of use cases.

▶ Identifying key business events in the domain of interest to see which activities occur as a result of each event. The events here are external actions that occur periodically (e.g., "At 5pm each evening a summary of the day's transactions is produced"), or as a result of some stimulus (e.g., "When a teller suspects that a check may be fraudulent, they immediately inform a supervisor"). Each such event is a potential use case.

As an illustration of the use cases that will be defined, Figure 8.2 shows a use case for a customer making a cash withdrawal from his or her account. Note that the use case involves a number of actors (customer and teller) carrying out sequenced actions with each other and the system (Savings System).

The use case technique has a number of benefits. In particular, the defined use cases are often used to confirm understanding of the requirements documents, and to engage future users of the system in a dialog to ensure there is a common understanding of how the system will operate.

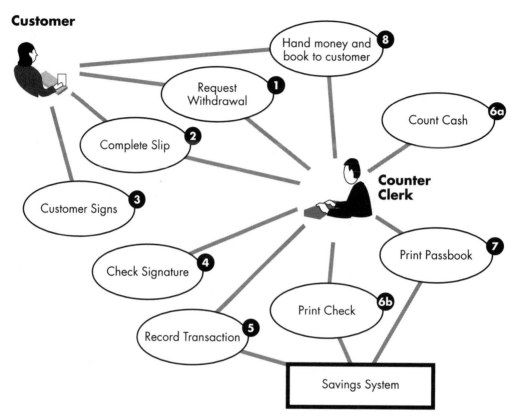

FIGURE 8.2.   An example of a use case.

Business Type Modeling

In business modeling the goal is to identify all the business items that will be of interest later on in describing the domain. For most development organizations trained in traditional structured design techniques, a good starting point for this is to consider the information to be managed. One approach is to identify all the business types that the new system will have to keep track of. Later in the design phases it will be necessary to keep records about instances of these business types, or have access to records about instances of these business types.

In a traditional development approach it is likely that the target for all data management is a single database, and a database schema is developed to describe the data. In a component-based approach the persistent data may be in many forms, managed by a number of components and packages, or be embedded in many databases and file stores. Hence, it is more appropriate at this stage to simply consider the conceptual information to be managed and refer to them as business types. This is a subtle, but essential, distinction. Beginning this design activity with the goal of creating a single database schema may lead to an inflexible design unable to reuse existing legacy systems and packaged applications responsible for their own data management. Later on, the exact form and location of this data can be determined, and business types may become records in relational tables, etc.

A number of steps are involved in business type modeling. First, the main concepts in the domain of interest are identified, and a type model showing how these concepts relate to one another is sketched out. At this stage it is necessary to simply define the main concepts in the form of a "conceptual map" [5]. An example of such a diagram is shown in Figure 8.3.

Second, this conceptual map is refined into a non-redundant type model, which describes the data that the new application will need to persistently manage. This is much like a traditional entity relationship model, except entity types are simply called *types*, and relationships are called *associations*. This is illustrated in Figure 8.4. At this point some details of those types and associations can be added. This includes the main properties of each type, and the cardinality of the associations.

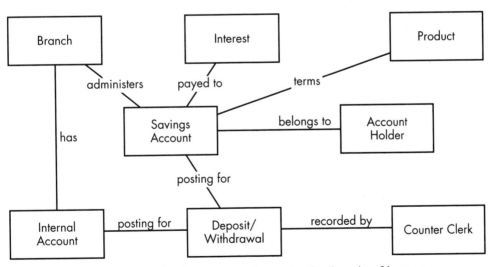

FIGURE 8.3. An example of a conceptual map for the domain of interest.

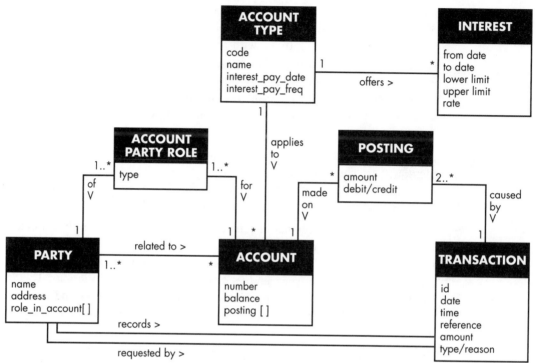

FIGURE 8.4.   An example of a type model.

Third, the type model is refined into a *business type* model, which identifies the (type of) business elements that the application needs to persistently manage. Not all types in the previous model will be business types: some types are likely to be repeating or conditional collections of attributes, which would not be recognized as real-world things by the user representatives. Those should be eliminated from the model. An example of a business type model is shown in Figure 8.5.

At this stage the properties of business types are also considered in more detail. In particular, a set of structured data types may be defined as the base types for the properties defined. This is also illustrated in Figure 8.5.

The resulting business type model provides a list of business types for the domain of interest, the associations among the business types, and some of the specific data items the application needs to record, or be able to derive, about each business type instance.

Additionally, the business type model is refined as the use case modeling takes place and understanding of the domain evolves. Each new use case may provide additional business types, or add detail to those already discovered.

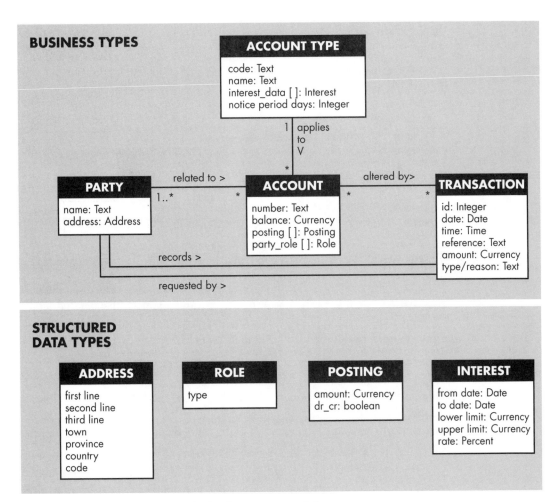

FIGURE 8.5.   An example of a business type model.

Once the basic system requirements are understood and documented, we can proceed with designing the components that will support the behavior of interest in this domain. The aim is to arrive at a coherent set of interface definitions suitable for provisioning from existing assets, or for implementation. In straightforward design scenarios, the analyst may be able to begin listing interface details immediately. However, further analysis is frequently required to understand the particular responsibilities of each interface in more detail. Analysis activities such as component architecture modeling and context modeling may be carried out to create a deeper understanding of these responsibilities.

For this example we consider four activities to be essential in defining the architecture of the system:

▶ *Component architecture modeling* where a collection of related components are proposed and refined;
▶ *Context modeling* to understand the scope of the system being developed;
▶ *Interface modeling* in which the business structures and actions are assigned to specific interfaces;
▶ *Interface definition* in which the interfaces are described in detail.

Component Architecture Modeling

The aim of component architecture modeling is to identify all the components that will be used to build the application, and identify the dependencies between these components. A component architecture diagram is used to depict a number of components and their relationships.

At the start of a design it is typical to draft a candidate component-based application architecture as a framework for further design activities. This will initially be a conceptual notion of the components and their relationships, as the specific interfaces they contain have yet to be defined. As the other design activities progress, this architecture will be refined and details of the interfaces supported by the components will be elaborated as required.

It is often useful to distinguish at least two different kinds of component architecture. Each has its own benefits when considering the design of a component-based system.

The first kind of component architecture is the component specification architecture. This describes the specification-level dependencies that exist between the components. It essentially describes a set of constraints governing *every* valid implementation of that system. For example, a component specification dependency could be used to model the fact that in every implementation of this system the component responsible for accepting an order must make use of the company-wide standard component for credit card validation.

The second kind of component architecture is the component implementation architecture. This describes the implementation-level dependencies that exist between components. It describes some of the component relationships that exist in a particular system design. For example, a component implementation dependency could be used to model a design for a system that describes the action of accepting a cash withdrawal that makes use of a separate customer component to check the customer's credit status. It expresses the choice made during design about how to implement the required behavior.

Obtaining a first-cut component specification architecture is by no means a straightforward activity. However, one way to approach this is to first propose a set of independent business components. These can be derived from the business type model. Initially, one component per business type may be proposed. However, business types that are highly interdependent can be combined into a single component if necessary. This occurs when the business types have multiple cross-component associations, or the use cases indicate that frequently executed operations require access to multiple business types. For example, a single account component may be used if the business type model contains separate types representing savings accounts, checking accounts, and commercial accounts.

Finally, if the organization has defined any component architecture standards, they should be examined to ensure that the proposed architecture conforms to it. For example, there may be some standard components to be used by all component-based applications such as error logging, or security management. These should be included in the proposed architecture as necessary.

For our example system, an initial component specification architecture is illustrated in Figure 8.6.

In Figure 8.6, the component specification architecture illustrates a number of important ideas that may be helpful in understanding a component-based solution and can be represented in such a model. These include:

▶ *Components can have dependencies on other components without identifying the interfaces.* This is useful in cases where two components are related, but at this stage you do not wish (or are unable) to be more specific about the interfaces. This relationship can be refined later in the design process.
▶ *Components can offer multiple interfaces.* Each interface may be closely associated with a particular role or facet of that component.
▶ *Components can be classified depending on the kinds of services they offer.* The classification illustrated shows that some components are part of the technical infrastructure, some offer business functionality, and some are more closely linked to the specific application being developed.
▶ *Components can be related according to an architectural style.* The way components are related can follow a particular pattern. Each pattern has

certain advantages and disadvantages with respect to maintainability, performance, and replacement of components. The example shown is sometimes called a "radial" or "hub" pattern because one component ("Savings System") acts as the central coordinator of all actions. Other styles are more hierarchical, or cyclic, in nature.

This initial component architecture acts as a touchstone for future analysis activities, providing guidance on partitioning decisions that will be made. As the analysis progresses, the component architecture will be refined and expanded to incorporate discoveries with respect to a better understanding of the domain.

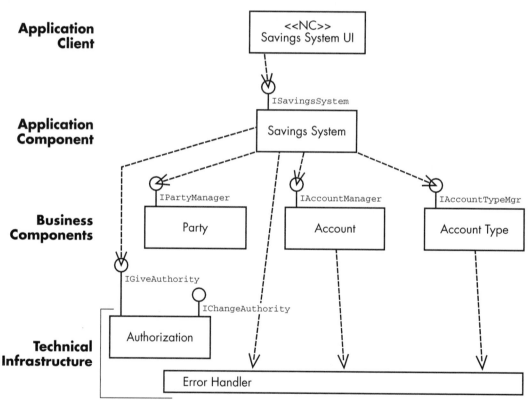

FIGURE 8.6.   An example of a component specification architecture.

Context Modeling

Once a candidate component architecture has been created, the behavior of the system can be analyzed in more detail. As we specify the behavior of the system, alternative ways of allocating our business structures and actions to specific interfaces are examined to choose a suitable design. The first step in this process is to define the scope of the functionality to be provided by the system in support of the business. This is achieved through context modeling.

In a sense, this can be considered a logical continuation of the domain analysis activities already carried out as part of business type modeling. However, the goal in context modeling is to include a description of the proposed system as a key part of the model and understand how the system works within the context of the defined business types.

Context modeling focuses on the system being developed, and the responsibilities of the components that make up that system. By performing context modeling, we obtain a deeper understanding of the desired component behavior. The result is a detailed analysis of what each component must do, without stating how that behavior will be implemented. This behavior is expressed via the component's interfaces. Full details of those interfaces are defined in a later set of activities.

A context model can be used to describe a complete system in the context of a business domain, or can be scoped to describe a particular component and its context. In either case, a context model describes a collaboration between domain types and the system to be implemented in terms of one or more interfaces. Consequently, it describes the system and its business context. An initial context model can be derived from use cases, domain models, or lists of component responsibilities (using familiar techniques such as CRC cards [6]). In deriving a context model from a use case, each actor in the use case becomes a domain type, and the "system" is depicted as a particular system interface.

An example, illustrated in Figure 8.7, shows a context model scoped to a component. It shows that, in the action of creating an account, the system makes use of operations on a number of interfaces. The calls to these operations are sequenced. Similar models could be drawn for other actions affecting each of the components to obtain a more complete understanding of the interfaces and their responsibilities.

In Figure 8.7 we see that responsibilities for each type can be defined based on the collaborations that are defined. For example, because the saving system may request a new account to be created, the IAccountMgr must offer behavior to create an account. This figure also illustrates renaming of

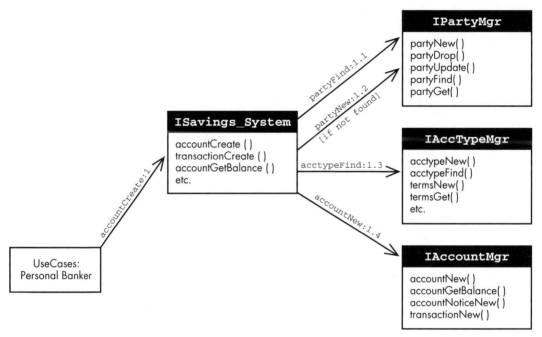

FIGURE 8.7. An example of a context model.

types offering behavior using the common convention of the prefix "I" to indicate that these types are interface types.

Interface Modeling

The goal of interface modeling is to obtain a set of candidate interfaces, and begin to describe the details of those interfaces. An interface is used to describe the common behavior of some set of objects. As a result, the interface must be described in sufficient detail to allow potential users of those objects to discern the objects' behavior by examining the interface description. This means that the interface must be described accurately, completely, and rigorously.

A good starting point is to reconsider the results of context models defined earlier, together with each of the business types previously defined as candidate interfaces. Many of the behavior-bearing types were identified as interface types in those models. Each of these interfaces can be further defined by describing three kinds of information:

▶ Attributes for recording information about the state of instances of the interface;

► Operations supported by that interface providing access to the behavior the interface offers;

► Invariants constraining the allowable states of objects supporting that interface.

In defining this information, the interface must also state the information that it "remembers" and can refer to in these definitions. This is called the interface type model. It primarily consists of the business types that the interface manages [7].

For example, Figure 8.8 is a diagram of a number of the interfaces for our scenario. It illustrates that the interfaces contain a type model describing the information each interface "remembers" and, hence, can be referenced in the definition of attributes, invariants, and operations for that interface.

In Figure 8.8, we also see invariants defined for relationships that must be maintained between instances of the interfaces. In this case, they are defined using a (semi-)formal notation. In other cases, they may be annotations in structured English. The description of each of the interfaces must be completed with attribute and operation information.

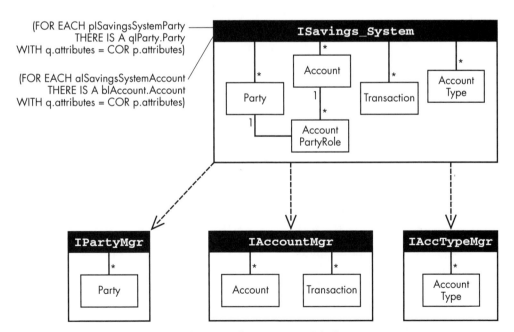

FIGURE 8.8.   An example of an interface type model diagram.

Interface Definition

Having obtained a deeper understanding of the roles and responsibilities of each of the interfaces, the details of those interfaces can now be completed. At an earlier stage, the initial interface type model was created, followed by definition of the operations supported by the interface. At this stage there are three main activities to perform.

First, the signature and behavior of each operation is considered. For each operation, its parameters are defined making use of appropriate types. The behavior of the operations is described using pre-conditions and post-conditions. Each pre- and post-condition pair defines aspects of the behavior of the operation in terms of the state that will result from execution of the operation (the post-condition) given the initial state described (the pre-condition). These may be written in a formal notation such as the Object Constraint Language (OCL), or informally using structured English text.

Second, additional invariants must be defined as they apply to the interface. These invariants help to simplify the description of the operation behaviors by factoring out common state definitions for the interface as a whole. Particular attention is often paid to cross-interface associations, which can be defined through the use of invariants.

Third, the interface type model is completed so that it is compatible with the operation parameters, invariants, and pre-condition/post-condition pairs defined. In a sense, the interface type model forms the vocabulary to be used in their definition. References to objects not a current part of the interface type model are added.

As illustrated in Figure 8.9, the accountNew() operation has parameters name and add, and returns a new account number, acc#. There are three pre/post-conditions defined. One, when the credit check succeeds (creditOK) indicates that a new account number is generated. The other two, badCredit and duplicateCustomer, indicate that a default account number is returned when the credit check fails, or the customer name and address already exists in the system.

This completes the interface definitions. However, due to the important role these interfaces play in the assembly of applications, it is typical that a great deal of feedback will come from those responsible for implementing the systems offering this behavior, and those responsible for using, or consuming, this behavior. With this feedback the interface definitions are refined to meet the requirements received from these implementation teams.

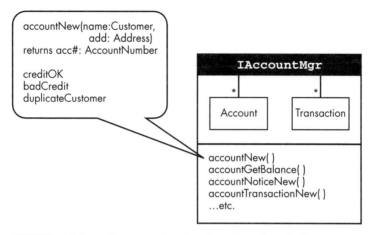

FIGURE 8.9.   An example of an interface description.

The completed sets of component and interface definitions are used as the basis for the implementation of the system. In a pure top-down approach, provisioning the solution would not commence until the architecture of the system has been completed. In reality, of course, many aspects of the solution may have been decided before the architecture was defined (e.g., due to the need to conform to corporate development standards), or may have been started while the architecture definition was taking place (e.g., development of technology prototypes). In any case, the result is an interleaved development process in which architecture definition guides provisioning decisions, and provisioning experiences are used to inform and refine the architecture.

There are four main activities taking place in provisioning the solution:

► Component implementation;
► Component wrapping;
► Component assembly;
► System deployment.

Component Implementation

In a component-based approach, the goal of component implementation is to convert a component specification into a conforming component implementation. To do this, the component specification must be refined from its abstract view of the component as a provider of services into a deployable software unit delivering those services.

To develop the implementation requires a number of activities to be carried out. They include:

▶ *Designing the implementation of the component.* Even with a component specification completed, there may still be significant effort required to design the internal behavior of the component implementation. The task may begin by producing internal implementation objects that correspond with the specification types for the component. Subsequently, the implementation objects may be combined, or decomposed, as the developer believes is appropriate.

▶ *Implementing the business logic necessary to support the behavior defined in the component specification.* The specification contains details of the operation names, their signatures, and the changes of state that each must support. The developer now develops the logic necessary to implement that behavior in the chosen technology.

▶ *Designing the persistent storage model.* The component specification does not provide details of the persistent storage required for the component. The developer is responsible for designing a persistent storage model capable of returning the information defined in the component specification. In reality, however, the specification types defined can be used as candidate persistent objects (or tables if a relational database is to be used). However, the developer is free to refine the persistent storage model within the context of the component specification.

▶ *Creating the user interface for the component, if applicable.* Many components are defined independently of any user interfaces required to access their services. However, some default user interface may be necessary to test each of the operations supported by the interface. In other cases the user interface is closely tied to the component and must be created when the component is implemented. Here, an interface design tool is used to implement the interface according to the organization's design standards, and employ good user interface practices. Many of the design artifacts produced during component specification may be useful during user interface design, particularly use case models and interface interaction diagrams.

Many implementation technology choices exist. In our illustration the chosen component implementation approach is to use the Java language, packaging the component as an Enterprise JavaBean (EJB). A Java development tool is used to implement the business logic. Persistent storage is supported through a relational database employing a Java Data Base Connection (JDBC) interface. The implementation is then packaged as an EJB.

In many cases the developer is required to be responsible for each of these four activities, with little help from the support tools and environment. With the latest generation of commercial products, such as Sterling Software's COOL:Joe, however, many of these tasks are automated or assisted through the use of wizards and templates.

Component Wrapping

Rather than implementing all of the functionality defined in the component specifications, much of it may already be provided in existing systems, or as third party components. In many cases it may be a viable alternative to reuse this existing functionality. In practice, however, the candidate functionality may be executing on a different platform, written in another language, or packaged in an incompatible form. It will almost certainly not be an exact match for the specified functionality.

To use this existing functionality, two activities must be carried out. First, the developer must decide how to make the match between the existing functionality and the services defined in the component specification. One option is to change the component specification to match the existing functionality. To take this approach requires the component architecture to be revisited, and the implications of these changes assessed within the broader system context. Another approach is to create a mapping between the component specification and the existing functionality. This additional mapping logic may be a straightforward task, or it may require detailed coding to take place.

The second activity is to develop the component wrapper providing access to the existing functionality. This wrapper must implement any mapping that has been defined, and allow the functionality to be delivered as a separate, deployable unit in the appropriate component technology. In our example this would involve writing EJB wrappers in Java for the existing functionality. This could be achieved, for example, even if the existing functionality was an existing program in a language such as COBOL, or a component developed in another component technology such as COM.

Component Assembly

Following implementation, the set of components must be assembled into a complete application. This requires connection between the client-side applications and the server-side components. In many cases, this assembly is made much more straightforward through the use of a "coordination" component, as illustrated in the example shown in Figure 8.6. That component acts as the coordination point for assembly.

In a web-based application, the assembly process is targeting a combination of application server and web server. As a result, component assembly will require creation or generation of servlets, Active Server Pages (ASPs), or Java Server Pages (JSPs) to tie together the static and dynamic elements of the client. The choice of which approach is web server technology-specific. However, in each case, the static layout and text information on the web pages must be combined with dynamically generated content obtained from calls to other components.

As the assembly activities progress, a great deal of effort will be placed on testing the resulting system. As well as testing that the functionality is as expected, many of the non-functional aspects of the system must also be examined. Addressing issues such as performance, security, and availability may require that all component specifications and implementations be revised.

System Deployment

Finally, the system can be deployed to the appropriate infrastructure and platform. The target technology will typically provide some form of deployment support to assist with this activity. For technologies supporting EJB, this is managed through the concept of a deployment descriptor. A deployment descriptor is a description of the deployment-specific characteristics of the application that may vary from one installed instance of the system to another (e.g., security, access control, and transactional behavior). Use of deployment descriptors allows customization of application behavior at runtime without having to change the software itself.

8.5   Summary

The task of provisiong an enterprise-scale solution for the Internet using component-based techniques has many interesting aspects that are different from traditional application development. In this chapter we have highlighted these differences through an illustrative example project from requirements definition to deployment. To do so we devised a typical application development scenario and followed a process indicative of many component-based development approaches.

The goal of this chapter has been to draw together many of the ideas in previous chapters to help visualize the steps of a component-based approach. While this illustration has been sufficient to highlight a number of key aspects of component-based development, it is clearly incomplete in many areas. There are many steps that were discussed at a high level that, in practice, may require detailed analysis and thought. This knowledge comes from practical experience in the application of component-based approaches and can be obtained from vendors, consultants, and academics specializing in component-based design and implementation. With the help of these experts, your organization will be better prepared to develop robust enterprise-scale solutions for the Internet age.

PART FOUR

A Look to the Future

THE BUSINESS IMPERATIVE: MOVING QUICKLY INTO THE DIGITAL AGE

In this book we have examined a number of the key underlying approaches, technologies, and standards that will fuel the current generation of enterprise solutions for the Internet age. These are centered on components and component-based design approaches. In this final part of the book we expand on these ideas and consider the elements likely to have a major impact on enterprise-scale solutions over the next few years. To do this, we consider the business drivers that form the basis of funding decisions, and the technological advances that will be fundamental to future solutions.

This part of the book is organized around two basic themes:

▶ This present chapter considers the business drivers shaping the investment strategies of organizations building and acquiring enterprise-scale software solutions in the Internet age. This defines the business imperative for Information technology over the coming years.
▶ The following chapter examines current technology directions and trends in the area of components and component approaches in response to these business needs. This leads to a discussion of longer term research initiatives that will influence future generations of enterprise-scale software tools, technologies, and solutions.

9.1   INTRODUCTION

According to an ancient Chinese proverb:

"A journey of a thousand miles begins with the first step."

In many ways this is true of the current journey being undertaken by many organizations as they take the path toward enterprise-scale solutions in the Internet age. Most organizations recognize the need to change all too clearly. They see new competitors in their markets, they have identified opportunities to offer new products and services to larger markets, and they have discussed the potential for information technology to create efficiencies in the way in which they conduct their business—from streamlining back-office functions to improved front-office customer services. Information technology is seen as a major element of meeting these needs. In many people's eyes it is the defining factor in their ability to execute efficiently and effectively in the rapidly evolving business landscape.

For most established organizations, however, their response to these opportunities and threats has been much more cautious. A majority of companies now have some form of web presence allowing them to advertise their products and solutions globally to anyone with a web browser and an Internet connection. A number are also beginning to track visitors to their sites, collect information about the visitors and the information they examine, personalize the web pages for different kinds of users, and use the Internet to generate leads for potential new sales of products and services. Unfortunately, that is as far as many organizations have come on their journey to realize their goals for enterprise-scale solutions in the Internet age. With a few high-profile exceptions, most organizations are still not using Internet technologies as a fundamental part of the way they conduct their businesses. It can be argued that to be successful over the next decade requires organizations in every business domain to take a number of steps towards the use of Internet technologies to transact business over the web, and to redefine their key business processes based on the use of these technologies.

Confirming the current state of Internet use is a September 1999 survey from *InformationWeek* magazine. In that survey they found that more than 65% of the organizations they questioned had no long-term strategy for how they plan to use Internet technologies within their organizations as part of the information technology infrastructure for delivering enterprise-scale solutions. Furthermore, they were uncertain about the direction technology is heading for, and felt unable to make long-term plans for how they will exploit the opportunities they foresee.

To understand these issues in more detail requires an examination of the business drivers that form the basis of the requirements for future information systems. The success of these systems will be evaluated within the context of these business issues. Over the next few years there are two key business drivers that will dominate future enterprise-scale solutions.

The first is the push toward greater exploitation of Internet technologies in support of e-business. As frequently reported in the media, market economics are being redefined in many business domains due to the opportunities being created by Internet technologies. These technologies will be a major factor influencing boardroom decisions over the next few years.

The second issue is the continued trend toward outsourcing of information technology services. This is a trend that has been building momentum for some time. Yet recently there have been a number of interesting changes in this approach that may greatly influence traditional "buy versus build" decisions for enterprise-scale solutions.

9.2   E-ANYTHING AND E-EVERYTHING

The major driver in many business domains today is the use of Internet-based technologies to open new market opportunities, deliver improved services to customers, and streamline internal business processes [1, 2]. In its broadest sense these changes are most often called *e-business*.[1] The upheavals being seen in many industries reveal that e-business is changing the underlying economics of business. Through the use of innovative e-business strategies, traditional businesses are being transformed by nimble new competitors offering cheaper value propositions, bringing them to market more quickly, and attracting large interest from consumers. In order to compete, established companies themselves are undergoing complex and painful transitions to build new business practices and their supporting technologies.

As a consequence, we are seeing complete transformations of existing business practices in the light of these new opportunities and threats. In particular, many of the cornerstones of business practices for the past decade are

---

[1] Aspects of these approaches may also be referred to as e-Commerce, e-Supply-Chain, e-Strategy, or e-Somethingelse!

being challenged. Understanding these changes and their impact on business in the Internet age will be the primary focus of corporate decision making for the coming years.

There are many areas where existing business practices are being rethought. These changes to business practices have a direct influence on the kinds of information systems necessary to support them. In particular, there are five key changes worthy of note [3]:

▶ Many companies have survived by building vertical industries that allow them to control the complete product process including research, design, manufacturing, marketing, distribution, and support. This was in an attempt to manage costs, control schedules, and ensure quality products. The new Internet economy has seen the breaking down of this trend toward specialization, and the creation of virtual organizations capable of integrating the best-of-breed solutions in fast, flexible ways. Many established organizations are rethinking their corporate core competencies and looking to partner with specialist organizations to obtain the rest. As a result, information systems must become more flexible and open, making it easier to combine systems from a number of suppliers to create integrated solutions across a range of functions.

▶ Traditionally, the value of an organization has largely been measured in terms of its physical assets such as office buildings, manufacturing plants, equipment, and a large staff of people. These were considered a primary issue in understanding the ability of an organization to function. Internet technologies have brought the speed of communication and collaboration necessary to change many people's thinking in this area. It is now possible to create businesses based on intangible assets such as design skills, knowledge of market trends and directions, and the ability to put to work unused capacity or underused resources. Whole new businesses are being created to take advantage of these possibilities. In many cases they have very few physical assets, yet their intellectual capital, brand awareness, and flexibility mean that the stock market values them in excess of the more traditional businesses. Many of these new businesses are reliant on information technology to manage information, look for common patterns in existing data, and provide greater access to all aspects of the business process. Consequently, information systems will continue to be driven to provide greater innovation and new services to meet these evolving needs.

▶ The ability of an organization to drive profit has always been related to an organization's size and its position in the marketplace. As the organization grows larger, its physical assets become more difficult to manage, changes are more costly to implement, and profit margins often decrease. In the new economy, where intangible assets dominate, the converse may be true. The incremental costs of growing an organization may actually decrease with size. And at a certain point, one or two companies may dominate a particular market at very high profit margins. As a result, getting into a market early and gaining mind share is increasingly seen as a key attribute, in some cases more important than current operating profit. In such an environment, the speed at which information systems can be delivered and changed becomes a dominant factor. As a result, the pressure on information technology departments for increased turnaround of solutions will increase. Systems must be developed and deployed quickly, yet be robust and scalable to support large transaction volumes and worldwide access to information.

► The difficulties of obtaining accurate, up-to-date information have led to a number of assumptions in the way in which businesses interact with customers and each other. For example, a great deal of customer loyalty to a product is based on the difficulty for a consumer to research alternatives, understand the trade-offs involved, and make a smooth transition from one product to another. As product advertising was often the primary source of consumers' information, organizations were, to a large extent, in control of their market's access to information and could predict their buying habits. With Internet technologies, many of the problems with information access are removed. Much more information is available than ever before, and in a much more timely manner. Furthermore, agent and brokering services are routinely available to connect consumers with suppliers, or to find the cheapest supplier of services for given criteria. This flexibility for consumers is further increased with the removal of many of the geographical constraints of making informed decisions and obtaining products. This forces established organizations to rethink the pricing, packaging, and distribution of their products and services. More and more frequently the limiting factor in making these changes will be the information systems supporting the business. Information technology departments will find they have greater visibility within organizations as they make changes in their services and solutions. This may provide increased resources, but with the burden of increased responsibility for solutions.

► For many business domains there was a relatively high cost of entry for any organization interested in competing in that space. This was caused by the need for acquisition of tangible assets, the time required to establish supply-chain relationships, and the slow pace of gaining market share and customer loyalty. The new virtual organizations are seemingly appearing overnight. They are using Internet-based technologies to create a virtual supply-chain, advertising globally without investing significantly in direct marketing and its associated infrastructure, and gaining market share by offering the most competitive prices. The enormous opportunities for new businesses to quickly appear in an existing market present a major challenge for established organizations. To respond to this will require a range of new solutions, in addition to new features and services to be added to existing systems. This will result in many changes to existing development practices, requiring greater use of processes and techniques for rapidly developing and deploying new systems.

Unfortunately, while many opportunities for new kinds of business are offered, there is also a great deal of hype and over expectation surrounding e-business. Many organizations are attempting to join the e-business revolution without the skills, understanding, and achievable business goals necessary for success. In fact, a study by software industry analysts, Gartner Group, predicts that as many as 75% of e-business projects will fail because of a lack of understanding of technology and poor business planning [4].

In their study, Gartner described a number of the most common reasons that e-business projects will fail. These reasons included a lack of planning regarding how the e-business project would impact the business as a whole, poor tracking and management of the project and its underlying technologies, inflexible solutions that were unable to integrate with existing systems, and insufficient awareness of competitor solutions to ensure the solution provided the anticipated impact in the marketplace.

These issues highlight a number of major challenges facing information technologists in their aim to support the business goals of their organizations. To address these challenges, we are beginning to see a fundamental change in the internal organization and politics of many companies. In the new "real politik" of the Internet age, information technology is viewed as an essential contributor to achieving a business advantage. As a result, there is frequently a much closer relationship between those involved in business development and those required to support these initiatives within the company's information technology infrastructure.

9.3   THE END OF SOFTWARE DEVELOPMENT?

There are many business pressures on the information technology departments of most organizations to deliver more solutions faster than ever before. Furthermore, these solutions must be flexible to changes in business practices, rapidly evolving hardware and software platforms, and business domains undergoing a variety of mergers, acquisitions, and realignments. Over the past two years the diversion of IT resources to year 2000 projects has further increased the pent-up demand for new IT solutions.

These requirements are difficult enough to satisfy. However, they are further exacerbated by the current shortage of available skills, the difficulty of reeducating highly trained staff, and the high costs of personnel. All of these reasons point to the need for alternative approaches to satisfying the insatiable need for information technology solutions. With the need to also increase the value of IT services to an organization's ability to create new business solutions, many people are beginning to suggest that software development within IT departments will end [5]. The role of an organization's IT department will be to manage the integration of existing solutions, and to provision new solutions from third-party suppliers. Predictions are that the worldwide IT services industry will grow to more than $630 million by the year 2003 [6].

This thinking is encouraging many organizations to outsource certain aspects of their development process. A number of goals drive an outsourcing approach to provisioning software solutions. First, outsourcing can increase predictability of costs as an aid to the planning and budgeting of software projects. Second, an organization can manage the long-term total cost of ownership of a solution by assigning responsibility for maintenance to a third party at a known, fixed cost. Third, flexibility can be improved by reducing internal information technology assets and allowing new skills and resources to be acquired from external vendors and consultants as needed.

A number of different strategies are being attempted in the goal to outsource solutions, each with its advantages and disadvantages. These approaches include the following:

> ► A common approach taken by large software development organizations to reduce costs is to set up offshore development offices, or to hire specialist developers in lower cost locations across the world. For example, a number of large software companies have located offices in countries such as India and Russia to produce software at less expense than in

many parts of the U.S. or Western Europe. While this approach has reduced development costs and allowed development to take place during an extended working day due to time zone differences, it has also introduced a number of problems. In particular, managing remote offices in diverse parts of the world has often introduced a number of cultural, communication, coordination, and configuration problems. These have frequently manifested themselves in product quality problems, difficulties in managing product schedules, and product support concerns.

► A strong emphasis in many industry domains has been toward greater use of purchased packages and commercial off-the-shelf (COTS) solutions [7]. This has most clearly been seen in areas such as financial management, customer relationship management (CRM), and enterprise resource planning (ERP), where there are a number of well-known packages on the market. The goal in many organizations has been to replace homegrown solutions with purchased third-party packages. This moves the burden of maintenance and upgrade of the solution to the third-party supplier, reducing ongoing costs for the system. This approach has been successful in a number of scenarios, most notably when the function to be supported is ancillary to the main purpose of the organization. In such cases, it often makes financial sense to delegate responsibility of that function to a specialist third-party supplier, allowing the organization to concentrate its internal resources on areas that allow it to differentiate its services from those offered by its competitors.

However, this solution may also come with a number of unforeseen costs. In particular, it is often found that the cost of purchase of the package is dwarfed by the cost of the services needed to install, customize, and maintain it [8]. This is particularly true when the package does not closely match current practice, or performs only a relatively small subset of the functionality required.

► Rather than buy a packaged solution, another approach is to use systems integrators (SIs) and independent software vendors (ISVs) to provide customized solutions tailored to the organization's needs. A large number of SIs and ISVs have emerged in response to the need to provide customized solutions. Typically, they specialize in one of two ways. The first way is to specialize within a particular application domain. For example, an ISV may build up domain knowledge in the financial services industry, and offer a family of solutions supporting various functions within that domain. Alternatively, they may specialize in the application of a specific technology. For example, an SI may choose to support Microsoft-based solutions using technologies such as Microsoft's SQL Server and the Visual Basic language.

Unfortunately, this flexibility comes at a cost. Many of the SI and ISV organizations are small in size, and work on tight profit margins in a competitive market. This can often lead to a high level of instability in many of these solution providers, which translates to occasional quality problems in the solutions, lack of capacity for support and post-installation services, and a possibility that the solution provider may go out of business altogether.

► With the rapid change in skills required to develop and maintain large-scale systems, many organizations are hiring consultants and service providers to develop and maintain application solutions. In the past, the loss of control and difficulties of managing external contractors had often been a cause for problems with this approach. However, the pressures on IT departments are currently so great that many organizations are reviewing their earlier hesitancy. In particular, the advantage of using an external contractor is that an organization can hire expert skills in a domain and a technology of importance without the overhead of training and managing internal staff. In a vibrant job market with extensive staff turnover, turning to specialist consulting organizations becomes even more attractive. Often this approach provides an organization with a more flexible approach to growing its available IT resources with the help of the consulting organization.

Unfortunately, this approach too has its drawbacks. Most notably, without careful management, it is found that essential skills are often delegated to the consultants. The expected flexibility of this approach is lost when it is discovered that the business cannot function without the consulting organization's services.

► In recent months there has also been growing interest in the idea of "leasing" application solutions. In a strange flashback to the days of timeshare solutions, a number of solution providers are hosting applications that an organization accesses via Internet-based technologies and pays a fee based on its use of that application [9].

A number of companies now offer hosted Web-enabled applications. The attraction is that a customer's application runs over the Internet with high performance and security, but without complicated middleware software to be installed and managed at the customer's site. The latest advances in distributed, web-based technologies are combined to offer customers 24x7 application availability, fast access to database services, robust virtual private networking (VPN), firewall security, and high bandwidth availability. Additionally, the pricing model is a simple, usage-based program that enables customers to achieve enterprise-scale with vendor-managed upgrades and no software maintenance.

It seems likely that hosted solutions will be a major growth area over the next few years. However, these standardized solutions will not be suitable for those organizations requiring customized functionality, or those with extensive needs to integrate solutions across a number of business processes.

Each of these initiatives is having an interesting impact on the development of enterprise-scale solutions in general, and the future shape of IT departments in particular. Most notably, the role of a typical IT department changes from one of developing applications to that of managing the provision, integration, and evolution of software-intensive solutions.

As a result, the importance of integration technologies and techniques within the software industry has been significantly increased. The technology directions of most significance over the next few years are likely to be those that improve our ability to integrate existing systems, deliver applications with greater openness and flexibility, or encourage greater flexibility in the way in which solutions can be customized and evolved over time.

9.4   SUMMARY

As a result of the Internet and its associated technologies, many of the traditional assumptions about business techniques and business economics have been reassessed. Organizations around the world in every industry are asking themselves how they must change to take advantage of the new opportunities of the digital age. Consequently, the Internet is driving a new set of requirements for future information systems supporting these businesses. Often, a significant element of an organization's future survival is dependent on the speed at which information systems can be assembled to support new business initiatives.

However, providing Internet-based e-business solutions also has consequences for the operation of the business and the qualities of the software-intensive systems that support it. One issue of particular note is that

Internet-based systems are highly visible to a large potential market every minute of every day. This global reach is perhaps their biggest appeal. Unfortunately, it may also be their Achilles heel.

Once assets are made available in a global fashion over the Internet, and a company's business processes are connected with those of other partners and suppliers, there is a much higher cost to "downtime." When a system is unavailable due to being overloaded for system upgrade or for maintenance, a great deal of business, confidence, and goodwill is lost. This was graphically illustrated recently when unscheduled outages in a major auction portal resulted immediately in a dramatic fall in that company's stock price. Numerous other examples also exist—a major telecommunications company had costly loss of service for several hours, a bank in Singapore posted accounts in error due to system overloads, and a major financial services provider needed to take their systems offline in order to make software updates. These outages equate to customers and dollars lost.

Consequently, the business imperative is to move business into the digital age with an information technology infrastructure that:

▶ Quickly supports new business initiatives;
▶ Provides robust, scalable support with worldwide access to resources;
▶ Exhibits sufficient flexibility in design so that it can adapt to the changing business environment.

The Technology Response: Flexible Services and Solutions

Current business drivers place major challenges on the shoulders of IT professionals to produce scalable, robust solutions that are flexible to changes over time—yet to do so at a faster rate than ever before. How can this be achieved?

The key is to ensure that the right business problems are being addressed in the most open, flexible ways possible using appropriate tools and technologies. In this chapter we look at technology advances currently taking place in the domain of enterprise-scale solutions. These technologies will form the backbone of the next generation of enterprise-scale solutions. We then explore some of the key research initiatives likely to influence future generations of products and techniques.

10.1   Introduction

The Internet age has brought with it a number of new challenges in the way we design, build, and evolve the software that drives this revolution. The key driver for this is exploiting new business opportunities. These opportunities drive requirements for software design processes to enable the development of software-intensive applications that:

► Can be developed quickly to meet time-to-market demands;
► Support the ability to deal with highly varied kinds and quantities of access to data;
► Exhibit the flexibility to allow frequent changes as the environments in which the applications operate evolve.

Experiences from building distributed systems over the past decade lead to the conclusion that the *only* way to achieve these goals is with solutions that offer three fundamental characteristics.

First, the solution must be based on a multitiered architecture. To obtain the flexibility required in the face of many business and technology changes, a clear separation of functionality to multiple tiers offers greater insulation from the impact of those changes. Experience with client/server architectures, and the interest in application servers have provided many lessons in this regard.

Second, use of components and component-based design approaches is necessary to support integration and assembly of many pieces. A major challenge is to quickly develop complex systems that scale. This requires reuse of parts of existing systems, and outsourcing of purpose-built packages. Integrating these pieces demands a view of application development based on the assembly of these pieces into a workable design that can be evolved cost-effectively over time.

Third, component standards must be used to provide openness and flexibility. To make the use of multitiered architectures and components manageable and practical, a component standard is required. This provides interoperability among vendors of infrastructure services. Furthermore, it facilitates a marketplace for components, skills, and solutions.

In summary, any enterprise-scale e-business solutions must be implemented utilizing multitiered distributed component architectures.

To investigate these concepts in more detail, we now consider the key elements that will make these solutions successful. First, we review the infrastructure and platform technologies that will form the basis of future systems. Second, we examine the role of standards in creating a flexible solution to enterprise-scale systems. Finally, we discuss the role of tools in enabling solutions to be created and managed. The chapter is concluded with a brief review of key research directions and their impact on future enterprise-scale solutions.

10.2   INFRASTRUCTURE AND PLATFORM TECHNOLOGIES

Over the past few years our understanding of how to design enterprise-scale solutions has matured significantly. Early successes with client/server architectures were quickly followed with a recognition that such an approach in some scenarios suffers from severe limitations. Recently, these limitations have become all too apparent, with support required for large numbers of browser-based clients, the need to target different web-based infrastructure technologies, and the struggle to integrate with a wide variety of back-end servers and application systems.

In response to this, a new set of ideas concerning the appropriate design of enterprise-scale solutions in the Internet age has begun to emerge. These ideas result in a basic architecture that will significantly influence thinking in web-based solutions for the next few years. This is supported by a growing number of products from vendors specializing in various aspects of these solutions. Based on the ideas of N-tier architectures, enterprise-scale solutions in the Internet age will have five clearly distinguished sets of services, or servers,[1] as illustrated in Figure 10.1.

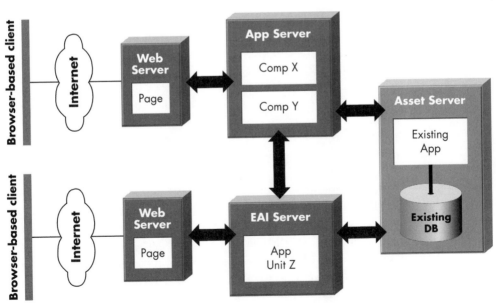

FIGURE 10.1.   The five key elements of future enterprise-scale systems.

---

[1] In this context, a "server" refers to a set of services that may be implemented in hardware, software, or a combination of both.

As shown in Figure 10.1, the typical architecture of future enterprise-scale solutions involves a wide variety of services at a number of different levels. The following five key elements can be distinguished:

▶ *Web services.* To enable a variety of web-based clients requires web servers capable of delivering the content using standards such as the Hypertext Markup Language (HTML) and the Extensible Markup Language (XML). Navigation between pages and initial data validation is typically performed on the web server to reduce communications traffic and limit requests to the other servers. A number of web server products are available at low cost, as freeware, or are now bundled as part of the machine's operating system.

▶ *Application services.* The main business logic of an application captures the workflow typical in the domain, and manipulates business data as required to support that workflow. These rules will be implemented in meaningful, reusable units as components. Application servers support the deployment and assembly of these components by supporting a component standard such as EJB or COM. Many application server products are available with different characteristics in terms of price, scalability, usability, and performance.

▶ *EAI services.* As pieces of enterprise-scale systems will be derived from many sources, it is becoming common to establish a single approach to integrating these pieces. This involves the use of an Enterprise Application Integration (EAI) server. The EAI server provides a set of technologies for translating from one piece of the system to another. It provides a focal point for all integration code, reducing the complexity of complex system integration scenarios. Many EAI products have recently become available. These were initially based on proprietary standards, but lately many have converted to XML as a standard interchange mechanism.

▶ *Reused assets and services.* Organizations have a large number of existing IT assets accumulated over a long period of time. This includes applications, packages, databases, and screen designs. These represent many years of effort, and cannot simply be replaced. As a result, it is essential to find ways to provide access to these assets and offer their functionality as services to the rest of the system being produced. A range of techniques has been developed to achieve this, including approaches such as wrapping and mining. Many products are available to assist with these techniques. Indeed, many of the existing middleware and transaction monitor products now offer wider capabilities to support these approaches.

It is useful to think of each set of services as being managed and controlled by a specific kind of server dedicated to that task. This approach offers the maximum flexibility in terms of replication of services, use of technology from multiple vendors supporting appropriate standards, reuse of existing skills in specialized areas, and evolution as the business needs change.

10.3   STANDARDS ACTIVITIES

Standards play a key role in an effective and efficient solution to the development of large-scale systems. It is through standards that openness and flexibility of distributed systems is achieved, and a community of skilled people supported by cost-effective tools and techniques is created. A number of standards activities are working toward greater interoperability and interchange of information among enterprise solutions. These standards will be critical to the future of robust, flexible systems. There are two interesting aspects of the current standards activities worthy of note:

► The standards activities that are likely to have the greatest impact over the next few years are being driven by interested parties within the industry, and supported by lightweight standardization efforts by formal bodies such as the World Wide Web Consortium (W3C) and the Object Management Group (OMG). This is in sharp contrast to standards efforts in the 1980s. Those efforts were dominated by large government-sponsored bodies within the military, and international groups such as the International Standards Organization (ISO) and the Institute of Electric and Electronic Engineers (IEEE). The increased speed of the change of technology has encouraged the industry to form their own streamlined standards activities to create a measured level of consistency and uniformity within various markets. Rather than wait for large standards bodies to set the direction for a particular technology, advanced practices within certain industry domains has been the focal point for new approaches in a range of areas.

► The latest standards focus on solving well-defined problems within the context of the wide area of technology necessary for assembling enterprise-scale solutions in the Internet age. The emphasis appears to be on simple mechanisms for solving key problems, with an openness to extend those mechanisms in useful ways specific to each domain of application. As a result, there are interesting standardization activities taking place in areas such as user interface design and presentation, information modeling, data communication, middleware services, platform functionality, and so on. In the past, many standardization efforts were much too broad in their goals and domain of application. This often led to a slow standardization process and to standards that were complex in nature, making them difficult to interpret, implement, and maintain.

There are a number of key standards that will play a major role in enterprise-scale solutions over the next few years. These are briefly reviewed here.

XML

The Extensible Markup Language (XML) is a relatively simple tag-based language that can be used to describe and communicate information between senders and receivers [1, 2]. The XML document format embeds the information within tags that express the information's structure. XML also provides the ability to express rules governing the structure of the information. These two features allow automatic separation of data and metadata, and allow generic tools to validate an XML document against its grammar. XML is an open technology standard of the World Wide Web Consortium (W3C).

One of the reasons that XML has gained so much popularity so quickly is that it provides a simple solution to a range of different problems. Most notably, XML can be used in three different situations [3]:

► In building and maintaining web-based information systems, XML provides a markup language similar to Hypertext Markup Language (HTML), but with the ability to explicitly define the structure of the data being displayed. This allows intelligent techniques for analysis and manipulation of the information to take place as part of its processing and display. In particular, with its associated style language (XSL), a developer of information systems is able to keep display-specific formatting instructions separate from the data manipulation instructions.
► In the exchange of structured documents between systems, a standardized approach based on the Standard Generalized Markup Language (SGML) is popular. SGML is an international standard for the definition of device-independent, system-independent methods of repressing texts in electronic form. However, SGML is complex and difficult to implement and support. XML offers a simpler approach in which only a core set of concepts is defined. The user extends XML with the tags appropriate to each domain-specific need. This approach has proved to be much easier to implement and support, in addition to being more in step with the use of a variety of web-based technologies for document manipulation and display.

▶ Many distributed applications require interchange of data to provide integration and coordination between the various pieces. XML offers a standardized approach for defining these integration schemes. Its simplicity, and the ease with which it can be extended, allow it to be used in a wide range of integration scenarios in many domains. In addition, standard XML development and parsing tools can be used to create these common formats, and can readily be embedded within tools that need to perform import or export of the XML notation.

This final scenario is particularly relevant for building enterprise-scale distributed systems. Due to its simplicity, XML can encode a wide variety of information structures. The rules that specify how the tags are structured are called a Document Type Definition (DTD). An XML DTD defines the different kinds of elements that can appear in a valid document and the patterns of element nesting that are allowed. Within different user communities there are many standardization groups attempting to create standard DTDs to allow greater sharing among solutions within that domain. For example, in the financial services, insurance, and utilities domains there are attempts to create standard DTDs that will improve interoperability between systems from different suppliers and vendors. Similarly, agreements on standard DTD are being sought among vendors of tools supporting the design and implementation of enterprise-scale solutions. Such agreements will allow design models and artifacts to be more easily transferred between tools from different vendors.

EJB and the CORBA Component Model

Some of the most intense activity in the standards arena over the past few months has been in defining a set of consistency rules and guidelines for server-side components in an N-tiered architecture. Much of the focus of this activity has been centered on the Enterprise JavaBeans (EJB) standard—now subsumed within the Java 2 Enterprise Edition (J2EE) platform. This standard provides a description of an architectural model for Java-based distributed systems in which the infrastructure services required by any application are defined in a standard way. A container in which business-level components live provides these services. This separation between standard container services and domain-specific business components is key to a simplified approach to designing enterprise Java applications.

Although incomplete, the EJB 1.1 standard has received widespread support. For example, within a year of its release there are already at least a dozen books available on building enterprise Java applications in line with the EJB specification, and more than 20 vendors already claim (partial) support for the EJB specification in their server products.

A primary element of the EJB specification is the definition of the interface to an EJB container. In essence, this is an abstraction of the lower-level Java services, but because it is abstract it can be implemented in a technology other than the Java services themselves. For example, many of the early EJB-based application servers layer this interface above an implementation of the Common Object Request Architecture (CORBA) services. This has allowed them to rapidly support the EJB standard on top of a mature, existing product.

In fact, one of the reasons for the rapid popularity of EJBs is this strong relationship between the existing CORBA standard and products, and the emerging EJB standard. One way this relationship is being further strengthened is with the creation of a true component model for CORBA based on the EJB standard. For some time, the Object Management Group (OMG) has recognized the need for defining a component standard above the CORBA infrastructure. With the popularity of the EJB specification, the OMG has moved ahead with the creation of such a standard. It differs from the EJB specification in four main ways [4]:

▶ It provides a simplified abstraction of the CORBA services. By building on the EJB specification, the CORBA component model provides a language-neutral API for building and assembling components with common infrastructure services. One of the benefits of this is that it promotes interoperability among server vendors by specifying a standard way in which to use CORBA services to implement the EJB container API.

▶ It supports an extended concept of a component. A rich set of component concepts is supported in the CORBA component model based on the notion of ports and channels. A component defines the events it emits and consumes, together with the interfaces it provides and those it uses. Each source or destination for interfaces and events are modeled by the generic concept of a port. Connections between ports establish a channel with specific semantics (e.g., a channel may be defined to be exclusive to those ports).

▶ It distinguishes between four types of components with different semantics based on the kind of life cycle and persistence required for the component. *Entity components* are expected to have long-term persistence, and will typically be involved in transactional behavior. Management of the persistence is delegated to the container. *Process components* are also persistent, but have no client-accessible primary key. *Session components* have no container-managed persistence, and have transient states that the component must manage. *Service components* are stateless.

▶ It allows packaging and deployment elements to be defined as part of the definition of components. XML descriptors are used to describe the packaging and deployment of the components. Additionally, an assembly descriptor describes component dependencies as port connections from one component to another.

The EJB and CORBA component model standards are likely to have a major influence on enterprise-scale solutions over the coming years in two main ways. First, these standards define the basic structure and vocabulary for an architectural style of building distributed systems. This style, involving containers, ports, channels, and assemblies, will undoubtedly become the common language for designing, documenting, and discussing distributed systems architectures. They will become part of the common lexicon for software engineers for the foreseeable future.

Second, as the market for enterprise-scale distributed systems continues to mature, there will be many more solution providers focused on supporting these technologies. This direction can already be seen in a number of recent developments: the emergence of component-based solution-provider organizations offering design advice and consulting practices based on EJB technology (e.g., The Theory Center—*www.theorycenter.com*), the growth of third-party providers of components written to maturing component standards (e.g., ComponentSource—*www.componentsource.com*), and an emerging marketplace for brokering organizations requiring components with those capable of designing and building them using appropriate standards (e.g., Flashline—*www.flashline.com*).

10.4   TOOL DIRECTIONS

For application development tool vendors there are a number of important challenges ahead to provide appropriate support for future enterprise-scale application solutions. In the near term, there are specific product releases and enhancements that will be made. In the longer term, the results of specific research activities will begin to influence tool features.

Currently, there is a great deal of attention focused on the areas of components, component technologies, and component approaches to software development and maintenance. Many companies have fundamentally reorganized their provisioning of software-based solutions to take advantage of these products and techniques. Consequently, it is critical to look at current directions in these areas and pose the question: What are the most significant advances being made in the area of component approaches in support of enterprise-scale software solutions? To address this question, we must consider a number of related areas of software development, and their support for business drivers shaping their growth and direction.

In terms of near term strategies, there are two important initiatives focused on improving the CBD support offered by tool vendors. The first involves improved integration of tool capabilities across the CBD lifecycle. The second involves the release of new kinds of tool capabilities more specifically directed at provisioning enterprise-scale solutions through components.

Enhanced Product Integration in Support of CBD

For organizations to truly embrace CBD, they need to rethink how they develop, deploy, and maintain software-intensive solutions. The impact of this reappraisal can have a profound effect on all stages of their software development life cycle. As we consider the implications for application developers, this immediately results in new requirements for organizations providing application development tools and technologies. More specifically, it leads to questions concerning the range of support application developers need, and the consistency of that support across the activities involved in CBD.

These concerns are at the heart of a number of vendors' product offerings in support of component-based approaches. Such products are intended to address many of the activities involved in application development and maintenance. The challenge is to do so in a consistent, seamless way across the lifecycle for a range of users employing a variety of development styles and techniques. The current trend is toward improved, integrated support for CBD across a set of tools supporting different aspects of the development lifecycle. The target of these integration efforts requires at least four dimensions of integration to be addressed. Different approaches are taken in each dimension to provide the necessary cooperative behavior:

> ► *Data integration.* The strength of many existing tools over the past decade has been the completeness and consistency that has resulted from maintaining a conceptual data model controlling all persistent data management. This aspect of the tools will remain. The concentration of additional effort in this regard will be on extending the underlying data models used to represent component concepts as cleanly and consistently as possible across the tools. Many small improvements will be instigated that will improve the quality and consistency of the models

recorded. In addition, by reshaping these models, there will be efficiency improvements in the transformation between various component representations.

▶ *Control integration.* Using a suite of tools effectively in concert requires the ability to easily navigate from one tool to another at appropriate points in the development lifecycle. As experience with CBD grows, the patterns of use that are typical in developing component-based applications become better understood. This presents opportunities to improve the navigation among tools to support those ways of working. In some cases, the changes necessary may be as simple as reorganizing menu options, or redesigning toolbars. In other cases, much deeper changes are required, demanding functionality to be duplicated in multiple tools, redistributing functionality across tools, or replacing inappropriate behavior. All of these kinds of changes may be appropriate as the interaction among the tools is considered. Standards such as XML will be influential in allowing tools to offer this level of interoperability.

▶ *Presentation integration.* The surface behavior and appearance of the tool set can have an immediate and compelling impact on its ease of use. This problem is particularly acute in tools that have been developed at different times, by different people over an extended period of time. Many opportunities for improvement have been recognized across product suites, and even more will be obvious as end-user organizations gain experience with CBD activities. User experience, coupled with usability studies carried out by human-computer interaction experts will result in many improvements in the consistency of user interaction across CBD tools.

▶ *Method integration.* Many interesting (and heated) debates have taken place over the years concerning the need for strong method support within tools on the one hand, and method-neutral tool support for greater flexibility on the other hand. The approach in many enterprise-scale product suites has been to offer strong method support for users who require it, while allowing many customizations and shortcuts for those who don't. It seems likely that this flexible approach will continue in CBD tools. In particular, for users who wish to carry out CBD activities, there is a need for specific, detailed advice and guidance on the best ways to use the tools in support of the methods. Organizations new to CBD can follow the guidance and make effective use of CBD in a controlled way. However, more experienced users will be encouraged to try new and innovative ways to use the products, giving access to tool functionality to allow organizational or individual customization of methods as necessary.

A New Generation of Component Design and Implementation Tools

Improvements to existing products and services for those wishing to adopt a CBD approach remain a high priority for many tool vendors. However, they are also looking to new areas and new opportunities in the marketplace. In particular, a new generation of software engineers, brought up on object-oriented analysis techniques and implementing their systems in languages such as C++ and Java, are facing challenges all too familiar to those experienced in the enterprise application development world. These software engineers are realizing that:

► Scalability of the solutions they develop is not an incremental process— building large-scale systems in languages such as Java is by no means the straightforward task often implied;
► Much of the solution they are developing is not directly implementing the business logic of their application domain, but rather it is concerned with synchronization of behavior across the application, interaction with persistent data stores, and communication with the operating system's underlying services;
► Complex and difficult choices are available in terms of the target architecture and platform for their applications, and these choices frequently have subtle (and not so subtle!) implications for the operation of their solution;
► Slogans such as "write one, run anywhere, access everywhere" associated with technologies such as Java are difficult to live up to given the vagaries of a heterogeneous computing base.

These challenges have direct parallels to similar issues from the mid-1980s that were the inspiration for the approach adopted by a range of popular tools and environments. The principles on which such tools were based included extensive use of abstract models of the solution domain, generation of implementations from these models, and centralized control of model elements to ensure consistency, synchronization, and visibility of project progress across large teams of developers [5].

Consequently, it seems natural to look at the problems faced by the new generation of application developers to see if those principles can be applied. Furthermore, the application of these principles leads to new products that will provide significant productivity and quality improvements for developing robust, enterprise-scale solutions using object-oriented analysis techniques, languages, and approaches.

Soon to be available from vendors such as IBM, Sun, and Sterling Software is a new generation of application development tools. These embody the basic principles of previous generations of tools, but within the context of the following enhanced characteristics:

▶ *CBD as the primary approach to provisioning solutions.* These tools can be primarily considered the core of a component-based solutions approach. It is expected that developers will be constructing applications from pieces, not as monolithic systems. All of the models, tools, and techniques supported by the tools will be focused on this as the primary provisioning paradigm.

▶ *Consistent with de facto component standards.* A number of interesting and important standards for CBD have become popular. These include many discussed in this book—the Unified Modeling Language (UML), Java Beans, Enterprise JavaBeans (EJB), the Microsoft Component Object Model (COM), and the Common Object Request Broker Architecture (CORBA). Support for such standards is integral to these tools. Some of them target a specific component standard, and offer services dedicated to creating solutions using that standard. Others attempt to abstract details of the component standard in favor of a later step in which the system is generated for a specific component standard. This latter approach ensures compatibility with the widest possible set of third-party components and tools.

▶ *Targeted at emerging platform technologies.* A new set of platform technologies is beginning to be used as the basis for future distributed systems. This will include technologies from Microsoft (COM and Distributed COM [DCOM], Microsoft Transaction Server [MTS], Microsoft Message Queue [MSMQ], and Windows NT), implementations of CORBA and its related services (e.g., IBM's Component Broker, and Iona's Orbix), application servers based on the EJB standard (e.g., IBM's WebSphere and BEA's WebLogic), and a variety of object-oriented and object-based databases from many vendors. These platforms are the primary targets of many new generation CBD tools.

▶ *Taking advantage of recent developments in software engineering practices.* Software engineers recently out of college are educated in a new set of techniques for software engineering based on object-oriented techniques. These are aimed at developing distributed, multithreaded applications in languages such as C++ and Java. The new tools build on these skills and allow developers trained in these techniques to quickly become effective contributors to a large-scale development project.

10.5   RESEARCH DIRECTIONS

Over the coming years enterprise-scale solutions will be impacted by a wide variety of new developments in software, hardware, and related technologies. These include at least the following:

▶ Continued improvements in hardware price/performance, together with miniaturization of hardware devices, is leading toward greater use of handheld devices, Internet appliances, and wearable computers.

▶ Significant advances in the communications infrastructure that will revolutionize distributed computing platforms in use toward pervasive broadband high-throughput networks. The high level of interest in standards such as the Wireless Application Protocol (WAP) is an indication of these developments.

▶ Mergers and alliances between computer, entertainment, and cable companies will bring a new generation of home entertainment devices and services. This will further increase demand for flexible, software-intensive solutions supporting a whole new generation of personalized multimedia services, rich content, and interactivity.

▶ More intelligent software systems (based on brokering) and agent technologies will allow software-intensive systems to be personalized to a user's needs, habits, and preferences.

Each of these advances (and many others) will impact the kinds of enterprise-scale solutions that must be designed, developed, and deployed. However, for this section we focus our attention much more narrowly and pose the question: For CBD-based solutions, where will the productivity and quality improvements come from in future years? To address this question, we briefly examine three key areas identified as paramount to the improved productivity and quality of future component-based approaches: the use of patterns and frameworks, more rigorous approaches to component specification, and enhanced modeling approaches for CBD.

Use of Patterns and Frameworks

Reuse has been a long sought-after goal in software engineering [6]. In object-oriented design and programming, reuse has been addressed through the concept of a "framework." This has proven to be a very useful way to reuse skeletal implementations of architectural designs while permitting customization to different contexts. However, pieces of code are by no means the only useful reusable artifacts; recurrent patterns are found in analysis models, specifications, interactions, and refinements. Moreover, the basic unit of encapsulation in object-oriented programming, a class, is not the most interesting unit for describing designs; it is the collaborations and relationships among components that constitute the essence of any design.

This thinking has led a number of researchers to more generally consider common solutions to problems via the notion of a pattern [7, 8]. A pattern is a description of the essence of a solution to a problem that can be applied within some context to guide the solution. Much attention has been focused on ways of describing patterns, techniques for applying patterns in different contexts, and producing catalogs of patterns for specific domains and technologies.

One aspect of this research is the notion of patterns and frameworks being applied to the design of component-based systems. The goal is to apply framework-like techniques to the modeling, specification, and implementation of component-based systems in a methodical way. The result is a set of domain models and requirements specifications from parts that themselves define skeletal and customizable models. The specifications for a particular problem should be constructed by applying the generic requirements and "plugging in" details for the problem at hand. On the implementation side, an implementation for the generic specification should be correspondingly customizable for the specialized problem specification.

Following this approach, the application of patterns and frameworks in CBD offers significant opportunities for productivity improvements. The knowledge embodied in previous development efforts can be readily applied in new contexts, greatly improving the speed with which solutions can be developed, and reducing the need for extensive testing.

More Rigorous Approaches to Component Specification

In following a CBD approach, it is useful to think of one component being the provider of a set of services, and another component consuming those services. As a result, the component approach to design can only be used effectively if it is possible to say a priori whether two components will work together. To do this requires a clear abstract description of a component, which can act as a form of "contract" between a component and any others that may wish to access its services [9]. This contract describes the interface to the component: what actions the component can carry out, what preconditions must be met before those actions can take place, what effect those actions have when carried out, and how to invoke those actions.

The goal of defining precise system specifications for software-intensive systems has been pursued for a number of years, resulting in a range of languages and techniques (e.g., [10]–[12]). Much of the attention of this work has been on appropriate semantics for describing the structure and behavior of a system's behavior. In many cases these languages and techniques have only been applied to domains such as real-time safety critical systems. However, with component-based systems, this requirement for well-defined "contracts" is a cornerstone of the approach.

The difficulty with applying formal techniques to CBD comes in deciding how to write these "contracts." In order to meet our needs, component descriptions must at the same time be both abstract and precise. They must be abstract to allow the component's behavior to be described in a way that is uncluttered with unnecessary details and not overconstrained with extraneous implementation details. They must also be precise to allow more meaningful analysis of their behavior as a basis for selection, evaluation, and integration.

Hence, components require precise abstract interface specifications separate from their implementations. This specification must be much more than simply a list of operations the component supports, because that is insufficient to allow us to understand exactly what the component does. The specification must also be completely separate from its implementation, as we may wish to change a component's implementation without affecting what it does from the point of view of a consumer.

To satisfy these goals requires more formality in the description of a component's specification than currently provided in most component-based development approaches. In approaches based on Java, for example, the interface to a component is obtained through a process known as introspection. Using this technique, details of a component's interface can be extracted automatically. However, that information is restricted to operation signatures. To use a component of any complexity typically requires significant trial-and-error use of the component to verify your initial intuitive understanding of the component's behavior.

Approaches such as Catalysis, however, take a more formal approach to component specification [13]. In Catalysis, a component is described by a specification, which defines a vocabulary to establish the context for the component's actions. The vocabulary is defined using a type model, expressed as a set of queries on that type. These queries, expressed formally as boolean expressions, enable operations to be described with some precision.

Unfortunately, developing component specification without appropriate tool support is both time consuming and error prone. Such a tool must take away some of the burden of defining these formal expressions, and help in the practices of validation, refinement, and conformance. Current tools allow these formal descriptions of component behavior to be captured only by means of textual annotations on a component specification. As such, they can be used in manual inspections of a component, but cannot be used as the basis for tool support in any way.

The goal of current research in this area is to investigate the use of formal approaches to component specification, and the use of those specifications as the basis for tools support in component-based development. Improvements will result in much more effective searching mechanisms for components, greater accuracy in assembling applications from components, and improved techniques for component testing.

Enhanced Modeling for Software Architectures

In recent years a number of researchers have focused attention on the software architecture of a system as an important topic in its own right [14]. They highlight the fact that a key aspect of any enterprise-scale solution is an understanding of the major pieces of that solution and their interdependencies. This architecture is often representative of a common architectural style characterizing many aspects of that system's performance, robustness, and maintainability [15]. As a result, a number of modeling notations, guidelines, and evaluation techniques have emerged based on a strong understanding of a system's software architecture.

Software architecture is a key concept in any component-based development project. At a conceptual level, components form a logical architecture for the system being considered. At a concrete level, components form a physical architecture defining the packaged software units and their deployment to a particular physical infrastructure.

In discussing techniques for CBD, attention is often turned solely to the conceptual level at which a system is conceived of as a set of interconnected functional units. However, once the basic component design is developed, it must be implemented in a physical design compatible with the operational requirements of the system. Satisfaction of these operational requirements is dependent upon the characteristics of the physical architecture of the target platform and the allocation of the functional components to that architecture. Unfortunately, these two levels of design, conceptual and physical, are all too often treated separately, with little thought to their integration until very late in the design and implementation life cycle. The consequence of this is that, having agreed on an acceptable conceptual design for a system, a great deal of time is spent finetuning, redesigning, and rebuilding existing components to satisfy the operational requirements.

Fortunately, a number of commercial tool vendor organizations have extensive experience with generating code from high-level models of applications for a variety of target platforms. In fact, it can be reasonably argued that code generation technology is the best available approach for creating enterprise-scale, robust, client-server applications—this technology is in use by thousands of customers worldwide. As a result, a wealth of knowledge has been developed concerning the strengths and limitations of different physical architectures for enterprise-scale solutions with high transaction throughput, many simultaneous users, and low system downtime.

A target for a number of current research efforts is to improve the utility and applicability of that knowledge by investigating ways of capturing it for use by designers in the early stages of the component-based development life cycle [16]. For example, it would be useful if the designer could express operational requirements of the system early in the design phase, and the system suggest potentially viable low-level physical architectures. Then, as the high-level design proceeds, any decisions which are likely to impact those operational requirements could be flagged, and alternatives suggested.

To do this requires techniques that describe the physical architecture in a way that is amenable to analysis, provide ways of mapping conceptual architectures of component-based systems to physical architectures, and document valuable heuristics about the strengths and limitations of various physical architectures for particular usage scenarios. However, once captured and used effectively within the development life cycle, the resulting applications are likely to be much more suited to the user's needs, more predictable in its operation, and require significantly less tuning and customization.

10.6   SUMMARY

Business pressures are leading to increased expectations regarding the software-intensive solutions that form the cornerstone of many activities in a majority of the world's corporations. This has resulted in a remarkable increase in the range and variety of available technology for building enterprise-scale solutions. Consequently, many organizations are facing significant challenges with respect to how to make effective use of this technology within their constantly changing business environment.

CBD offers the possibility that organizations can incrementally take advantage of new technology innovations within the context of their substantial existing investments. Many technological advances in CBD can be expected over the next few years. In this chapter we have considered a number of changes in technology related to components and component-based approaches, and discussed how these changes will impact the future of enterprise-scale solutions in the Internet age.

As these demands intensify, designing robust, highly available systems will continue to be a major challenge to the software industry. Furthermore, successful improvements in the technology is essential. Industry analysts, Gartner Group, estimate that it is currently 10 to 15 times more expensive to have a system up 99.9% of the time than it is to have it up for 99% of the time [17]. It has even been argued that building enterprise-scale web-based solutions is much more complex than building client/server applications. Many industry and research initiatives are aimed squarely at reducing these costs, and improving the efficiency and effectiveness of enterprise-scale solutions using components.

Useful Resources on Enterprise-Scale Application Development

There are many different aspects to consider when developing enterprise-scale solutions in the Internet age. These involve a diverse set of business factors, strategic approaches, and technologies. One of the major tasks facing every organization is simply keeping up-to-date with the range of options available, the latest concepts and products, and the lessons from application of these ideas in practice. To assist with this, there is a wealth of information available from many different sources.

However, it is difficult not to be overwhelmed by the quantity of papers, journals, books, and articles on enterprise-scale application development issues. Here, we provide an annotated list of many of the references that we have found to be interesting and insightful over the past few months in gaining a deeper understanding on enterprise-scale solutions in the Internet age.

By necessity, this is a rather subjective reading selection, and is representative of the trends and technologies in favor as this book was being written. Please use this list as a starting point for developing your own set of important reference materials specific to your background, needs, and preferences. For the latest information, updates and additions to this list can be found at the author's own website at *http://www.CBDEdge.com*.

A.1   E-Business and e-Business Strategy

N. Negroponte, *Being Digital*, Vintage Books, 1996.

Although a few years old, this book remains an interesting perspective on the path of technology and the ongoing revolution taking place in the digital age. Negroponte has a clear, informed writing style, and draws on a great deal of experience. His vision for the future is compelling.

R. Kalakota *et al.*, *e-Business: Roadmap for Success*, Addison–Wesley, 1999.

An exploration of e-business impacts, and the need for all corporations to invest in a solid e-business strategy and roadmap. Lots of useful examples and anecdotes from industry are provided to illustrate the extent of the changes taking place, and the costs of being too late.

"E-Commerce," Definitive Guide Series for IS Executives, 1999. *http://www.quidnunc.com/knowledge/eCommerce/eCommerce.htm*.

A very readable introduction to the e-revolution currently taking place. Describes the impact of the major technologies on all our lives, and the changes that business must make to compete. An eye-opening article on why the Internet age will change everything!

C.V. Callahan and B.A. Pasternack, *Corporate Strategy in the Digital Age*, May 1999. *http://www.bah.com/greatideas/pptdata/index.htm*.

Describes the major Internet trends that are having impact on business based on a survey of 525 executives. A good overview of the current directions and the emerging business models in response to these trends.

G. Dalton, "E-Business," *InformationWeek*, June 7, 1999.

A useful summary of the results of a survey of 250 IT managers and their attitudes and expectations from the Internet. Case studies and the impact of the changes on those organizations are observed.

"Building Your E-Business," *InformationWeek*, June 21, 1999.

A discussion of the technology and approaches supporting e-business. An interesting discussion of performance issues, and a look at the architecture of barnesandnoble.com. Although not very deep in its analysis, it provides a valuable case study.

J. Akerley, M. Hashim, A. Koutsoumbos, A. Maffione, *Developing an E-Business Application for the WebSphere Application Server*, IBM, 1999. *http://www.redbooks.ibm.com.*

> Excellent introductions to the web programming model and the technologies that support it. A detailed home banking example is created for the IBM WebSphere application server. Although many of the details are specific to a technology, the overall approach and concepts are much more widely applicable.

A.C. Picardi, "Software Megatrends of the New Millennium," IDC Bulletin #W19065, May 1999.

> A view on the trends and causal factors that will drive software investment for the first few years of the new millennium. Concludes that the U.S. and Europe will remain dominant in the technology world for at least the next few years.

A.2   COMPONENTS AND COMPONENT-BASED APPROACHES

P. Allen and S. Frost, *Component-Based Development for Enterprise Systems*, Cambridge University Press, 1997.

> A detailed discussion of CBD backed by guidance and best practices from the SELECT approach to component-based development. Contains good discussions of a business-driven approach to CBD, and a set of steps for component modeling.

C. Szyperski, *Component Software: Beyond Object-Oriented Programming*, Addison-Wesley, 1998.

> An examination of a range of component technologies starting from a programming language perspective, but addressing a number of component technologies. This book has a very strong section on component concepts.

R. Sessions, *COM and DCOM: Microsoft's Vision for Distributed Objects*, John Wiley Press, 1997.

> A review of the Microsoft approach to building enterprise applications. It discusses COM/DCOM, but mainly addresses how the combination of Microsoft technologies can be used collectively to architect robust, scalable applications for the enterprise.

A.W. Brown (Ed.), *Component-Based Software Engineering: Selected Papers from the Software Engineering Institute,* IEEE Computer Society Press, 1996.

A set of papers discussing some of the fundamental technologies supporting CBD. Looks at aspects such as software architecture, distributed systems, and commercial off-the-shelf (COTS) integration. Good background information for understanding technology trends and strategies.

A.3   ENTERPRISE APPLICATION INTEGRATION

J. Highsmith, *Application Integration—Part 1*, Application Development Strategies, June 1999.

A good overview of the current state of the technologies, approaches, and vendor products supporting Enterprise Application Integration (EAI). Describes the different approaches to EAI and how vendors line up in each approach.

D. Skeen, "The Seven Myths of EAI," Distributed Computing, May 1999.

A very useful summary of why EAI is a major opportunity for enterprise-scale solutions. Discusses the fact that EAI is not just a hacked together solution with a few connectors, but an architected approach to leveraging existing assets.

"Hurwitz Group EAI Market Segmentation," Hurwitz Group, April 1999.

A somewhat lightweight overview of EAI, but an interesting market segmentation. Looks at EAI as five main layers of integration: platform, data, component, application, and business process. Discusses vendors in relation to these layers.

"Component Software Integration," The Open Applications Group, 1999.

The Open Applications Group Inc. (OAGI) is a non-profit industry consortium looking at business component interoperability. This white paper explains their vision for interoperability and how standard components and interfaces achieve this. An interesting high-level view of the architectural approaches.

"From Application Server to Application Integrator: Building the Application Services layer," 2nd quarter 1999 Trend Teleconference, Meta Group, June 1999.

Excellent set of slides plus notes on current trends in the application integration market. A very useful analysis of the current directions and the role of application servers in the future architecture of systems. Concludes that EAI solutions must be architected, independent of a specific application server, and part of a broader, enterprise-scale solutions strategy.

D.S. Linthicim, *EAI Without the Hype*, Enterprise Development, July 1999.

A good overview of the different approaches currently being supported in a variety of products for EAI. It provides a discussion of the six major categories of the EAI solution: database-to-database, federated database, brokered, composite applications, process automation, and a mixed approach.

A.4   DISTRIBUTED SYSTEMS ARCHITECTURES

R. Fichera, *Infrastructures for Web-Enabled Applications: Foundations for the 21st Century*, Giga Thematic Planning Assumption, April 1999.
http://www/gigaweb.com/scripts/forwarder.dll/Get.s/gnpa/T-0499-002.htm.

A detailed overview of the current state of web-based technologies and their role in distributed systems in the Internet age. A good categorization of the market for web tools based on the needs of power users, 4GL developers, and 3GL developers.

S. Garone, "IDC's Definition and Segmentation of the Application Server Market," IDC Bulletin #W19043, May 1999.

A good overview of the application server market, and a segmentation of the products available. The analysis looks at three approaches: data-centric, processing-centric, and application-integration-centric. It then looks at their scalability and how proprietary the solution is.

M. Gilpin, "Distributed Application Platforms," Giga Thematic Planning Assumption, June 1999.

This review of the distributed systems market starts by looking at the latest trends for application servers and the impact of Java technologies. The paper then provides a categorization of the market based on the scale of the solutions supported, and the complexity of the applications produced.

P. Harmon, J. Highsmith, K. Dick, "Application Servers: Hip or Hype?," Cutter IT Journal, January 1999.
http://www.cutter.com/ads/fulltext/1999/01/index.html.

A great market assessment and analysis providing a review of application servers as an approach, a categorization of Internet application servers, and a review of different EAI strategies.

A.5   TECHNOLOGIES FOR ENTERPRISE-SCALE SOLUTIONS

R. Orfali *et al.*, *The Essential Distributed Object Survival Guide*, John Wiley Press, 1997.

> An introduction to distributed objects, concentrating heavily on the CORBA approach. It provides an extensive introduction to CORBA for software managers and novice distributed systems builders. It is a good starting point for those looking for an introduction to distributed systems with CORBA.

R. Orfali *et al.*, *Client/Server Programming with Java and CORBA*, John Wiley Press, 1998.

> This book describes how CORBA can be used with Java to build distributed systems that operate over the web. A good introductory text on this topic.

D. Chappell, *Understanding ActiveX and OLE*, Microsoft Press, 1996.

> A management level overview of the OLE and ActiveX landscape. It explans in detail the basic concepts behind the technology, the technology details themselves, and their application for building distributed systems for the Microsoft platform.

D. Rogerson, *Inside COM*, Microsoft Press, 1997.

> A detailed book for those requiring a full explanation of how COM works. For those who want to have an understanding of what is under the covers of COM.

R. Monson-Haefel, *Enterprise Java Beans*, O'Reilly, August 1999.

> A very good introduction to EJB and building systems with this standard. The early part discusses the need for and approach of EJBs. The rest of the book looks at how applications are built using EJBs.

M. Gilpin, "Enterprise JavaBeans: Moving into the Mainstream," Giga Thematic Planning Assumption, April 1999.

> A high-level paper discussing the role of EJB and its likely impact in the market. Most useful for its detailed overview of the different Java technologies and their relationships.

"Enterprise JavaBeans: A Shark in the Proprietary Pool," Executive White Paper, Aberdeen Group, June 1999.
http://www.software.ibm.com/webservers/aberdeen9906.html.

> This paper describes three models of application development and their characteristics: web computing, enterprise computing, and Java computing.

Positions EJBs as the consolidation of these three. Looks at IBM WebSphere as an example EJB server.

J. Bosak and T. Bray, "XML and the Second Generation Web," *Scientific American*, July 1999.

A great introduction to XML and its importance in the next generation of web technologies. Provides enough background to place XML in context.

"Java Server Pages," Sun, July 1999.
http://java.sun.com/products/jsp/whitepaper.html.

A great overview of Sun's JSP technology. Provides background and a number of examples.

K. Brown and G. Craig, "Using Java Server Pages—Servlets Made Simple," Java Report, August 1999.

An excellent introduction to JSP and servlet technology. Provides a simple set of examples for the reasons for JSP separating presentation from logic. Compares the approach to the model-view-controller (MVC) pattern.

A.6   INDUSTRY AND PRODUCT DIRECTIONS

S. Garone, R.V. Heinman, S. Hendrick, "IBM's Application Development Strategy for the 21st Century," IDC, January 1999.
http://www.software.ibm.com/ad/analysts/idcad21c.html.

A great overview of the different IBM initiatives in the Java arena and their relationships. This document provides an excellent case study for how a large software organization is attempting to move forward into the digital age.

"Turning Enterprise Java Beans into Functional Applications," Hurwitz Group, May 1999.
http://www.inline-software.com/proddesc/hur-wppr.htm.

Discusses the overall architecture of an EJB application. The paper then discusses the InLine Assembly Line products as key to making it all work. This provides the packaging, assembly, configuration, and installation of EJBs into an application server environment as a plug-in to a Java IDE.

G. Flurry, "The Java 2 Enterprise Edition," *Java Developers Journal*, December 1999.

> A discussion of the goals and elements of the J2EE. This is the Java platform for distributed systems that ties together many existing Java initiatives with a programming approach and a set of validation and testing capabilities. This paper provides a good, short review of the main features.

J.P. Morganthal, "Microsoft COM+ Will Challenge Application Server Market," NC Focus Research Bulletin, May 1999.
http://www.microsoft.com/com/wpaper/complus-appserv.asp.

> A useful, short overview of COM+ and Microsoft's positioning of Windows 2000 as an application server platform. Few short descriptions are available on COM+. This provides a very good positioning of the various pieces of the COM+ initiative and its goals.

D. Kiely, "Microsoft Tackles Distributed Computing," *InformationWeek*, June 28, 1999.

> A discussion of Microsoft's DNA approach. Basically, it says that at its heart DNA is Microsoft's description of how to build N-tiered applications using a collection of Microsoft technologies. It builds on that to provide extra value in bringing some communities together to make that task easier.

A DETAILED CBD MODELING EXAMPLE[1]

In this section we provide a case study that illustrates the application of component-based modeling techniques and addresses many of the difficulties and challenges faced by today's software development organizations. Through this case study, many of the detailed techniques discussed earlier in the book are highlighted in the context of a project employing component-based development concepts.

It is important to emphasize, however, that this case study is illustrative of the kinds of modeling ideas, notations, and steps typical of a project using component-based techniques. Many variations from these steps are possible as dictated by the specific context within which the project takes place—goals, skills, timescales, available assets, etc. In particular, this case study concentrates on the earlier stages of the project when gathering requirements, analyzing the domain, and creating an initial component architecture. These stages are emphasized here because they provide the groundwork for a component-based development project, yet are frequently the most misunderstood and misapplied.

In this case study we begin by looking at the overall background and basic context for the case study. We then continue by sketching out an initial enterprise component architecture for the proposed solution. This provides a

---

[1] This case study is extracted from a paper by Paul Allen entitled, "CBD in Practice." The full paper is available from Sterling Software at *http://www.sterling.com/cool*. This case study is provided here with permission from the author.

context for considering the application to be developed using components. Finally, we consider how to evolve the initial application to provision components through a number of evolutionary steps. In particular, we illustrate how to apply the requirements, architecture, and specification phases of CBD in an iterative and incremental fashion. While the emphasis is on analysis and modeling activities, a number of salient comments about implementation and deployment are provided throughout the case study.

The rest of the case study uses a Catalysis-inspired approach to component modeling as refined within the Sterling Software technologies and solutions. This makes use of an extended form of the Unified Modeling Language (UML) notation to describe modeling artifacts, and should be familiar and straightforward to anyone proficient in object-oriented analysis techniques.

The approach used throughout the case study is intentionally informal and discursive. In particular, a number of design alternatives and options are discussed in many cases. These will provide illustrations of the kinds of decisions that must be made during CBD, and lead to a number of heuristics for good design.

B.1   INTRODUCTION

This case study considers a vehicle hire company, Harry's Vehicle Hire (HVH), and the development of a software-intensive system to manage the rental activity that supports the primary function of the business.

Some of the key aspects of HVH include:

- ► HVH is part of Harry's Enterprises.
- ► There are currently ten HVH branches, with expansion plans for four more in the next eighteen months.
- ► A key element in the company's business strategy is to partner with other vehicle hire firms to share and outsource services.
- ► Information technology, particularly e-commerce and e-business, is recognized as a central enabler of the business strategy.
- ► Other services within Harry's Enterprises involve valet and chauffeur services, as well as fleet hire.

B.2   ENTERPRISE COMPONENT
ARCHITECTURE DESIGN

A first-pass enterprise component architecture is modeled for maximum flexibility and ease of application integration. The focus is on core business domain components: Invoices, Requisitions, Parties, and Vehicles as indicated in Figure B.1. Code Tables, Address Formatting and User Security are business infrastructure components. Error Handler and Recovery and user security are technical infrastructure components. Address Formatting is used exclusively by Parties, at this stage. The other infrastructure components are used globally by any business component; by convention, their client dependencies are omitted from the diagram.

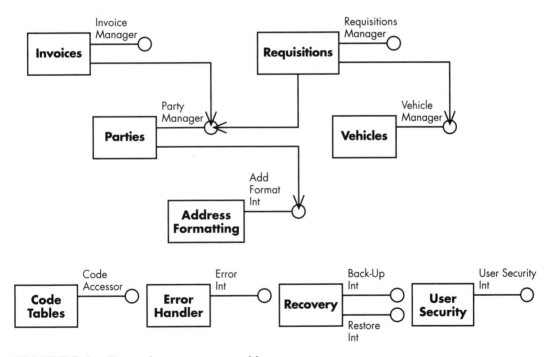

FIGURE B.1   Enterprise component architecture.

The overall provisioning strategy is to reuse existing applications and to purchase packaged software where possible. Software is only to be custom built where there is a significant business advantage to be gained. Specific provisioning strategies are as follows:

COMPONENT	PROVISIONING STRATEGY
Parties	Existing application integration project using existing system modeling and component design tools
Vehicles	Outsource to component supplier
Invoices Requisitions	Wrap existing Cobol application
Address Formatting Code Tables User Security	Purchase and extend from component framework
Error Handler Recovery	Purchase standard component

B.3   APPLICATION DEVELOPMENT

This example assumes that an application is to be developed with maximum reuse of existing components, but with no requirement to deliver the application itself as a component. The prime driver of such projects is a tight deadline in which to deliver useful business functionality. There is simply no time to engineer interfaces for the application itself. This is a situation many developers find themselves in today.

However, even on such "tight projects," it is still useful to perform a limited degree of component-based analysis to ensure the right components are being reused and as an insurance policy for the future. Such applications are commonly the subjects of upgrades, extensions, and further variants. Once the application has been delivered successfully, it may be possible to upgrade the application itself to the status of a component.

Requirements

Following a period of intensive discussions with the project sponsors, a detailed statement of requirements for the project is agreed. These fall into three main areas: functional requirements, non-functional requirements, and project requirements.

Functional Requirements:

► Efficient service to customers reserving vehicles over the telephone. Currently, this takes too long and is inefficient, resulting in lost business.
► Sales agents must have effective access to quotations (according to vehicle type and seasonal variations) and sales support information (for example, special offers and customer loyalty schemes).

► Longer term, the system must be capable of extension to direct reservations by customers over the Internet.

► Accurate scheduling of vehicles for collection by customers. In particular, there have been problems with booking failures and double bookings.

► Efficient service to customers collecting vehicles. Currently, this takes too long and is inefficient.

► Efficient service to customers returning vehicles. Currently, this takes too long and is inefficient.

► Timely production of invoices on vehicle return. Currently, too many invoices are either produced too late or lost in the paperwork.

Non-functional Requirements:

► Availability: Maximum 60 minutes downtime per month during opening hours.

► Response Time: < 5 seconds for all transactions.

► Integrity: 100% accuracy of accounting data.

► Security: All transactions and databases need access controls, so only authorized employees can update or view account and customer information.

Project Requirements:

► Must be built incrementally, with tested increments delivered every six months or less.

With these broad requirements in place, analysis activities can begin, aimed at obtaining a detailed understanding of the domain of interest. To achieve this, the main concepts in the application's domain are sketched out on a type model as shown in Figure B.2. This is primarily a "concept map" of the domain, identifying all business types that the new application must keep track of.

Understanding the domain and requirements can be augmented by the use of a business modeling tool, which provides the detailed business process modeling support, particularly critical for Internet development. Use cases work well as a bridgehead between business process modeling and interface specification. A popular technique is to use thread diagrams to identify processes as shown in Figure B.3. Processes are organized into "swim-lanes" depicting the responsible business roles. (In this case each process maps to a corresponding use case and each swim-lane maps to an actor). Of course, this example is deliberately simplified for brevity of explanation, but it is included here as it is increasingly relevant for Internet technologies that span easily across business roles in the form of organization boundaries.

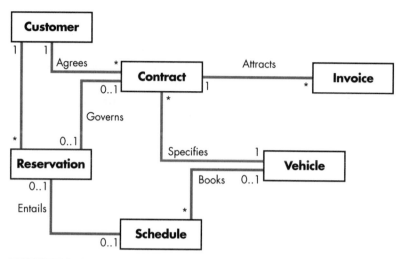

FIGURE B.2   A first-cut business type model.

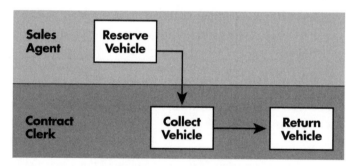

FIGURE B.3   Business process thread diagram.

Additionally, the main actors and use cases are identified and diagrammed as shown in Figure B.4.

Each use case is described in terms of its intent and its steps, with particular attention paid to those that involve an end-user exchange with the new application. Some examples follow.

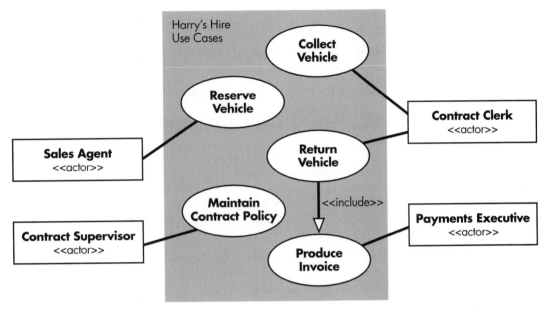

FIGURE B.4   Use case diagram.

Use Case Name	Reserve Vehicle
Use Case Intent	To reserve the most appropriate and available vehicle for a customer.
Use Case Description	1. *Identify customer.* A customer search is used to find customer details for confirmation with customer. Customer credit is checked.
	2. *Establish hire requirements.* A suitable vehicle type is found and details, including hire rate, are agreed. The reservation period is entered, and a suitable vehicle is found for the period.
	3. *Secure reservation.* The vehicle is booked for the requested period. A reservation is made, securing the vehicle for the customer. The reservation number is displayed.

Use Case Name	Collect Vehicle
Use Case Intent	To support collection of a vehicle by a customer according to reservation.
Use Case Description	1. *Identify reservation.* Reservation number is used to find reservation for customer.
	2. *Stipulate contract.* Contract details are agreed and set up. Contract number is displayed.
	3. *Agree hand-over details.* An entry sheet is printed showing vehicle mileage, service details, valet, and safety details. The contract is agreed and the entry sheet printed for signing by customer.

Use Case Name	Return Vehicle
Use Case Intent	To support return of a vehicle by a customer according to contract.
Use Case Description	1. *Identify contract.* Contract number is used to find the contract.
	2. *Check compliance to contract.* A return checklist (keys, documents) is checked. Return information is entered, including any damage or accident details.
	3. *Calculate settlement amount.* The return mileage and deposit is used to calculate the final balance for invoicing.
	4. *Produce invoice.* An invoice creation service is invoked. The invoice printed.

Knowledge of system requirements and use case descriptions is used to refine the "concept map," in particular by adding attributes, developing types and associations, and removing redundancy (see Figure B.5). Requirement prototypes are used to help verify the use cases.

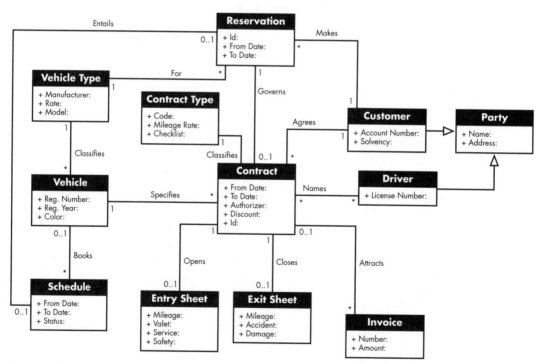

FIGURE B.5   Business type model.

By modeling collaborations within that domain, domain knowledge is further refined. Collaboration models help build an understanding of the domain in which the new software will run. Collaboration models can be applied at a high level, as a precursor or alternative to use case modeling. Here, the technique is used at a lower level, shown in Figure B.6, to analyze the domain of the Reserve Vehicle use case with respect to the Type Model. The ellipses represent actions involving the types with which it is connected via line paths. These actions are later refined by assigning them to specific interface types.

Project Architecture

Having gained an understanding of the domain, we need to identify all the interfaces that will be used to assemble the application, to identify the dependencies between these interfaces, and to scope the part of the application that must be built. In Figure B.7, three existing interfaces are identified, leaving the business types Contract Type, Reservation, Contract, Entry Sheet, and Exit Sheet within the scope of the application to be built. A useful technique is to

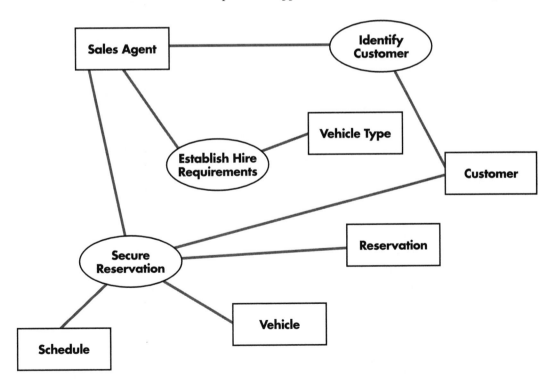

FIGURE B.6   Collaboration diagram.

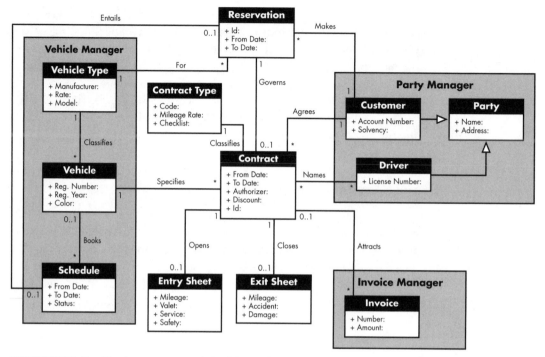

FIGURE B.7   Business type model with candidate components overlaid.

group business types into candidate components, using overlays to suggest a
separate interface for each component, as illustrated. In this case, the interfaces are suggested from the provisioning strategy. Of course, this is not a formal diagram, it is intended merely to illustrate the thought process involved in
the manner of a whiteboard discussion when considering a candidate set of
components.

Use cases and collaboration models are used alongside the business type
model to help identify interface responsibilities. They are also used to help
identify associated existing systems and interfaces. In the collaboration model
shown in Figure B.8, note how the action Secure Reservation in Figure B.6 is
refined into the two actions, Schedule Vehicle and Create Reservation, in
Figure B.8.

Reusing prototypes from previous projects and modifying these to meet
the requirements under study can also be particularly fruitful for identifying
existing interfaces. Available existing services are measured against requirements detailed in the Requirement Definition. In this case, it is decided that
existing interfaces Party Manager and Vehicle Manager are sufficient to sup-

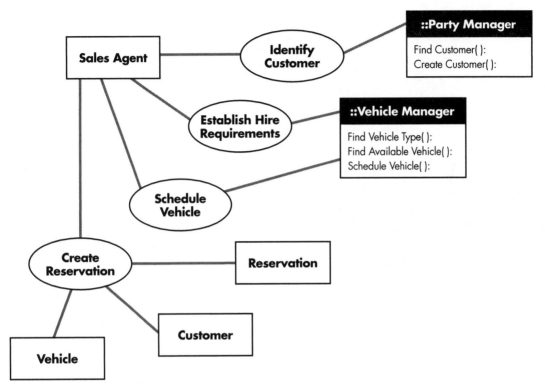

FIGURE B.8   Collaboration diagram with interfaces.

port three of the actions. The remaining action, Create Reservation, lies within the scope of the application build.

A first-cut project architecture is prepared, as shown in Figure B.9, initially by assuming one business component for each business type interface.[2] All software units used to compose the application are included; non-component software units are prefixed <<NC>>.

---

[2] The initial architecture is best described in terms of component implementations, working back to derive practical specification architecture with interface dependencies that will constrain the implementations. In the example, it is assumed that the specification and implementation architectures are in direct correspondence.

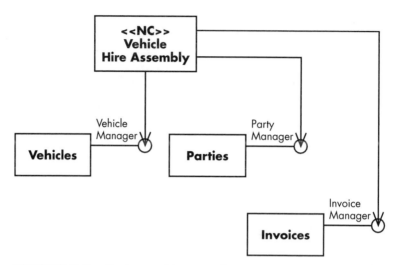

FIGURE B.9   Project architecture diagram.

Specification

Existing interfaces to be used in the assembly are inspected and verified for compliance with the system requirements. Types falling within the scope of the assembly are declared. It is also necessary to understand the associations that must be maintained with integrity between these types and types falling within the scope of business interfaces.

User interface prototypes and workflow diagrams are created. Primary Windows, and the primary flow between those Windows, are declared. If a business process model was prepared, then the major flows between business activities will be known, enabling efficient links between different windows/use cases to be designed.

Implementation

The implementation involves user interface design, coding, assembly, and various testing stages, including integration testing with existing interfaces.

A wide range of technologies may be chosen for application implementation. For example, a tool such as Sterling Software's COOL:Gen may be used to build Windows user interface designs for the Vehicle Hire system. Similarly, with a COOL:Gen approach, Java proxies are generated which enable the business types to be developed in Java with access to Invoice Manager, Parties, and Vehicles interfaces.

B.4   COMPONENT PROVISIONING

An increasingly common approach in organizations that do not want to take the time to provision components from scratch is to evolve software to component status. This is referred to as the "bottom-up" or "components-as-you-go" approach.

In other cases, requirements definition and analysis phases may start with a much broader brief: to expose common requirements across several business areas without the benefit of previously developed software. This is referred to as the "top-down" or "components-in-advance" approach.

In all cases it is necessary to specify behavior of interfaces within the context of a well-designed architecture before determining or verifying implementation strategy. By pinpointing required interfaces, the most appropriate provisioning strategy can be identified for each interface. This is particularly important where there is a need to integrate diverse applications and technologies using a mix of build, buy, reuse, and outsource implementation strategies. This example illustrates a typical mix of the top-down and bottom-up approaches.

Requirements

The Requirements Definition for Harry's Vehicle Hire described earlier includes a functional requirement:

▶ Longer term, the system must be capable of extension to direct reservations by customers over the Internet.

The system was very well received and partners have also expressed an interest in buying a more generalized version. A new project requirement is therefore raised:

▶ The system must be capable of extension of all features to meet the needs of any vehicle hire business, and consideration must be given to the needs of equipment hire in general.

No further types are discovered, so the type model developed earlier suffices. A further use case for Internet reservations is added to the use case model, developed earlier, as shown in Figure B.10. Contract Clerk resolves to two separate roles: Welcome Agent and Return Clerk. By identifying different roles in this way, we increase the chances of achieving a good set of reusable

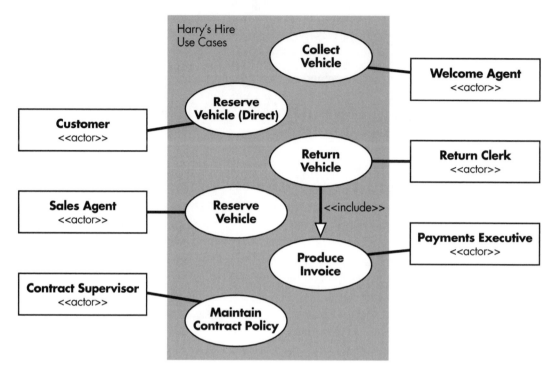

FIGURE B.10   Refined use case diagram.

interfaces that are not constrained by existing procedures but that correspond to business roles, regardless of existing constraints.[3]

Further analysis reveals some common behavior, as shown in Figure B.11. Scheduling is in fact a generic requirement for all types of equipment and vehicles. Factoring out a separate Schedule Equipment use case with another role, Scheduler, suggests a separate Schedule Manager interface that will be investigated further in the project architecture phase.

Similarly, Provide Quotation turns out to be a generic requirement for all sales situations, both by salespeople in the office and customers over the Internet. This suggests reuse of the Find Vehicle operation from the Vehicle Manager interface.

---

[3] Though it should be noted that in this particular example we choose not to assign separate interfaces for these two roles.

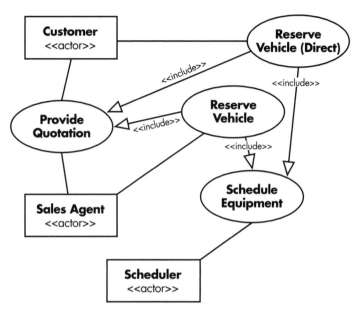

FIGURE B.11   Use case diagram showing "uses" and "extends" relationships.

Project Architecture

Evolving the project architecture is a complex task requiring a deep understanding of many aspects of the system and its use. In particular, it involves weighing up various, often conflicting, factors and making trade-offs as illustrated below.

Business type interfaces are identified using both the business type model and knowledge of use cases and collaborations, as shown in Figure B.12. Earlier, three interfaces were identified: Vehicle Manager, Part Manager, and Invoice Manager. A fourth interface, Schedule Manager, is now added for the generic scheduling requirement, identified in the previous section. Use of a component framework is to be considered for implementation of this interface.

A separate interface, Reservation Manager, is introduced to cater to the two reservations use cases. Although there is just one business type, Reservation, that needs to be managed here, Reservation is very much a core type of the Vehicle Hire business. Any business rules that are local to the reservation business are well catered for by a separate reservation interface. Reservation has structural dependencies on Vehicle Type and Customer that are reflected in single multiplicity associations to these two types. It is therefore worth considering including reservation management as a responsibility

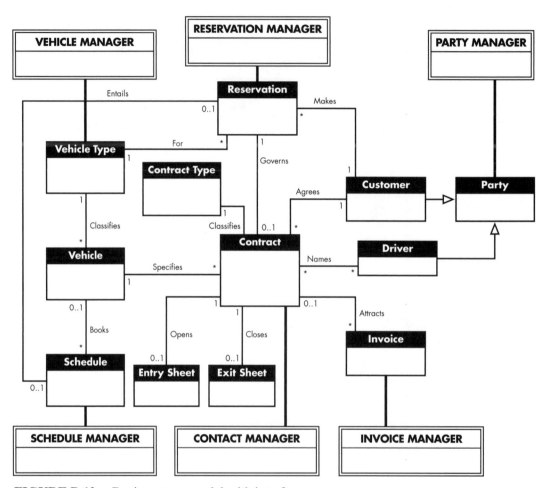

FIGURE B.12   Business type model with interfaces.

of the Vehicle Manager or Party Manager interfaces. However, in this case, it is decided not to do so, as it would compromise the stated requirement for flexibility.

Contract has structural dependencies on Vehicle, Driver, and Reservation that are reflected in single multiplicity associations to these types. It is therefore worth considering including contract management as a responsibility of the Vehicle Manager, Party Manager, or Reservation Manager interfaces. Using Vehicle Manager or Party Manager would place a circular dependency (something to be avoided) on Reservation Manager. So, again in this case, it is decided not to do so.

We might instead consider including contract management as a responsibility of Reservation Manager, either collapsing the Contract Manager interface into the Reservation Manager or allowing Reservation Manager to delegate responsibility to Contract Manager. However, the structure of the business type model suggests a separate Contract Manager interface to cater for the use cases Collect Vehicle, Return Vehicle, and Maintain Contract Policy. Note that although Collect Vehicle and Return Vehicle are superficially "about vehicle," their main intent centers on contractual matters. Moreover, Contract Type, Entry Sheet, and Exit Sheet are all exclusively related to Contract: the four types are cohesive within the domain of contracts. Finally, there is the extensibility requirement to cater for all types of hire, suggesting a decoupling of contract and reservation management. Any business rules that are local to the contract side of the business can be encapsulated through a separate. So, on balance, it is decided to use a separate Contract Manger interface.

Interface dependencies can be usefully modeled using an interface dependency diagram, prior to packaging into component specifications. However, in this example, it is decided to group interfaces one-to-one with component specifications, so the component specification architecture is modeled directly.

Clearly, the decisions made in creating the project architecture have an impact on the enterprise architecture, which must be assessed and verified. The enterprise component architecture evolves, as shown in Figure B.13. Note, in particular, that if design and implementation of Vehicles is to be outsourced, as indicated in the first pass of the enterprise component architecture, then the developers designing the Vehicles component are constrained by the dependency of Vehicles on Schedule Manager.

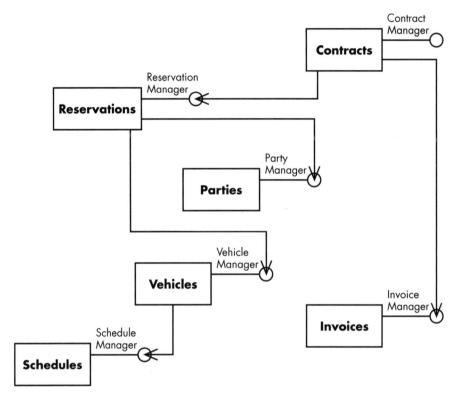

FIGURE B.13   Refined enterprise architecture diagram (partial).

Specification

Details of the interfaces can now be considered. Interaction diagrams help to assign responsibilities to interfaces. An interaction diagram is constructed for the reserve vehicle use case, as shown in Figure B.14.

Interface types are specified with the help of interface type models, as shown in Figures B.15 and B.16. Operations are shown in the lower portion of the box representing the interface. Types that the interface must remember are declared within the middle portion of the box representing the interface. This includes types that allow association navigation to types falling within other interface specifications. A type can appear in any number of interface specifications. For example, Reservation Manager needs to remember all Reservation attributes plus its associations to Vehicle Type, Customer, and Schedule.

Precise operation specification is achieved by writing a set of pre- and post-conditions for each operation. A pre-condition is an assertion that will be

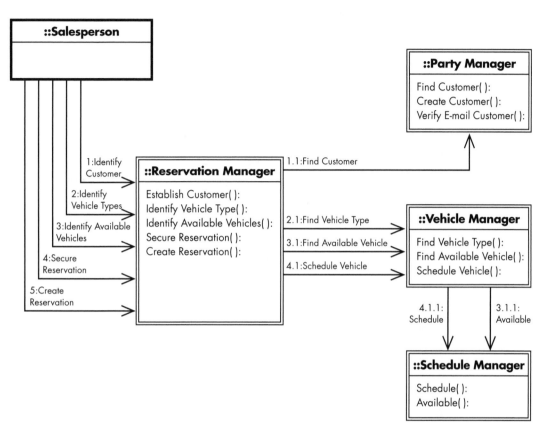

FIGURE B.14   Interaction diagram.

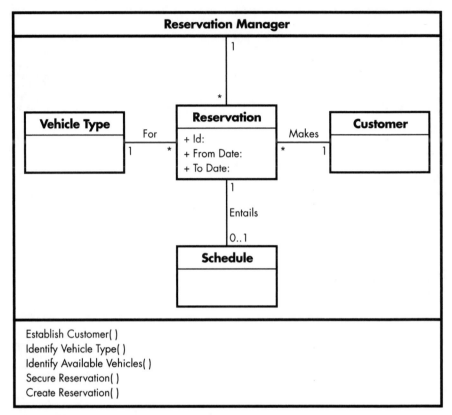

FIGURE B.15   Interface type model for Reservation Manager.

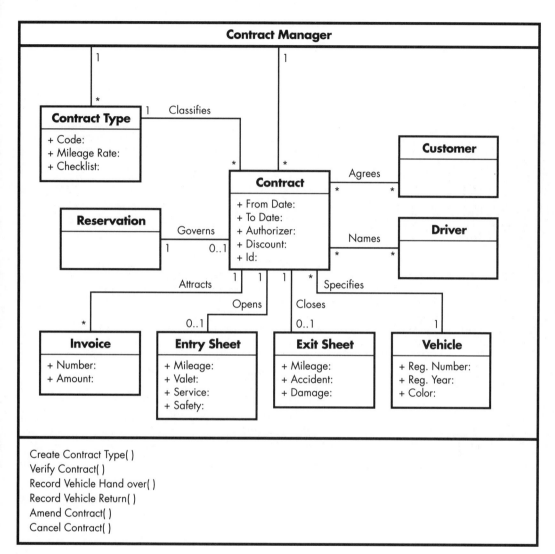

FIGURE B.16   Interface type model for Contract Manager.

true prior to execution of an operation. A post-condition is an assertion that will be true following an execution of the operation, given that the pre-condition was true. Each operation is specified using pre- and post-conditions, as illustrated in Figure B.17.

In this case, for the operation Create Contract Type, two pre- and post-condition pairs are shown. The first describes what happens when this new

```
Create Contract Type(in n:string, in id:number, S:number, return r:Result)

pre     NO Contract Type q EXISTS IN Contract Types WITH q.code = id
post    Contract Type p is CREATED IN Contract Types WITH
        p.code = id
        p.mileage = s
        p.checklist = n

pre     Contract Type p EXISTS IN Contract Types WITH p.code = id
post    r.error code = 12
```

FIGURE B.17 Example of pre- and post-condition pairs for Create Contract Type.

contract does not yet exist—it is created. The second describes what happens when the contract already exists—an error code is returned.

Implementation

With all elements of the components and their interfaces described in detail, implementation of those components is now considered. The implementation involves internal design, coding, assembly, and various testing stages, including integration testing with existing interfaces.

The existing internal designs for the previous software assembly implementation are evolved using appropriate implementation tools and techniques. With Sterling Software's COOL:Gen, for example, implementations are coded in action diagram language from which error-free component modules are generated. Design patterns and action diagram templates are used to improve productivity further. The persistent storage design is automatically created from the internal type model. The component implementation must support all of the operations described by the interfaces of that component. The semantics of each operation are constrained by the pre- and post-conditions defined for the operations on the interfaces.

The components will be implemented and assembled by teams of developers, often working in parallel to speed up the development life cycle. In this case, Reservations is designed and tested first, as Contracts depends on Reservations. The implementation in all cases takes into account integration and deployment testing.

REFERENCES

CHAPTER 1

[1] IDC, "Programmer Development Tools Synopsis: 1999 Worldwide Markets and Trends." IDC Report #19187, June 1999.

[2] J-M. Jézéquel and B. Meyer, "Design by Contract: The Lessons of the Ariane." *IEEE Computer,* vol. 30, no. 2, January 1997.

[3] "The Dawn of e-life," *Newsweek*, October 11, 1999.

[4] V. Basili, F. McGarry, *et al.*, "The Software Engineering Laboratory—An Operational Experience Factory," *Proceedings of the Fourteenth International Conference on Software Engineering,* Melbourne, Australia, May 1992.

[5] M. Paulk, B. Curtis, M. Chrissis, and C. Weber, *"Capability Maturity Model for Software, Version 1.1,"* Software Engineering Institute, Carnegie Mellon University, CMU/SEI-93–TR-24, February 1993.

[6] ISO 9000 Series Standards, International Standards Organization (ISO), *http://www.iso.ch/9000e.*

[7] F. Brooks, *The Mythical Man-Month*, Addison-Wesley, 1995.

CHAPTER 2

[1]   G. Booch, "The Future of Software," a set of presentation slides, 1996. *http://www.rational.com*.

[2]   D. Garlan and M. Shaw*, Software Architectures: Perspectives on an Emerging Discipline*, Prentice-Hall, Englewood Cliffs, NJ, 1995.

[3]   D. Garlan *et al.*, "Architectural Mismatch: Why It's Hard to Build Systems From Existing Parts," *Proceedings of the 17th International Conference on Software Engineering*, pp. 170–185, ACM Press, 1995.

[4]   P.C. Clements, "A Survey of Architectural Description Languages," *Proceedings of the 8th International Workshop on Software Specification and Design*, Paderborn, Germany, May 1996.

[5]   "ASSET: Source for Software Engineering Technology," see *http://source.asset.com*.

[6]   J. Solderitsch *et al.*, "The Reusability Library Framework: Leveraging Software Reuse," November 1992. *http://source.asset.com/stars/lm-tds/Papers/sses-rlf/symp.html*.

[7]   A.W. Brown, D.J. Carney, and M. McFalls*, Proceedings of the SEI/MCC COTS Symposium*, SEI/CMU Technical Report, January 1995.

[8]   K.C. Wallnau *et al.*, "Correcting, Identifying, and Avoiding Interface Mismatch: Theory and Practice," Software Engineering Institute, Carnegie Mellon University, Pittsburg, PA. Submitted to ICSE '97, August 1996.

[9]   G. Valetto and G. Kaiser, "Enveloping Sophisticated Tools into Computer-Aided Software Engineering Environments," pp. 40–48*, Proceedings of the 7th International Workshop on CASE*, IEEE Computer Society Press, July 1995.

[10]   A.W. Brown (ed.), "Component-Based Software Development," IEEE Computer Society Press, 1996.

[11]   E. Yourdon, "CASE Update," *Application Development Strategies*, vol. 8 no. 10, October 1996.

[12]   P.C. Clements and L.N. Northrop, "Software Architecture: An Executive Overview," pp. 55–68 in IEEE Computer Society Press, 1996.

[13]   R. Orlafi *et al.*, *The Essential Distributed Object Survival Guide*, John Wiley Press, 1996.

[14]   J. Seigel, *CORBA: Fundamentals and Programming*, John Wiley Press, 1996.

[15] "WebCenter: Internet for the Enterprise," Sterling Software White Paper, Version 3, Sterling Software Part Number 264117-0001, December 13, 1996.

[16] A.W. Brown *et al.*, *Principles of CASE Tool Integration*, Oxford University Press, 1995.

[17] The Unified Modeling Language (UML), *http://www.rational.com/uml*.

[18] D. D'Souza and A. Wills, *Objects, Components, and Frameworks with UML: The Catalysis Approach*, Addison-Wesley, 1999.

[19] C. Dellarocas, "Towards a Design Handbook for Integrating Software Components," *Proceedings of the 5th Symposium on Assessment of Software Tools (SAST97)*, IEEE Computer Society Press, June 1997.

[20] J. Robertson, E. Subrahmanian, M. Thomas, and A.W. Westerberg, "Management of the Design Process: The Impact of Information Modeling," Technical Report, Engineering Design Research Center, Carnegie Mellon University, Pittsburgh, PA, EDRC 06-179-94, 1994.

CHAPTER 3

[1] R. Kalakota *et al.*, *e-Business: Roadmap for Success*, Addison–Wesley, 1999.

[2] D. Amor, *The e-Business Revolution*, Prentice-Hall, 1999.

[3] C.V. Callahan and B.P. Pasternack, *Corporate Strategy in the Digital Age*, Boor Allen Hamilton, May 1999. *http://www.bah.com/greatideas/pptdata/index.htm*.

[4] "From Application Server to Application Integrator: Building the Application Services Layer," *2nd Quarter 1999 Trend Teleconference*, Meta Group, June 11, 1999.

[5] B. Cameron, W. Deutsch, J. Gatoff, and M.H. Hillman, "Packaged Application Strategies," The Forrester Report, Vol. 3, no.3, Forrester Research Inc., June 1998.

[6] K. Girard, "Botched Software Project Plagues City Payroll," *CNETNews.com*, December 2, 1999.

[7] P. Harmon, J. Highsmith, and K. Dick, "Application Servers: Hip or Hype?," *Cutter IT Journal*, Cutter Information Corp., 1999.

[8] S. Garone, "IDC's Definition and Segmentation of the Application Server Market," IDC Bulletin, International Data Corporation, 1999.

[9]   M. Gilpin, "Internet Application Integration," *Application Development Trends*, October 1999.

[10] D.S. Linthicum, "EAI Without the Hype," *Enterprise Development Journal*, July 1999.

[11] A.W. Brown *et al.*, *Principles of CASE Tool Integration*, Oxford University Press, 1995.

[12] D. Skelton, *The Seven Myths of EAI*, Distributed Computing, May 1999.

[13] D. Rogerson, *Inside COM: Microsoft's Component Object Model*, Microsoft Press, 1997.

[14] R. Monson-Haefel, *Enterprise JavaBeans*, O'Reilly Press, 1999.

[15] J. Seigel, "What's Coming in CORBA 3?," *Java Developers Journal*, October 1999.

CHAPTER 4

[1]   D. Phipps, "Workgroup AD in the Next Century: Death and Rebirth," Gartner Group Research Note, 29 November 1999.

[2]   S. Garone and S. Cusack, "Components, Objects, and Development Environments: 1999 Worldwide Markets and Trends," IDC Report #19112, June 1999.

[3]   A.W. Brown and K.C. Wallnau, "The Current State of CBSE," *IEEE Software*, September 1998.

[4]   P. Allen, *Realizing e-business with Components*, Addison-Wesley, August 2000.

[5]   D. Garlan, R. Allen, and J. Ockerbloom, "Architectural Mismatch: Why it's Hard to Build Systems Out of Existing Parts," *Proc. of the International Conference on Software Engineering*, April 1995.

[6]   D. Parnas, "On the Criteria for Decomposing Systems into Modules," *CACM* vol. 15, no. 12, pp. 1053–1058, December 1972.

[7]   D. Parnas, "On the Design and Development of Program Families," *IEEE Transactions on Software Engineering*, vol. 2, no. 1, March 1976.

[8]   R. Prieto-Diaz and P. Freeman, "Classifying Software for Reusability," *IEEE Software*, 1987.

[9]   B. Cox, *Object Oriented Programming—An Evolutionary Approach*, Addison–Wesley, 1986.

[10] A.W. Brown and K.C. Wallnau, "Engineering of Component-Based Systems," *Proceedings of the 2nd IEEE International Conference on Complex Computer Systems*, Montreal, Canada, October 1996.

[11] D. Kara, "Components Defined," *Application Development Trends*, June 1996.

[12] P. Allen, "Using Components to Improve Your Business," *Component Strategies*, July 1999.

[13] J. Daniels, Objects and Components, Sterling Software, February 1999.

[14] C. Szyperski, *Component Software: Beyond Object-Oriented Programming*, Addison–Wesley, 1998.

[15] B. Meyer, *Object-oriented Software Construction*, Second Edition, Prentice-Hall, 1999.

CHAPTER 5

[1] A.W. Brown and K. Short, "On Components and Objects: The Foundations of Component-Based Development," *Proceedings of the 5th International Symposium on Assessment of Software Tools (SAST97)*. pp. 112–121, IEEE Computer Society Press, 1997.

[2] J. Cheesman, "What is a Component?," Sterling Software Internal Working Draft, April 1999.

[3] J. Cheesman and J. Daniels, "The Unified Component Model," Tutorial slides, Presented at *Object-Oriented Programming, Systems, Languages, and Applications (OOPSLA)*, 1999.

[4] J. Cheeman and J. Daniels, *The Unified Component Model*, Addison-Wesley, October 2000.

[5] "Unified Modeling Language Specification," Object Management Group, Version 1.3, OMG, June 1999.

[6] B. Meyer, *Object-oriented Software Construction*, Second Edition, Prentice-Hall, 1999.

[7] Microsoft, "Component Description Information Model (Cde)," See *http://www.microsoft.com/repository*, July 1997.

[8] Sterling Software, "Sterling Software Component Standard," Version 3.0, See *http://www.cool.sterling.com/CBD*, 2000.

[9] D. D'Souza and A.C. Wills, *Objects, Components, and Frameworks with UML—The Catalysis Approach*, Addison-Wesley, 1998.

[10] A.W. Brown and B. Barn, "Enterprise Scale CBD: Building Complex Computer Systems From Components," *Proceedings of STEP'99*, pp. 82–93, IEEE Computer Society Press, August 1999.

[11] J.B. Warmer and A.G. Kleppe, *The Object Constraint Language: Precise Modeling with UML*, Addison-Wesley 1999.

CHAPTER 6

[1] G.A. Moore, "Crossing the Chasm: Marketing and Selling High-Tech Products to Mainstream Customers," *Harper Business*, 1999.

[2] G. Booch *et al.*, *The Unified Modeling Language User Guide*, Addison-Wesley 1999.

[3] J. Rumbaugh *et al.*, "The Unified Modeling Language Reference Manual, Addison-Wesley, 1999.

[4] I. Jacobson *et al.*, *The Unified Software Development Process*, Addison-Wesley, 1999.

[5] G. Booch (Ed.), *The Best of Booch: Designing Strategies for Object Technology*, SIGS Publications, 1997.

[6] H-E. Eriksson and M. Penker, *UML Toolkit*, John Wiley Press, 1998.

[7] P. Bernstein *et al.*, "The Microsoft Repository Version 2, and the Open Information Model," March 1999. Available at *http://www.microsoft.com/repository*.

[8] R. Sessions, "Component-Oriented Middleware," *Component Strategies*, October 1998.

[9] "The Object Management Architecture (OMA) Guide," 1998. OMG, Available from *http://www.omg.org*.

[10] J. Siegel, *CORBA Fundamentals and Programming*, John Wiley Press, 1998.

[11] "CORBA Services," 1999. OMG, Available from *http://www.omg.org*.

[12] J. Siegel, "What's Coming in CORBA 3?," *Java Developers Journal*, October 1999.

[13] R. Sessions, *COM and DCOM: Microsoft's Vision for Distributed Objects*, John Wiley Press, 1997.

[14] D. Box, *Essential COM*, Addison-Wesley, 1997.

[15] D.S. Platt, *Understanding COM+*, Microsoft Press, 1999.

[16] D. Flanagan, *Java in a Nutshell*, O'Reilly Press, 1999.

[17] C.Horstmann, *Core Java 2, Volume 1: Fundamentals*, Prentice-Hall, 1999.

[18] S. Asbury and S.R. Weiner, *Developing Java Enterprise Applications*, John Wiley Press, 1999.

[19] C. Austin and M. Powlan, "Writing Advanced Applications for the Java Platform," Sun Microsystems, December 1999. Available at *http://java.sun.com.*

[20] Sun Microsystems, Enterprise JavaBeans Standard, Version 1.1, 1999. Available at *http://java.sun.com.*

[21] E. Roman, *Mastering Enterprise JavaBeans and the Java 2 Platform, Enterprise Edition*, John Wiley Press, 1999.

[22] G. Flurry, "The Java 2 Enterprise Edition," *Java Developers Journal*, December 1999.

CHAPTER 7

[1] A.W. Brown (Ed.), "Component-Based Software Engineering: Selected papers from the Software Engineering Institute," *IEEE Computer Society Press*, 1996.

[2] P. Allen and S. Frost, *Component-Based Development for the Enterprise: Applying the Select Perspective*, Cambridge University Press, 1998.

[3] D. D'Souza and A.C. Wills, *Objects, Components, and Frameworks with UML—The Catalysis Approach*, Addison-Wesley, 1998.

[4] M. Kirkland, *Designing Component-Based Applications*, Microsoft Press, 1998.

[5] P. Clements (Ed.), *Constructing Superior Software*, McMillan Press, 1999.

[6] P. Kruchten, *The Rational Unified Process: An Introduction*, Addison Wesley, 1999.

[7] I. Jacobson, *The Object Advantage: Business Process Reengineering with Object Technology*, Addison Wesley, 1995.

[8] B. Boehm *et al.*, "Developing Multimedia Applications with the WinWin Spiral Model," *Proceedings European Software Engineering Conference*, November 1997.

[9] M. Arellano and J. McGlaun, "Eating Elephants: EWA Flies High with Component-Based Development," *Distributed Computing*, November 1999.

[10] A.W. Brown and B. Barn, "Enterprise Scale CBD: Building Complex
      Computer Systems From Components," *Proceedings of STEP '99*,
      pp. 82–93, IEEE Computer Society Press, August 1999.

[11] Sterling Software, The Sterling Software Component Standard, Version 3.0,
      2000. See *http://www.cool.sterling.com/CBD*.

[12] J. Cheeman and J. Daniels, *The Unified Component Model*, Addison–Wesley,
      Summer 2000.

[13] P. Coad and M. Mayfield, *Java Design: Building Better Apps and Applets*,
      Second Edition, Yourdon Computing Press, 1999.

[14] M. Fowler, *UML Distilled: Applying the Standard Object Modeling
      Language*, Second Edition, Addison Wesley, 1999.

[15] H-E. Eriksson and M. Penker, *UML Toolkit*, John Wiley Press, 1998.

CHAPTER 8

[1]   P. Coad and M. Mayfield, *Java Design: Building Better Apps and Applets*,
      Second Edition, Yourdon Computing Press, 1999.

[2]   J. Ackerley *et al., Developing an e-business Application for the WebSphere
      Environment*, IBM, July 1999. available at *http://www.redbooks.ibm.com*.

[3]   R. Sessions, *COM+ and the Battle for the Middle Tier*, John Wiley and
      Sons, 2000.

[4]   J. Dodd, "CBD Express," Sterling Software Internal paper, July 1999.

[5]   T. Buzan, *Use Your Head*, BBC Books, 1989.

[6]   D. Bellin and S.S. Simone, *The CRC Card Book*, Addison-Wesley, 1997.

[7]   D. D'Souza and A.C. Wills, *Objects, Components, and Frameworks with
      UML—The Catalysis Approach*, Addison-Wesley, 1998.

CHAPTER 9

[1]   R. Kalakota *et al., e-Business: Roadmap for Success*, Addison–Wesley,
      1999.

[2]   M.K. McGee, "Outlook 2000: E-business Initiatives Will be IT Executives
      Key Focus This Year," *InformationWeek*, January 3, 2000.

[3] R.M Melinicoff, "The eEconomy: It's Later Than You think," *Outlook Magazine,* Anderson Consulting, June 1999.

[4] Gartner Group Bulletin, *www.gartnergroup.com*, October 1999.

[5] R. Whiting, "Software Morphs into a Service," *InformationWeek*, October 11, 1999.

[6] R. Seeley and J. Vaughan, "IT to Outsourcers: Help!," *Application Development Trends*, October 1999.

[7] A.W. Brown, D.J. Carney, and M.D. McFalls, (eds.). *Proceedings of the SEI/MCC Symposium on the use of COTS in Systems Integration.* Technical Report CMU/SEI-95–SR-007, Software Engineering Institute, Carnegie Mellon University, Pittsburgh, PA, September 1995.

[8] B. Cameron *et al.*, "Packaged Application Strategies: Analyzing the Impact of Packaged Applications on Business Performance," *The Forrester Report*, vol. 3, no. 3, June 1998.

[9] "Application Service Providers (ASP)," Spotlight Report, Cherry Tree and Co. October 1999. Available at *http://www.cherrytreeco.com.*

CHAPTER 10

[1] E.R. Harold, *XML Bible*, IDG Books Worldwide, 1999.

[2] R. Deadman, "XML as a Distributed Application Protocol," Java Report, October 1999.

[3] M. Goulde, "Is XML the Answer? Depends on the Question," *Application Development Trends*, October 1999.

[4] D.S. Frankel, "CORBA Components – Alive and Well," Java Report, October 1999.

[5] A.W. Brown *et al.*, *Principles of CASE Tool Integration*, Oxford University Press, 1996.

[6] R. Prieto-Diaz and P. Freeman, "Classifying Software for Reusability," *IEEE Software*, 1987.

[7] E. Gamma *et al.*, *Design Patterns: Elements of Reusable Object-Oriented Software,* Addison Wesley, 1995.

[8] C. Larman, *Applying UML and Patterns: An Introduction to Object-Oriented Analysis and Design*, Prentice Hall, 1997.

[9]   B. Meyer, *Object-oriented Software Construction*, Second Edition, Prentice-Hall, 1999.

[10]   M. Woodman and B. Heal, *An Introduction to VDM*, McGraw-Hill, 1993.

[11]   J. Davis and J.C.P. Woodcock, *Using Z: Specification, Refinement, and Proof*, Prentice-Hall, 1996.

[12]   J.B. Warmer and A.G. Kleppe, *The Object Constraint Language: Precise Modeling with UML*, Addison-Wesley, 1999.

[13]   D. D'Souza and A.C. Wills, *Objects, Components, and Frameworks with UML—The Catalysis Approach*, Addison-Wesley, 1998.

[14]   C. Hofmeister, *Applied Software Architecture*, Addison-Wesley, 1999.

[15]   D. Garlan and M. Shaw, *Software Architectures: Perspectives on an Emerging Discipline*, Prentice-Hall, Englewood Cliffs, NJ, 1995.

[16]   L. Bass *et al.*, *Software Architecture in Practice*, Addison-Wesley, 1998.

[17]   D. Marshall, "EJB and its Role in e-Business," *e-businessEdge*, January 2000. Sterling Software, Available at *http://www.sterling.com/cool*.

INDEX